Praise for Captain Richemonte

Not only does Robert Stermscheg translate Karl May from German into English, he gifts the modern English world with 19th Century German sensibility, zeitgeist, and idiom. Through Stermscheg's brilliant lens we engage with swashbuckling action, romantic characters, and the evil bad guy of our worst nightmares. We are swept into human depravity and glory. History repeats if we forget. Bringing Karl May to the modern reader refocuses our myopia and reminds us, we are not that much different from our near ancestors.

—Nicola Cameron, author of *Leoshine, Princess Oracle*

A thought-provoking read for fans of historical fiction.

This story has it all… intrigue, humor, love, betrayal, and difficult choices. The reader experiences events from the perspective of different characters with unique perspectives. Stermscheg draws readers in with his powerful descriptions and well-rounded characterizations, bringing *Captain Richemonte* and events from history to life.

—Ruth L. Snyder, author, coach & Wall Street Journal bestselling author

Robert Stermscheg has done it again. With his characteristic mastery of language, he has brought the work of 19th century German author Karl May to English readers. In this latest book, Captain Richemonte, darker themes weave a complex tapestry of espionage, intrigue, and irrepressible love. Set within the rich cultural background of a bygone era, the author reminds us that while history does repeat itself, it does so in an infinite variety of fascinating ways.

—Ron Hughes, voice narrator, pastor

CAPTAIN RICHEMONTE

HUSSARS LOVE
PART IV

Karl May
Robert Stermscheg

CAPTAIN RICHEMONTE
Copyright © 2023 by Robert Stermscheg

Unabridged translation of the original text by Karl May (1842–1912).
First published 1883–1885 in *Deutscher Wanderer*, in serial format.

All rights reserved. No part of this publication may be reproduced, stored in a retrieval system, or transmitted in any form or by any means—electronic, mechanical, photocopy, recording, or any other—except for brief quotations in printed reviews without prior permission from the author or his publisher.

This book is licensed for your personal enjoyment only. This book may not be re-sold. If you would like to share this book with another person, please purchase an additional copy for each recipient. If you're reading this book and did not purchase it, or it was not purchased for your use only, then please delete and purchase your own copy. Thank you for respecting the hard work of this author.

Distributed to the trade by the Ingram Book Company.

Cover design: Travis Williams

Photo Credits

Front Cover:
Main image: photo by Janko Ferlič/Unsplash
Stone tunnel: "underground" © 2015 Escli/Adobe stock
Oil lamp: photo by Imphilip © Tao Jiang/Adobe stock
Brick factory with chimney: photo by Imfotograf/Adobe stock

Back Cover:
Stone tunnel: "underground" © 2015 Escli/Adobe stock
Author portrait: Robert Stermscheg

ISBN 978-1-7753559-5-3 (paperback)
ISBN 978-1-7753559-6-0 (eBook)

This novel is dedicated to all the fans of Karl May.

ACKNOWLEDGEMENTS

I would especially like to thank my father, John Stermscheg, who instilled within me the desire to explore the works of Karl May.

At the risk of being repetitive, a huge shoutout to my wife, Toni Abiusi, who continues to support my writing endeavours.

To Ralf Harder, for making the original text available on the Karl May Gesellschaft (KMG) website.

To Gord and Tricia Kell, for their advice and encouragement in the writing process.

To my editor, Evan Braun, who continues to surprise me with his skill and invaluable suggestions. Thanks for all your hard work.

To Travis Williams who came up with the wonderful cover.

To all of you, thank you. Your encouragement has not gone unnoticed and continues to motivate me.

FOREWORD

I believe all of us have appreciated the way gifted authors, such as Alexandre Dumas, James Fenimore Cooper and Karl May have opened up a whole new world to our imaginations through their portrayal of life. I have read and re-read many of Karl May's travel narratives and novels and I can honestly say that I have never tired of them. His prolific writings have taken me from the plains of Europe to the endless sands of the Sahara, even to the Rocky Mountains.

As I contemplated this fourth translation project, *Captain Richemonte*, I felt that I had attained a considerable amount of experience after writing the first book, *The Prussian Lieutenant*, *The Marabout's Secret, and Buried Secrets*. Once again, the challenge I faced was in remaining faithful to May's original work while conveying the story in modern English. Also, Karl May's novels, interspersed with French and Arabic references, were penned in German over a century ago. It was not my intention to critique or edit Karl May's political views; rather I wanted to convey to the reader what May had written, thereby conveying his knowledge of the times.

I often encountered obscure idioms, such as:

These idioms stemmed from an era that has long ago faded into the mists of time and when resurrected, needed to be explained to give them relevance. It took a considerable amount of time to chase down some of them, and I hope it leads the reader to a clearer understanding and lend it the authenticity it deserves. See the translation notes for details.

This fourth book, *Captain Richmonte*, is quite different from the previous three. It has a much darker tone, as evidenced by the cover. The protagonist, Richard von Löwenklau finds himself embroiled in mysteries. The unscrupulous Captain Richemonte, together with his ally,

Count Jules Rallion, concoct a daring plot to steal money from an unsuspecting American businessman. But Richemonte doesn't stop there. He's determined to wed his granddaughter Baroness Marion to Rallion's son, a man she despises outright. Still, all isn't lost, and May brings back the amusing landscape painter, Hieronymus Aurelius Schneffke, adding a little light to the dark theme.

This fourth book in *The Hussar's Love* series, reveals a number of situations, many of them shrouded in mystery. Appropriately, I've chosen the opening quote.

"Truth sits upon the lips of dying men"
-Matthew Arnold (1822-1888)

I think this is fitting, because Karl May draws us into graveyards replete with ghosts, dingy taverns that sport sinister men, and into secret meetings that harbor collaborators and highwaymen. From secret passages below Castle Ortry to Castle Malineau, where Hieronymus Schneffke stumbles across a painting with its own secrets, you will have to pay close attention to keep up to the drama. Coupled with engaging dialogue, the tension and darkness that we've experienced previously is balanced by Schneffke's humor, leaving the reader rooting for the hapless painter.

In any event, to quote my friend Victor Epp, another May aficionado:

"May his [Karl May's] spirit walk with you on this marvelous journey."

Robert Stermscheg
May 2023

CONTENTS

1	Amelia and Madelon	1
2	A Spy Returns	19
3	The Old Cavalry Master	27
4	The Plant Collector	47
5	New Discoveries	55
6	Rallion Demands Certainty	73
7	Marion's Ally	83
8	A Forest Encounter	93
9	Richemonte's Ultimatum	107
10	An Underground Passage	117
11	Two Conspirators	125
12	Doctor Bertrand	141
13	An American Businessman	149
14	A Horrible Deed	171
15	A Timely Escape	191
16	The English Lady	203
17	The Portly Painter	225
18	Nanon Forges Ahead	235
19	Charles Berteu	249

20	The Old Mill	273
21	The Steward	283
22	The Pastel Painting	305
23	Berteu's Plans	317
24	Schneffke's Friend	335
25	An Unusual Proposal	343
	Translation Notes	355

"Truth sits upon the lips of dying men"

-Matthew Arnold (1822–1888)
'Sohrab and Rustum' (1853)

CHAPTER ONE

AMELIA AND MADELON

In the spring of 1870, Berlin was bathed in spring-time splendour, its stately architecture prominent everywhere in the city. Bernard de Lemarch, a count in France's nobility circles, nearly felt at home in the heart of Prussia's capital. He was aware of the magnificent examples of Baroque and Renaissance architecture that seemed to be pressing in on him from all sides.

Bernard sighed. This wasn't Paris. The grandeur of his surroundings was nearly lost on him, no longer appearing as a count, but masquerading as a landscape painter. He had temporarily laid aside his title and adopted a commoner's name, an assumed name—Haller. He sauntered down the busy street, having replaced his cherished pearl-handled walking stick with a cumbersome, plain-looking painter's easel. He had to remind himself he was not in Berlin for a casual holiday but acting in the capacity of Napoleon's vanguard. In short, he was a spy.

He swallowed, supressing the bitter taste in his mouth, his mind replaying his recent encounter with the recluse, Underhill. He clenched his teeth so he wouldn't curse out loud. He'd been uncermoniously thrown out, *him*, a count. *I have to control my temper*, Bernard reasoned. *I'll best that spiteful Underhill soon enough. Perhaps my fellow painter Schneffke will have more luck.* The memory of Schneffke sipping black ink, which he had mistaken for Portuguese Tinto, at last brought a smile to his lips.

Bernard reined in his wandering and briefly stopped at a local coffee house. He took a seat in a quiet corner and surveyed the throng hurrying past. Aside from the bustling pedestrians, he observed horse-drawn carriages transporting their passengers to important meetings. As his mind drifted to the mission still ahead, he held out hope that Madelon Köhler would deliver and facilitate the important introduction to the Löwenklau family.

He was well aware that tensions were on the rise between Germany and France. Napoleon III needed to find a way of appeasing the growing unrest in his country, and what better way than to deflect his inability to reign than by provoking a long-standing nemesis, Prussia.

Bernard thought about the accolades to come from his superiors, *if* he proved successful in obtaining sensitive military information. He stood up, straightened his suit and headed back to his residence, his renewed confidence evident in his purposeful stride down the sidewalk.

◦✠◦

In another part of the city, in one of Berlin's fashionable neighbourhoods, Amelia von Löwenklau stood outside Madelon Köhler's suite. Amelia had recently returned from a trip and was looking forward to a visit with her good friend, Madelon. She quickly appraised her appearance in the glass's reflection before she rang the bell.

Amelia was in her mid-twenties, and the blonde hair pulled back in a bun accented her fine cheekbones and nearly flawless complexion. Satisfied, she smiled to herself and pressed the buzzer. When there was no response, she supposed that Madelon was out, perhaps engaged with her landlady, Ingrid Schüller.

Deciding to check for herself, she took the stairs to the next level and knocked on Schüller's door. When a maid opened the door for her, Amelia found her intuition had served her well. Both ladies were inside the apartment, happy to see their friend again. Naturally, Amelia joined them.

"Don't be surprised," Frau Schüller commented, "if a certain gentleman were to join us shortly."

"Ingrid, do you mean your son?" asked Amelia.

"No, I was referring to my new tenant."

"Ah, so you've managed to rent out your suite."

Schüller, a recent widow, nodded. "Yes, just yesterday, and happily I might add."

"What does this new tenant do for a living?"

"Oh," she replied with an air of importance, "he's an artist."

"An actor, perhaps a writer?" Amelia offered.

"No, he's a painter."

"I see," Amelia sighed, a little disappointed. "I'm not very fond of them. They strike me as a rather peculiar lot."

"Oh, but Herr Haller seems to be a considerate, upstanding gentleman," Madelon insisted.

"Yes," the landlady eagerly agreed. "He left that impression with me also."

The name caught Amelia's attention. "Did you say his name is Haller?"

"Why, yes."

"Where does he come from?"

"From Stuttgart, I believe," Ingrid replied.

A strange feeling passed through Amelia. "Does he strike you as distinguished?"

"Without question," Madelon said.

"Does he exhibit a somewhat formal or military bearing?"

"Now that you mention it, yes, he does so. He carries himself like an officer in civilian attire. Do you know him?" Madelon asked.

Amelia shook her head. "No. But it has been my experience that a man whom one considers to be upstanding at first glance often has a military look about him."

"You would be surprised to learn how much Herr Haller resembles our very own Sergeant Franz." Madelon offered. The similarity between Haller, a landscape painter, and Schneeberg, a non-commissioned Prussian officer, didn't escape Madelon's keen eyes.

"Do you mean my brother's servant, Franz?" asked Amelia, a slight crease forming on her forehead. "How interesting."

With the first mention of Haller's name, Amelia's mind turned to her brother's letter, warning her of the arrival of a French vanguard by that same name. Now that there was talk of his resemblance to Franz, she was forced to think of the painter whom she had met three times, though in different circumstances.

"Yes, they share a close resemblance with each other," Ingrid confirmed.

"Hmm, perhaps I will get to see him soon. But first," Amelia said, her tone growing serious. "I need to make you aware of something… vital."

Schüller frowned. "Why Amelia, you have that look about you. Is it very important?"

"It is. But you must both promise to keep it to yourselves."

"A secret!" Madelon exclaimed, clapping her hands together. "How wonderful, how interesting."

"Yes," Amelia noted. "An… important secret. You love your home country, don't you, my dear Madelon?"

"Very much so."

"More than your present country, Germany?"

The lovely girl moved her head from side to side, as if weighing her answer. "How can I decide between the two? France is my birthplace, my fatherland, but Germany has become my home. I love both, France patriotically, and Germany affectionately."

"Well, if I may be so bold, I would like to pose another question. Would you do anything to harm your adopted country?"

"No, never!"

"Then please tell me, has Herr Haller already spoken with you?"

Madelon reflected. "Yes, last night, at the supper table."

"Did he take the opportunity to make inquiries about my family?"

Ingrid and Madelon looked at each other. They remembered that Haller had requested that they not disclose his manner of questioning.

"Please be up front with me," implored Amelia. "I want to hear the truth."

The landlady made up her mind first. "Very well, I have to admit that he asked about the Löwenklau family."

"Specifically, about my brother?"

"Yes."

"Did he inquire about where he is stationed?"

Frau Schüller nodded. "Yes, he did."

"And did he ask if it would be difficult to gain admittance to the family?"

"Why, yes."

Amelia sighed audibly. "Then you no doubt mentioned my occasional visits with you."

"Yes," confirmed the landlady, somewhat baffled. "But how do you know all this?"

"I surmised it, that's all. And you, my dear Madelon, probably indicated that we are good friends."

"Yes, I've told him as much," replied Madelon. "Was it a mistake?"

"Oh no! I surmise further that he asked you to facilitate an introduction with my family."

Even though Madelon had turned red, she answered truthfully. "Yes, I did promise him that."

"Is he pleasant to talk to?"

"Of course."

"Hmm. Well, that doesn't surprise me. A man who can so quickly gain my Madelon's sympathy must not be underestimated. Even so, I'm afraid he's more than just an opportunist; he's a dangerous man."

"Oh no. He's not dangerous," Madelon refuted.

"Look, you're already defending him. Anyway, I'm not changing my mind. He's a dangerous individual," Amelia proclaimed, looking serious. The two women looked at their friend with concern on their faces.

"What grounds do you have to make this claim, Fräulein?" Ingrid asked.

"Very valid ones."

"Do you know him?"

"If he's the one I've heard about, then yes. Still, I need to be sure. Did he travel here directly from Stuttgart?"

"No," the widow replied. "He told us that he was also in Dresden."

Amelia hesitated, still thinking. "What about Tharandt?"

"Yes, he was there too."

"Was he there by himself?"

"No. He mentioned meeting a fellow artist along the way, a short, portly fellow, a peculiar character."

"Didn't he tell you we had already met?" When Schüller shook her head, Amelia continued. "Picture the following scene: I was travelling with my aunt on a holiday, and we happened to take a stroll through the Tharandt forest. I was hoping the fresh forest air would invigorate and soothe her ailing spirit. We were sitting in a dale, discussing a particularly pleasant theme. I believe I was reading from Gerok's poem, *Palm Leaves*. Suddenly, we heard a man cry out, followed by loud sounds of cracking, rolling, and sliding. Frightened by the unexpected tumult, we jumped up and turned around. What do you think we witnessed?"

The two women had been following her account closely. "Well, what? Tell us, quickly," pleaded Madelon.

"Two people came sliding down the embankment, accompanied by stones, sand, and small clumps of earth. They didn't just fall slowly, either. They plummeted with the rapidity of an approaching avalanche. Think of two boys sliding down a hill on a sled and then picture them doing it on their rumps, without the sled."

Madelon cringed. "Oh, dear."

"One of them was tall and had a muscular build," Amelia went on. "He looked a lot like Franz, my brother's servant—"

"But that sounds like him. Yes, it must be," Madelon interjected.

"The man didn't stick around," Amelia added. "He hid himself behind some nearby bushes."

"Oh, how cowardly," Ingrid crowed. "How embarrassing."

"Well, the situation didn't exactly lend itself to heroics. Besides, that little downhill slide left his clothes in rather bad shape. I don't think he dared show himself in front of two ladies."

"What about the other one?" asked Madelon.

"He was short and rotund, fat actually, round like a ball. The man came rolling and tumbling down the hill, coming to rest at my feet. He greeted me with a compliment and proclaimed himself to be a painter. He proudly offered his name: Hieronymus Aurelius Schneffke."

"While sitting at your feet?"

Amelia had to keep herself from bursting into laughter. "Yes, at my feet."

"That must have been funny," laughed Madelon. "Anyway, that seems to be the same name Mr. Haller mentioned last night at the supper table. Did you see them again?"

"Yes. By coincidence, we happened to share the same first-class coach on the way to Dresden. During the train ride, the small, portly fellow finagled my aunt into a lively conversation and ended up pulling me in as well. By the time we reached Dresden, he declared his love for me."

Ingrid and Madelon looked horrified. "That must have been dreadful," the landlady remarked.

"No, not at all," noted Amelia. "Quite on the contrary. He expresses himself in such comedic fashion that you can't take him seriously, nor can you be annoyed with him. Just the other morning, Aunt Hedwig and I took a stroll toward Blasewitz. Suddenly, we heard horses approaching from the rear. We turned around, and who did we see?"

"The tall man, Haller?"

"Yes, accompanied by his *Sancho Pansa*."[1] Amelia smiled, recalling the incident. "The portly fellow wanted to ride past in a most dignified manner. Perhaps he had some equestrian tactic in mind, but he made the mistake of striking the horse's head with his whip. Naturally, the horse spooked and threw him off. You wouldn't believe it, but once again he landed squarely at my feet." The women shared a good laugh, albeit at the painter's expense. "It was most entertaining. We haven't laughed so hard for some time."

"Surely, the poor painter was mortified," Madelon added.

"Not in the least. I suspect it's rather difficult to embarrass that man."

"He sounds like a most original character," commented Ingrid. "And then?"

"He picked up his Calabrese hat and ran after the horse. Then today, when I was—"

"What?" Madelon interrupted. "You've seen him today already?"

"Both of them."

"That's true," reflected her friend. "Herr Haller left the house earlier. But where did you encounter them?"

Amelia smoothed her dress. "Madelon, I was getting ready to pay you a visit. I was about to go past our neighbor's gate when a carriage came rolling out. That's when I saw something big and round come flying across the lane with framed pictures scattering all over the ground. A large Calabrese hat rolled up to my feet, and who do you think was lying in the midst of the paintings?"

"Your rotund fellow?" Ingrid guessed.

"Yes, who else but him."

"But how did that happen?"

"He must have seen the approaching carriage at the last minute and tried to jump out of the horse's way. I suppose he miscalculated and lost his balance, sending his hat and pictures flying in all directions."

"That poor man," Madelon sighed with pity in her voice. "Was he hurt?"

"Not at all," smiled Amelia, remembering the scene. "He swore softly and looked about him. Then, when he spotted me, he greeted me from his prostrate position and declared himself to be one of the luckiest people alive since he had the pleasure of paying homage at my feet once again."

The two ladies, thoroughly enjoying Amelia's story, joined in with a hearty laugh.

"Surely he managed to stand up," Madelon said, still amused.

"Of course. He explicitly instructed Haller to gather up the pictures and—"

"What! Haller was with him?"

"Naturally. When it comes to awkward encounters, those two seem to be inseparable. Then came the best part. Haller hailed a porter and helped him gather up the pictures. That left Hieronymus alone with me and he wasted no time in announcing his affection for me yet again."

"Out in the open street?" ventured the disbelieving landlady.

"Indeed."

"And you, dear Amelia, did you just walk away?"

Amelia shook her head. "Not at first. Foremost, he wanted me to legitimize myself. He wanted to know my name, where I lived, who my parents were, and who knows what else."

"That was a little too bold. Yes, quite impertinent," said Ingrid.

"Perhaps. But you have to understand that all along he has confused me for a governess, a servant girl, or something like that."

"Dear God! How did he arrive at that conclusion?"

Amelia considered that for a moment. "I suppose because when my aunt and I were in the Tharandt forest, I wore my traveling clothes, not my formal attire."

"Mr. Haller certainly didn't mention any of this."

"I dare say he wouldn't. If he had, he wouldn't have portrayed himself in a very complimentary light. So, my dear Madelon, you've taken it upon yourself to introduce him to me?"

"Yes. As I've already told you, I made a promise."

"And when did you propose to carry out this promise?"

Madelon shrugged. "When he returns from his outing and finds you here with me. That would be the best opportunity."

"That could work. We will notice right away if he really is a polished individual."

"How so?"

"If he shows embarrassment or indicates that he has already seen me, it will be a poor reflection on his social skills."

"Now I'm really curious," Madelon admitted. "I wish I could find out right away."

"I, on the other hand, hope he tarries a little longer, since I still have an important disclosure to make to you both. I referred to him earlier as a dangerous man, and you were reluctant to accept it, dear Madelon."

"I haven't changed my mind."

"In that case, I want to emphasize a cautionary approach by stating that any association with him could prove dangerous. For all of us."

Madelon paled at her friend's remark. She knew Amelia well and realized that she wouldn't be making these accusations without valid reasons. She folded her hands with a resigned expression on her face.

"Then he must be a criminal," she said darkly, barely loud enough for her to hear.

"I'm afraid so. What he purposes to accomplish can only be rewarded by punishment and incarceration."

"And we held him to be a fine, upstanding gentleman," Madelon said. "How mistaken we have been. He has such kind eyes, such trustworthy features. His whole countenance speaks of goodwill."

"That hasn't escaped me, dear Madelon. And yet he is still dangerous. How else would you label someone who has the capacity to wreak havoc not just on one individual, but on a whole nation?"

Fear and confusion crossed Madelon's features. "The whole nation? I don't understand. Is he a disguised Russian anarchist... a social-democratic agitator... perhaps a conspirator involved in a political murder plot?"

"No, none of those things. Simply put, he is a spy."

Ingrid, who had left the conversation to the two young ladies, suddenly jumped from her loveseat. What she heard had struck her like a jolt. She, a faithful Prussian loyalist, a proud Berliner, now harboring a spy? The very thought alarmed her.

"A spy?" she exclaimed. "Is it really true?"

"Yes, my dear Frau Schüller," replied Amelia.

"You're certain about this?"

"Quite certain. You see," she explained, "I was forewarned about this painter, the one who calls himself Haller. I've been waiting for him, but I hadn't expected to find him lodged here."

"Who advised you?"

"My brother."

"I see. Well, that's good enough for me," said the landlady. "We all know how capable your brother is. The things he hears and talks about are carefully thought through and considered gospel by many. This Haller has to leave immediately. I will advise him as soon as he comes back from his walk. Yes, I will even notify the police of his scandalous intentions."

Amelia shook her finger at the older woman. "Frau Schüller, you'll do no such thing," Amelia replied solemnly.

"I won't?" Ingrid asked in surprise. "But why not? Should I knowingly allow a spy to live here and put me in contention with the authorities?"

"No. You're not going to drive him away, but you also aren't going to have him arrested. And you certainly won't come into conflict with the governing authority."

"Really? What should I do then?" asked Ingrid, feeling confused.

"Simple," Amelia said reassuringly. "You're going to allow him to live here, serve him well, and give him no indication that you know about his mission."

"But that's impossible," she said, shaking her head.

"Not at all. It is your duty and responsibility," Amelia replied, smiling at her friend. "Should I explain it to you?"

"Would you please, Fräulein?"

"Now then, without being a gossip, I can tell you that the ruling military body has the utmost confidence in my brother's abilities."

Schüller lifted her eyes proudly. "That's not gossip. It's common knowledge. Your brother knows about matters that other high-ranking officials can only dream of."

Amelia nodded. "Then perhaps I should inform you that a war is brewing between Germany and France."

"There is talk of it," Ingrid confirmed.

"The French regime wants to be careful by satisfying themselves that their military prowess is superior, or at least on par with ours. Naturally, they can't do so openly, so they revert to the only means open to them. They flood Germany with vanguards—spies!"

"And this Herr Haller is supposed to be one of them?"

"Absolutely."

"So, then he's French?"

"Of course."

"And he's not from Stuttgart?" asked the kind-hearted woman.

"No, not at all. The schemers in Paris know as well as we do that Richard enjoys his superiors' confidence and that he's been entrusted with sensitive materials concerning the situation between France and Germany. They speculate that the easiest way to glean information about the impending conflict is to get it from my brother directly. That's why Herr Haller, more accurately Count de Lemarch, is an officer in the French Guard and has been sent to Berlin to solicit vital information. His plan is to seek an introduction into the family, make himself out to be a loyal German, and then learn as much as possible."

"And that's why he inquired about you," Ingrid breathed, a light going on.

"Yes, I believe so."

"And despite what you've told us, I'm supposed to let him live here?"

"Without question. I myself will introduce him to our family."

Schüller looked horrified. "Isn't that rather dangerous? He *is* here to spy on us, after all."

"My dear, you're priceless," Amelia said with a smile. "We will allow him free rein to visit with our family and, as you say, spy on us. We, however, will supply him with outdated, erroneous, and altogether false information. Do you understand me now?"

The woman nodded. "Ah, now it makes sense to me. He will be deceived in the process."

"Of course. That's the plan. He will send reports back to Paris and lead his superiors astray, perhaps even Napoleon himself. In this way, we will take the trumps out of his hand and use them for our own gain."

"But what about the German authority?" Ingrid asked anxiously. "What will they think of me?"

"They have already been advised by my brother. As soon as Haller makes contact with the French embassy, arrangements will be made to have him watched. Believe me, it's much safer if they know where he is, rather than him working in secret. If you play it smart and leave him unhindered, you can be assured of future recognition."

The landlady considered this. "But what if he tries to get information out of me?"

Amelia fought hard not to laugh out loud. "Well, you're not privy to any state secrets, are you?"

"No, I suppose not. But I can't just sit here. I will have to say something about the current regime."

"That's fine. Just tell Herr Haller that we Germans are afraid of the French army, that we're out of sorts with the South Germans, that the Russians and English despise us, and that the Austrians haven't forgotten their thrashing on our account back in 1866. You can say that our soldiers aren't well-trained, and our officers are opposed to war. You can suggest nuances, like our gun powder is of inferior quality, the French marksmen are feared by all, or that their chassepots are more reliable than our own rear-loaders and no one wants to deal with the prospect of their *Mitrailleuse* cannons. Is that enough for you to work with?"

Ingrid and Madelon looked at Amelia in wonder.

"That was quite a litany," replied the landlady. "Well then, I will give it a try. So long as you reassure me that he will be granted access to your family, I can follow your lead."

"Carry on without any regrets. Haller will even be treated by our household as a guest." Amelia paused, looking at Madelon's suit with a frown on her face. "But my dear Madelon, I've only just noticed your outfit. You're dressed for a journey."

Madelon looked down at her traveling clothes before turning back to face her friend. "Indeed. I'm prepared to go on a trip. Our conversation so far has been of such interest that I didn't have the opportunity to fill you in."

"Where are you planning to go? Not far I hope."

"All the way to France, actually."

Now it was Amelia's turn to look shocked. "To France?" she asked. "At this time and so suddenly? Why, for God's sake?"

"I have just received a telegram from my sister, Nanon. Our caregiver has passed away and it's my duty to return for his funeral."

"Is your sister at Castle Ortry?"

"Yes, she has just returned there with Baroness de Sainte-Marie after a lengthy absence."

Amelia narrowed her eyes in thought. "Didn't your caregiver live near Etain?"

"Yes, at Castle Malineau."

"What a long, long trip. Will you be traveling with anyone?" When Madelon shook her head, Amelia looked at her in awe. "You're very brave. Does Baroness von Hohenthal know of it?"

"Yes. I have naturally written to her, disclosing the circumstances."

"My thoughts are with you for your sudden loss. And already you're preparing to leave. I had hoped to spend some time with you now that I'm back from my own travels."

Madelon looked sad for a moment, but then she managed a smile. "I won't be gone too long."

"I will have to be content with that. But I'm happy about one thing: you will see your sister again."

Madelon's face brightened. "It has been several years since I've seen her, and her letters are usually so short."

"Doesn't she write to you on a regular basis?"

"No, not too often. Oddly enough, her last letter was lengthy and quite interesting. It dealt with someone whose circumstances are coincidentally close to our own."

"That's curious," Amelia said. "Would you care to elaborate?"

"Why not? It concerns a poor plant collector from Thionville."

Instantly, Amelia became more attentive. She knew that Franz was employed as a gatherer of sorts, and that he was staying in Thionville. "That sounds intriguing," she said.

"It is intriguing. The poor devil has no parents; he's a foundling. Because he was found in the snow as a young boy, he inherited the name Schneeberg."

This confirmed to Amelia that the true subject of Nanon's letter was Franz. "Is your sister interested in his background?"

"Yes, very much so. We're both orphans. She was speaking to this plant collector recently and quite accidentally learned that he carries an identifiable sign that may make it possible to learn something about his parents. You see, Nanon once heard of a Parisian lady who at one time had twin boys. They were taken from her—kidnapped! The two boys were supposed to have the same identifying article in their possession, just like the one Schneeberg carries."

"Twin boys?" asked Amelia. "Who was this Parisian lady?"

"Unfortunately, Nanon couldn't recall her name. She has a friend in Paris who could supply her with the information, but she has taken a last-minute trip to Italy. My sister did recall, however, that the boys' mother was of German aristocratic origin. Given that information, it occurred to Nanon that more could be learned here in Berlin. That's why she wrote to me, so that I could make inquiries about a family which may have suffered the loss of twin boys, over twenty years ago."

Amelia's expression had transformed itself from one of mere curiosity to one of considerable tension. "Doesn't the letter say more about the mother?" she inquired.

"No, only that she still carries the burden of her loss to this day."

"Dear God!" Amelia voiced, leaning forward. "What is this sign that the man carries on him?"

"A lion's tooth. It's fastened to a thin golden chain."

Hearing this, Amelia jumped out of her chair. "Go on. Is there anything unusual about the tooth?"

"Nanon says it's hollow. She wrote that if you unscrew the golden base, two miniature pictures come into view."

"That's it! It has to be the one," Amelia exclaimed, joyfully clasping her hands together.

Speechless, the two women looked at her. Finally, Madelon ventured to ask, "Do you know something about this tooth?"

"Of course. More than you can imagine. I thought I had told you the story long ago."

"No, not one word."

"And about my aunt, Hedwig von Goldberg?"

"In regard to this subject, no."

"But you know that my aunt is still in mourning?"

"Yes, I do," Madelon said, understanding dawning on her face. "But I never knew the circumstances."

"Well, it was more than twenty years ago when she lost two boys, twins in fact. The boys simply disappeared, vanishing without a trace. All inquiries about what happened to them proved fruitless. My uncle Kunz promised high rewards to anyone who might have information concerning their whereabouts, but nothing came of it."

Madelon sat back, gasping. "Is that really the way it happened? So, it was Frau von Goldberg who was in Paris."

"Yes. She travels there quite often."

"Then it has to be her. We have found the mother. Oh Amelia, let me hug you."

Madelon and Amelia embraced each other, exhilarated over their discovery, while the widow Schüller cried softly, moved by the unfolding of the incredible story.

"How thrilled Nanon will be when I personally deliver the good news to her," exclaimed Madelon jubilantly. "And you, my dear friend, you have to rush to your aunt and bring her these good tidings. I will give you my sister's letter so she can read it for herself. I'll go fetch it right away."

Filled with excitement, Madelon stood to leave the room. But the older and wiser Amelia held her back.

"Wait just a moment," she pleaded. "This matter is far too important for us to act hastily. My aunt's grief over her loss has slowly subsided over the years. But if we're wrong, if somehow, we've drawn the wrong conclusion, can you imagine how heartbreaking all of this could be for her? We should carefully consider what we do know." Once Madelon had resumed her seat, Amelia leaned in. "So then, Schneeberg is in possession of one of the lion's teeth?"

"Yes."

"You mentioned that he gathers plants. Do you know for whom?"

"Why do you ask?"

"I have my reasons, dear Madelon. Please, tell me."

Madelon frowned, trying to recall the details of the letter. "I believe he's employed by a local physician, Doctor Bertrand in Thionville."

"Dear God! That's him. What a miraculous discovery. Our family has known him for so many years without realizing he was in possession of one of the teeth."

For a moment, Madelon looked shocked. "What! You know him?"

Amelia was barely able to contain her excitement. "Yes, and you do, too."

"How? I don't know anyone by the name of Schneeberg. And I've never been to Thionville. How could I have seen him?"

"Right here in Berlin. He's only been in Thionville a short time. I could easily explain the whole thing, but I'm not at liberty to do so—at least not for now. Tell me, didn't Schneeberg speak to your sister about having a brother?"

"The letter doesn't mention one."

"Does he have the left or the right lion's tooth?"

"Apparently it's the right tooth," Madelon said.

"Were there any letters or numbers printed on the miniature portraits?"

Madelon considered. "My sister didn't mention anything like that in her letter. Perhaps there were none."

"Then let me explain," Amelia offered. "A long time ago, my Uncle Kunz shot a large lion in Algiers. As was the Arab custom, he removed the eye teeth and later had them hollowed out. Each tooth was affixed to a golden base in the shape of a crown and hung on a fine chain around each of the boys' necks. Those were the boys who mysteriously disappeared. When there were no ransom demands or responses to Uncle Kunz's offer of reward, we thought the boys must have been killed. But now we have a lead, a new hope of finding at least one of them."

Madelon's eyes glimmered hopefully. "Indeed, I suspect this Schneeberg is one of the lost boys."

"It's quite likely. I suppose there's a remote possibility that one of these teeth somehow made its way into the hands of another child—but, like I said, that seems unlikely." She paused to collect her thoughts. "So, when are you leaving?"

"I'm scheduled to depart on the three o'clock train."

"Then there is still time," Amelia said. "Would you like to accompany me to see my grandfather and tell him exactly what you've related to me?"

"Of course! I would be happy to. Should I bring the letter?"

Amelia nodded earnestly. "Would you please?"

"I'll be right back."

With that, Madelon stood excitedly and set off to retrieve the letter.

CHAPTER TWO

A SPY RETURNS

Amelia and Madelon were just saying goodbye to Frau Schüller when the outer door opened, and Bernard de Lemarch walked in. Naturally, he recognized Amelia, and a fine, almost imperceptible redness colored his cheeks. Otherwise, there was no indication of his surprise or embarrassment by her presence.

"I'm going by the name Amelia Löwe," Amelia whispered to Madelon. Instead of questioning her friend, Madelon turned to face Haller.

"Ah, Herr Haller, already back?" she asked in a friendly manner. "I would have thought you might spend more time wandering about Berlin, to become more acquainted with the city's layout."

"I have plenty of time to do that later," Bernard replied, smiling. "I remembered you have to leave soon, Fräulein."

"You needn't have come back so soon on my account," she said, sounding reserved.

"I came to wish you a pleasant trip and speedy return," he said, his tone serious. It was clear he caught something in her manner, a stiffness he hadn't sensed before, and felt the need to address it through a solemn reply.

"It's nice of you to say so," she said. "Would you permit me to make an introduction? Herr Haller from Stuttgart, this is my friend, Amelia Löwe."

He bowed graciously before Amelia and, in his most unpretentious voice, continued, "At the moment, I envy your friendship with Fräulein Köhler."

Amelia looked at him quizzically. "Do you find our relationship so enviable?" she asked.

"Absolutely!"

"May I know the reason?" asked Amelia.

"Certainly," he said, then turned to face Madelon. "But I would rather answer by way of Heinrich Heine's[21] words:

O dearest, canst thou tell me why
The rose should be so pale?
And why the azure violet
Should wither in the vale.

"Who can say why the flower gives its fragrance?" he continued. "Who can explain why a person loves one and hates another?"

Surprised, yet pleased at his prose, Madelon interjected. "That's very true. Likewise, my disdain for you is inexplicable."

"Your words frighten me, Fräulein," he quipped.

She eyed him teasingly. "You don't look very afraid."

"No, but I'm surprised at your choice of words."

"You don't look like a man who frightens easily. A man of your trade should be accustomed to such things."

Bernard's cheeks paled ever so slightly. *What does she mean by that remark?* he thought to himself. *She couldn't possibly know my real identity as a spy, yet a career as a painter could hardly be misconstrued as a dangerous one.*

"On the contrary," he replied after a moment. "I have every intention of letting my *trade*"—he stressed the word—"lead me into the luminescence of life. This ensures that I, a novice painter, continue to improve the quality of my art. There is no provision for experiencing the depravity of life."

"I disagree with you," Madelon countered. "An artist, particularly if he wants to be diverse, is occasionally forced to don the cloak of humility and figuratively climb down into the dregs of society. Where there is light, there is also shadow. As an artist, you have to differentiate between the two and be prepared to tackle the seedier aspects of life."

"I see that you've contemplated the arts, Fräulein, and that makes me glad."

She smiled. "Then you will permit me to give it some more thought. But for now, I must be on my way. Good day, Herr Haller." Madelon bowed, intending to leave with Amelia. Bernard, however, stepped closer to block her exit.

"Forgive me, Fräulein," Bernard apologized, "but before you leave, I need to ask a quick question. I don't want to impose, but would it be possible for you to grant me just five minutes of your time?"

"For what purpose?"

"I would like to make a disclosure. I think you'll find it to be an important one."

Madelon looked at her friend, then turned back to face Haller. "Can't it wait until I have returned from my trip, Herr Haller?"

"As far as I'm concerned, it could wait without the slightest impact on me. However, in respect to you, it would perhaps be better for you to hear what I have to say before you leave."

"Still, couldn't you keep this news until I return? My time is so short today. I barely have five minutes to spare."

"Even if I were to disclose to you that the object of my plea concerns your family?"

Madelon stopped in her tracks and looked at him inquiringly. "My family?" she asked. "Aside from my sister, I don't have one."

He shrugged his shoulders. "Perhaps you do," he teased lightly. Bernard immediately noticed the change in her manner toward him. *Why is that?* he thought. *Has her friend Amelia spoken to her of our earlier encounters? That doesn't seem likely. How could Amelia have known I was living here? But one thing is clear—I'm not going to let her presume who or what I am. I'm not a man to be the brunt of someone else's jokes.*

"Perhaps I do?" she asked, repeating his words. "You see, my sister and I are orphans. My mother died a long time ago. Even our stepfather has passed away."

"But your real father could still be alive. Perhaps even your grandfather."

"Why delve into such conjecture, Herr Haller?"

"Perhaps I have grounds for these personal inquiries. Isn't it true that your father's first name was Gaston?"

Madelon hesitated before replying, "Yes. I've already told you as much."

"And your mother's name was Amély?"

"You know that as well," she said again, showing her impatience.

"Is the name Bas-Montaigne familiar to you?"

"Bas-Montaigne?" She considered the word, rolling it around on the tip of her tongue. "Dear God, yes! It's as though I have heard it spoken often, early in my childhood. What is its connection to me?"

His eyes twinkled. "Well, that name is closely connected to the words 'sweet kolibri'. But then, you don't have time for me." He watched her carefully, gauging her reaction.

"Please explain yourself. You are speaking in riddles."

"The explanation would take considerably longer than the time you've allotted me. Earlier, you were kind enough to share a few of your childhood memories. Ask Fräulein Löwe. She encountered two people who were in possession of several kolibri paintings. Perhaps this will in some way shed light on something that has eluded you for so long."

She narrowed her eyes in impatience. "You're being purposely vague, not to mention unpleasant. I sense you're holding back. You know something. You've learned something about my past and are reluctant to part with it."

"By no means do I want to appear unpleasant, Fräulein Köhler," Bernard insisted. "Since you've confided in me, I would like to disclose the little that I do know, in the hope that I might help solve your life's riddle. It seems providence has been kind enough to favor me with a nod in the right direction. I could be mistaken, but I think I've found someone who is closely connected to your past."

"Who could that be?"

"Please allow me to keep that to myself for now. I have to consider and evaluate certain matters very carefully. I was hoping our talk might help me clarify a few things, but I can see now that it was presumptuous of me to burden you at this time. No doubt you will return shortly, when we will have more time to properly address these developments."

The painter's tone sounded cold and withholding to Madelon's ears. She looked at him expectantly, his comments having stirred up old memories, many of them vague and unclear. Her curiosity was definitely aroused. She would have gladly given him a half hour, but his tone only pushed her further away.

"As you say, Herr Haller," she announced. "I will have to be patient and look forward to a time when I can give your words the attention they deserve. Goodbye."

She nodded to him and left, Amelia bowing slightly and following her friend out the door.

Bernard gazed at the closed door absentmindedly, thinking about the two departed women. Almost reluctantly, he turned his attention to the landlady.

"Has Fräulein Löwe mentioned our earlier meeting?" he asked her.

"Yes," Ingrid replied, unable to avoid the question.

"I see," he reflected. "We have seen each other repeatedly, although it wasn't I instigating the encounters. But how could Fräulein Löwe know that the man she met in the Tharandt Forest was the same man who resides here with you?"

"Isn't it obvious?" Ingrid asked, smiling. "It was your portly colleague, the one who got you into all those predicaments."

"How so?"

"Well, you mentioned him last night."

"I recall that, yes."

"Fräulein Löwe told us about him today. The two descriptions matched so closely that we were convinced they described you."

He nodded, accepting the very rational explanation. "Yes, that makes sense." Just then, Bernard noticed a fan on the divan. He pointed to it. "Who does this belong to? Perhaps Fräulein Köhler?"

"No. Her friend probably left it behind. Too bad."

"Does Fräulein Löwe come by here often?"

The older woman shook her head. "No, only occasionally. She will miss her fan."

"She couldn't have gone far," Bernard said, half to himself. "Perhaps I can still catch up to her." Haller nodded to the landlady, picked up the fan, and left in a hurry. Frau Schüller made no attempt to hold him back.

By the time Bernard reached the gate, the ladies were nowhere to be seen. He intuitively turned in their direction and, after covering a fair distance, he spotted Amelia and Madelon walking together. He quickened his pace. Just as they passed the gate where Hieronymus had taken his tumble with the kolibri collection, they turned into an adjacent house. As Bernard reached the gate, he heard a bell ring upstairs. They were probably still in the foyer. He rushed up the steps, just in time to see the outer door open. The porter, who was still holding the door, looked at him inquiringly, but Bernard ignored him and called out, "Fräulein! Fräulein Löwe, a moment please."

Amelia turned around at the sound of her name. As soon as she spotted Bernard with her fan in his hand, she came to a quick resolve. She stood in the hallway and motioned for him to step closer.

"Ah, Herr Haller," she said, pleased. "I've left my fan behind, and you've been so kind to return it to me. Please, come in."

Not thinking to look at the nameplate attached to the doorpost, he stepped inside. The servant bowed respectfully and closed the door behind him. Without realizing where he was, Bernard was now committed. He assumed they were merely visiting the governess' family.

Amelia took the fan out of his hand and thanked him with a smile. "Please," she said, "would you do me the honor of coming in?" Her hand was already on the door handle of the second door. He paled at the thought of intruding on the countess and therefore sought to excuse himself.

"I'm not dressed for a formal occasion, Fräulein," he hastened to explain. "Please, allow me to withdraw." He reasoned that he was about to enter Countess von Goldberg's salon. How could he appear before her after his deplorable introduction in the Tharandt Forest? Besides, he was wearing a simple walking suit, which was hardly appropriate for such a visit.

She smiled disarmingly. "Why?" she asked.

"How could I, a stranger, and dressed like this, pay a visit to General von Goldberg?"

"Von Goldberg? You're not in the von Goldbergs' house, Herr Haller. This is my house, my family's home."

"Then I've made an honest mistake. That's different then." *I needn't feel embarrassed to show up dressed this way in a commoner's household*, he thought.

"Then please, won't you enter?"

CHAPTER THREE

THE OLD CAVALRY MASTER

Amelia opened the door and stood on the right side of the entryway, with Madelon on the left. As Bernard walked between them into the salon, he noticed a peculiar look in Amelia's eyes, a look reminiscent of a card player in possession of a trump card. There was only one other person in the room, an older gentleman with silver grey hair and moustache, resting in a comfortable chair. The old man had the most venerable face Bernard had ever seen. His firm, yet fine sculpted features, lively eyes, and high, broad-shouldered physique all led him to the same conclusion, that this man must have been handsome in his youth.

"Grandpa, will you permit me to introduce this gentleman to you?" Amelia asked, addressing the stately-looking Cavalry Master Hugo von Löwenklau, the former favorite of the old Field Marshall von Blücher. "He was kind enough to return my fan, which I had forgotten at a friend's house."

"Go ahead, my child," Hugo invited.

She curtsied and nodded to her grandfather with a smile. "May I present Herr Haller, a painter from Stuttgart."

The old man's eyelids sank momentarily. Was it so that no one would notice his surprise at hearing the visitor's name? Almost immediately, his eyes opened again, fixed on the newcomer while examining him with a sharp, probing look.

"Welcome, Herr Haller," he said, nodding to him. "You have rendered my grandchild a significant favor. Please take a seat. And a hearty welcome, my dear Madelon. Does the gentleman know who I am, Amelia?"

"I shouldn't think so."

"Then announce me, child."

"Please, sir," Bernard cut in, waving his hand dismissively. "There is no need for formality. The lady addressed you as her grandfather."

"Indeed, I am her grandfather."

"So, Herr Löwe, then?"

"Löwe?" asked the old cavalry master, surprised. He cast a quick glance at Amelia, catching her disguised smile fading quickly. "No doubt this is another one of your little pranks," Hugo qualified, stroking the ends of his large moustache. "Am I right? Did you know, Herr Haller, that young, unfettered ladies are difficult to tame? My name is not Löwe, but Löwenklau."

Bernard's face visibly paled. "Löwenklau?" he questioned. "Fräulein Köhler introduced me to this lady," he said, pointing to Amelia, "as Fräulein Löwe."

"Then it's clearly a matter of a young lady's playfulness. Amelia, Amelia! I should punish you."

"I plead for mercy, dearest Grandpa. It was so amusing to be mistaken for a governess."

"You were mistaken for a governess?"

"Yes, Aunt Goldberg's governess."

"Who supposed such a thing?"

"This man," she smiled, pointing to Bernard. "And his friend, that funny little painter, Hieronymus Aurelius Schneffke. Remember, I told you about him yesterday."

Bernard felt like he was in a dream. But the burning in his ears reminded him that he was wide awake, trapped in an embarrassing situation. *How have I gotten myself into this?* he thought. *I, an officer in the French Guard! If they only knew my true identity.*

"Excuse me, sir," he nearly blurted out. "It wasn't I who mistakenly held this lady for a governess, but my bumbling colleague, Schneffke.

My meeting up with him was purely coincidental and any further contact between us will likely remain infrequent."

"On the contrary, Herr Haller," replied the old man. "It's not incumbent on you to apologize. That obligation clearly rests with these two irrepressible women. Unfortunately, I have no authority over that little Madelon, but the other one resides under *my* roof, and I will find a suitable punishment for her." He considered for a moment. "Perhaps one week of house arrest will curtail her desire to carry out more pranks on unassuming gentlemen."

"Grandpa! Am I really such a conniving madcap?"

"Herr Haller may decide your fate."

Bernard bowed respectfully to both women. "I plead for leniency," he said.

"Well, in that case, I will exercise my right and show leniency. But in no way on your account, you wild bird," he said, directing his gaze back at his granddaughter. "I dare not dismiss the plea of our guest. Löwe instead of Löwenklau. Who would have thought such a thing?"

"If you will permit me a question," Bernard interrupted, "is it Löwenklau or von Löwenklau?"

"Von Löwenklau, sir. I am a retired cavalry master."

Ah, here I am, Bernard thought, *in the very midst of the family I've desired to be introduced to. What a wonderful coincidence!* Bernard, of course, had no clue he was already known to all and that the 'playful girl' was merely toying with him. *I should be able to deal with her and the old man easily enough. If I more or less play along with her easygoing character and come into the old man's good graces by paying heed to his war stories and past military accomplishments, I should have great success.* Unknown to him, though, Amelia was by no means the prankster her grandfather was making her out to be—she was, in fact, a serious-minded woman—and neither was the cavalry master himself so unassuming as he supposed.

"So, a cavalry master by the name of Löwenklau," Bernard repeated. "You must be the well-known officer who distinguished himself during the Napoleonic War and shared friendship with the renowned Field Marshall Forward himself."

"Yes, I was fortunate enough to find myself in his favor. We certainly gave those Frenchmen a solid thrashing."

"And how! Let's hope they have learned something from it."

Hugo shrugged. "Hmm, perhaps, though history tells us that people become forgetful. We are only human, after all."

"Do you think the French are looking for revenge?"

"If they are, it's not because of the Napoleonic War. More likely, it's over Sadowa. But that would be unlucky for Germany."

This piqued Haller's interest. "Oh, why do you say that?"

"Because the French would cook our goose."[3.1]

"Speaking as a loyal German, I somehow doubt that."

"Do you suppose I am any less a patriot than you, Herr Haller? But then you're an artist and I am a former military man. As such, I see things quite differently. Even though I'm no longer involved in the regular affairs of the army, my grandson Richard gives me an opportunity now and then to listen to matters at hand and voice my opinion."

"Is your grandson also in the military?" asked Bernard, doing his best to sound casual.

"Yes, he's a cavalry master in the Ulanen regiment and currently assigned to the general staff. Unfortunately, he's away on a holiday just now. Some of his recent work for the high command confirms what I have suspected all along: we need to avoid a confrontation with France. His manuscripts and notes are probably still in his study. I would like to spend more time going over them, but my eyes have lost their acuity and are no longer as sharp as they once were. Sadly, Amelia doesn't have the patience to read me his detailed accounts and letters. I've become too used to being alone. The ladies would much rather spend an evening at a ball or the opera than with an old man. Perhaps you could avail yourself of your time and visit me once in a while?"

Bernard smiled upon hearing exactly what he'd been hoping for: an invite to his residence. According to the old man's words, there might even be an opportunity to read some of those documents.

"Many thanks, Cavalry Master," Bernard said quickly in acceptance. "I am a stranger in this big city, and it will take some time for me to get settled in the social circles. Your kind words mean a lot to me."

"I'm happy to hear it. You're welcome here as often as it pleases you. We can play chess, read, or simply enjoy each other's company. Amelia, do you have anything special in mind for tonight's supper?"

Amelia smiled at him lopsidedly. "I would think we're not going to starve, Grandpa."

"That's reassuring, isn't it," Hugo murmured, with a smile on his lips. "Herr Haller, if you're not already engaged, would you do us the honor of dining with us? I have to find a suitable way to remedy the prank that was played on you."

"I remain completely at your disposal, sir."

"Shall we say eight o'clock then?"

"Eight o'clock would suit me fine."

In the meantime, Hugo had risen from his seat, a sign that the current discussion was drawing to a close. Bernard, happy with the outcome, also rose.

"I ask for your leave," Bernard said. "My regards to the ladies and, once again, thank you, Herr von Löwenklau." He shook the old man's hand, kissed Amelia's offered fingertips, and nodded a friendly goodbye to Madelon before heading back out the door.

Once he was downstairs, he collected his hat from the porter and, feeling particularly satisfied, tipped the man with a thaler. *By God, that was a fortunate meeting*, he thought. *And to think I was concerned about making my way into this tight-knit family. But now everything is in place. It worked itself out so easily. After all, this old military man seems approachable enough. He holds me for a military ignoramus, from whom he need not keep his secrets. I suspect he longs for male company now that his grandson is away, and so will probably engage me in conversation without holding back. Victory is close at hand.*

⁂

"So that was the man you encountered in the Tharandt Forest," the old cavalry master observed once Haller had left. "And you had no idea who he was at the time?"

Amelia turned to her grandfather and sat down next to him. "No idea at all. How could I? We were never introduced."

"How did you become entangled with him again?" Hugo asked.

"Believe it or not, he has rented one of the suites where Madelon lives. You know, in Ingrid Schüller's house. I visit them occasionally and today, somehow, I left my fan behind." Amelia proceeded to explain the events of the day while Hugo listened attentively.

"That worked out very smoothly," he remarked once she finished. "Now then, we'll have to supply him with information so that he thinks olives taste like chocolate. I'm rather looking forward to this evening. Just make sure you do an excellent job with dinner. These Frenchmen are renowned for their refined palates."

"Unfortunately, it's possible I won't even be here tonight, Grandpa."

Hugo looked at her surprised. "Where else would you be?"

"Away on a trip."

"*Sapperlot*! Where are you off to now? You've just returned from a trip."

"I'll be going far, far away," she said apologetically. "All the way to France."

"Are you mad?"

"Not at all." She smiled and glanced over at her friend. "Madelon will be traveling as well."

"To France?"

"Yes, to her stepfather's funeral."

"And you think you're going to accompany her?"

"Yes."

The old man shook his head. "Nothing will come out of it, child. Nothing at all. I suppose Madelon has to go. After all, the man raised both girls and they owe him this gesture, to show their final respects. But how does this concern you, my dear?"

"You think I want to accompany her on her stepfather's account? That's priceless. No, no, I have an entirely different reason, one much more urgent. Isn't it, dear Madelon?"

Her friend threw her a mixed look, half-concerned and half-relieved. "But you haven't said a word to him of your real intentions," she reminded her.

"I wanted to wait until I could speak to my grandfather here, in private." Then, turning to face Hugo, she continued, "Yes, dear Grandpa, it's quite important that I embark on this journey. Think of it, one of the lion's teeth has inexplicably surfaced."

"A lion's tooth? I'm not following you."

"Here, read this letter," she announced, taking the envelope from Madelon's outstretched hand and handing it to Hugo. The cavalry master's eyes were by no means as weak as he had feigned earlier to Haller, and his mind was still sharp, always attentive.

He unfolded the letter and began to read. As he progressed down the page, his facial expression exhibited more and more tension. When he finished, Hugo rose from his chair and, without saying a word, began to pace back and forth across the room, as was his custom when he became preoccupied with extraordinary circumstances. Amelia knew better than to interrupt him, so she allowed him all the time he needed to organize his thoughts. Once he had found clarity and came to a decision, she knew he would openly share his thoughts.

The two women sat quietly, waiting for him to address them. At last, he stopped pacing and halted in front of them, striking his fists together.

"Isn't this incredible, Amelia?" he beamed. "Simply extraordinary!"

"God still performs miracles, Grandpa."

"Yes, indeed. Could it be him?"

"Perhaps. The inscription is missing though."

"That's what I was getting at," Hugo said. "Even if they were mentioned, the possibility still exists that the lion's tooth has changed hands and come into possession of strangers."

"Yes, the thought has occurred to me," Amelia said with a nod.

"Just think of it!" Hugo exclaimed excitedly. "We've been searching for the boys all these years only to find that one of them has been in our midst the whole time. Haven't I always insisted that Franz bears a striking resemblance to the general?"

"Always."

"And then there is something else, just as incredible. Have you taken a closer look at this painter, Haller?"

"Of course. I suppose you're referring to his resemblance to Franz?"

"Yes. It's uncanny," Hugo agreed. "They look exactly alike, like two eggs placed next to each other. Could it be mere coincidence, a trick of nature? I don't know how else that Frenchman could look so much like him."

"Even his voice sounds like Franz's."

"Have you noticed that too? I heard it right away," Hugo noted. "So, Richard's servant is supposedly in possession of one of the lion's teeth. The letter says it's the right tooth, which would make him the firstborn. But can we say anything to Kunz or Hedwig?"

"Impossible!" Amelia objected. "We need more proof, Grandpa."

Hugo nodded gravely. "You're quite right. The old wounds could easily reopen, and we still don't know for certain if we're in a position to make a convincing argument. We have to examine the tooth itself, as well as the miniature portraits."

"That is why someone has to travel there," Amelia persisted. Madelon nodded, agreeing with her friend.

"Richard is already there," he suggested, looking pensive. "We could notify him, write him a letter."

"Are you willing to trust such an important edict to the mail service, especially in these uncertain times, with a war looming?"

"You're right again, Amelia. Damned irritating—too bad it's so far away. So, Franz has confided in Nanon. If only he had confided in Richard."

"Perhaps he intends to," Madelon suggested.

"But that still wouldn't be enough," Amelia continued. "We have to determine two things: first, if the tooth is really genuine, and second, if Franz is one of the kidnapped boys."

"Right. Then there's that trapeze artist, Eloise. It's a damned shame she has died," Hugo acknowledged, referring back to Nanon's letter.

Amelia's eyes widened in agreement. "She could have clarified a lot of things."

"Or that Bajazzo,[3.2] that clown… he's got a lot to answer for. We have to get a hold of him. I still think it's worth sending a letter to Richard."

Amelia looked steadily at Hugo. "No! The best and surest course of action would be to send someone."

"But who? We can't possibly inform the Goldbergs, and a private investigator is out of the question. That leaves you and me. Should I embark on this journey, at my age?"

"Not you, Grandpa. *I* must go."

"What? Girl, you can't be serious. Such a winged creature, one that hasn't learned to fly properly, and now she wants to flap her wings all the way to France?"

She raised herself up to her full height. "Madelon wants to fly there, too."

"Perhaps but consider the danger."

"What danger?"

"There's danger everywhere. Look how it went for me."

"That all happened in wartime," she reminded him.

He gave her a slight nod. "Yes, but some of it occurred during a break in hostilities."

"Perhaps, but it *was* still war."

"And then there was your father, my only Gebhard, who journeyed to that damned country, never to return."

"I know," Amelia replied gently. "Still, that undertaking was as dangerous as it was adventurous."

"Even his trustworthy servant Florian didn't return. The devil claimed them both."

It dawned on Amelia that her grandfather was afraid of losing another family member. Richard was behind enemy lines, even though war hadn't been declared yet. That left only her, his other grandchild. "Grandpa, what we have in mind is neither dangerous nor adventurous."

"I fail to see it that way."

"All I have to do is to travel to Thionville and speak to Franz. I will avoid seeing Richard, so as not to expose him unnecessarily."

"You could end up drowning in the Mosel, just as Richard nearly did. Remember?"

"But I won't be going by steamship."

"Maybe the train will derail, and I'll never see you again."

Amelia took Hugo's face into her hands. "Grandpa, weren't you one of those fierce and feared Zieten Hussars?"

"Of course!" he confirmed, his eyes shining. "I dare say that the old Hussar's blood runs through your veins."

"Indeed! I am the daughter of a military family."

"That's true," he said. "I know you're not afraid of going on this trip."

"You're forgetting about Madelon," she said, motioning to her. "She will travel with me."

"Yes, she'll be a good companion. She could come to your aid if you're accosted by another portly painter," he joked, his earlier concern for her waning. This prompted a smile from Madelon.

Amelia appeared relieved. "By the way," she added, "do you know what else I've thought about?"

"As far as I know, you girls only think of one thing," he quipped.

"Really? You know us women that well? I'm sure you're wrong this time, Grandpa."

"All you young girls think about is marriage."

"Absolutely," she laughed, joined by Madelon. "That's what I meant."

"*Sacrement!* I certainly hope you're not thinking of going to France to marry one of those Frenchmen."

"Well, why not, so long as he's rich."

Löwenklau's face clouded. "What? That's totally out of the question. I won't tolerate a Frenchman in my family."

"Grandpa," she said kindly, "didn't you yourself bring a Mademoiselle back home? And so did my father… as well as Uncle Kunz."

"But it was a good woman in each case. That's different. After all, over there in France, it's the women who carry the responsibility of common sense and understanding, while here in Germany, it's us men."

"Thanks for the compliment," she said, feigning injury from his insult. "But now, I want you to calm yourself. Rest assured that I have no desire to find myself a French lover. But then, you should concern yourself with Richard."

"Him? Oh, we don't have to worry about him in that regard. He hasn't so much as looked at a woman. He won't go near them. He hasn't been to a ball or other social function in months. He doesn't waste his time on such pursuits."

Amelia raised an eyebrow. "Do you really think so? I beg to differ. I know him better than you do."

"Be quiet, little mouthpiece."

"What!?" She fell into another fit of laughter. "I forbid you to patronize me with one of Blücher's idioms."

"Blücher wasn't afraid to speak his mind and to act when it really mattered. Now we have to abide by this new parliament, which prefers to resolve issues in a salon rather than on a battlefield. The only sane one among them is Bismarck." He paused, realizing he had strayed from the subject at hand. "Where were we? Right, Richard's lack of a love interest. So, you're of a different opinion?"

"Quite different!"

"I suppose you have something tangible to support your position?"

"Perhaps," she said evasively.

"*Zounds!* So, you've noticed something. Out with it, girl."

"It's more than something I merely 'noticed.' In fact," she added, unable to hide her smile, "I learned it from the surest source—Richard himself."

The old cavalry master played with the ends of his moustache. "Did he let the cat out of the bag? Surely it was a prank, something not immune to your doing."

"A prank? Richard? He'd never do that."

"Are you implying that he's romantically involved? That he's interested in a woman?"

"Yes, something like that," Amelia said, still smiling. Madelon, who had been following the *téte-a-téte* with interest, leaned forward to catch every word.

"What does that mean?" Hugo asked. "Something like what?"

"Look, Grandpa. One can be romantic without being in love or having a lover."

Hugo waved his hand dismissively. "You're splitting hairs. What minute differences are you trying to conjure up?"

"Well, if he likes a girl, then she is his friend. A female acquaintance if you like. But still not his lover."

"Why not?"

"She could only be his lover if the feeling was mutual."

"Girl, have you been studying the philosophy of love? Have you suddenly become an expert?"

"Just a little."

"Through personal experience?"

Amelia leaned in and put a hand on her grandfather's knee. "Not yet, Grandpa, don't worry. But I have managed to observe a thing or two. Take a look at our dear Madelon, for example."

Hugo's eyes darted to Madelon, whom he had nearly forgotten still sat opposite them. "Aha! Do you have a friend, perhaps a sweetheart?" he asked.

Madelon blushed. "That remains to be seen."

"So, so. Who is the fellow?"

When Madelon failed to respond, Amelia jumped back in. "It's that painter, Herr Haller."

"Heavens! The same man who was just here?"

"Yes, him."

"Amelia!" Madelon pleaded, turning red and sinking deeper into the sofa.

"Yes, Grandpa, it's true. You should have seen her face when I called him a dangerous person."

Hugo's glance alternated between the two women. "Did she defend him?" he asked his granddaughter.

"And how! But getting back to Richard..." Out of the corner of her eye, Amelia saw Madelon flush with relief at the change in subject. "He shared something with me recently, though I've had to keep quiet about it."

"So, you promised him to keep it to yourself?" Hugo asked.

"Yes, not a word to anyone."

"Then keep your word, girl."

Amelia hesitated. "But the circumstances have changed, you see."

"Does that mean you've already blabbed about it?"

"Well, only to my aunt."

"There you have it," Hugo roared good-naturedly. "Not a word to anyone but you blabbed it to your aunt. Don't you know that it's the aunts you can confide in the least?"

"Well, she was quite thrilled to hear the news."

Hugo nodded vigorously. "Of course! What woman wouldn't be eager to catch a glimpse into a romantic secret?"

"She even agreed to come with me and have a look for herself."

"Who can make any sense out of all this nonsense, girl?"

"You, you… old Blücher. I was speaking about the place where Richard first saw his lady."

"Ah, so that's it. *Sapperment*! So, he fell for her? Well, who could have predicted that? Love is like mustard for the peppered pickles of life. One isn't palatable without the other. And that's what he talked to you about? I find that hard to believe."

"But it's the truth, Grandpa!" she protested.

Though the former cavalry master was normally quiet and reserved, he was unusually talkative this day. He was in fine form, a rarity since Margot's death and the loss of his only son.

"Hmm. You're not making this up, are you?" he questioned, searching her face.

"No, not in the least."

"Then I'm pleased. There is still hope for my grandson. Come here, Amelia. You deserve a kiss for that." He hugged her joyfully and kissed her on the mouth. It was a precious sight. Hugo, the old patriarch, still an imposing figure, and Amelia, the passionate, beautiful girl.

"Should I share with you a few of the details?" she teased.

"I thought you were supposed to keep quiet about it."

Amelia took a deep breath. "I know, but there's something I need to tell you. Let's start with the locale."

"Yes. So, where did they meet?"

"On the road between Dresden and Blasewitz."

"Really? Why out there, on the open road?"

"Didn't you first meet Grandmother in the street?" Amelia asked.

"Hmm. I hadn't considered that. You're right, of course." Turning to Madelon, he offered a fuller explanation. "She was being accosted by a couple of Russian soldiers. I simply acted on instinct and took her under my protection, later escorting her home. But how did it fare for my Richard?"

"He was on horseback," Amelia continued, "out for an afternoon ride with several fellow officers. She was riding in a coach, coming toward him. Fast, like the wind, they passed by each other, and yet he caught her eye, and in that brief moment he felt a stirring in his heart."

"Oh, dear child. Fast like the wind—stirring in his heart—what can come out of such a brief moment?"

She leaned back and ran her fingers through her hair. "Then you don't know our Richard."

"But my dear Amelia, you can only win another's heart by talking to them and looking into their eyes."

"Not always. Love, after all, is supposed to be a wonderful experience."

"And difficult to grasp, that's true. So, it happened that quickly? Has he seen or talked to her?"

She shook her head.

"And still he got caught on her fishing hook?" Hugo asked.

"Quite steadfastly."

"Then he's a fool, a dreamer, even a fanatic. We should feel sorry for him."

"Richard, prone to fantasies, a fanatic?" Amelia wondered, breaking up laughing. "Far from it, Grandpa. Yet he's no less caught up in it. From that day forward, he hasn't been able to stop thinking about her."

"What use is that? He's got to find her and talk to her."

"I know. And that's exactly what happened."

Hugo sighed in relief. "Thank God! Finally, we're getting somewhere." Then, as if remembering a detail, he qualified, "But he hasn't been back to Dresden since."

"It wasn't necessary. Love has its own ways. In his first letter from Ortry, he wrote to say that he had unexpectedly found his love there."

"In that place—Ortry. Oh no! Does she live there?"

"Perhaps."

A look of horror crossed the old man's face. "She can't belong to *that* man's family. Surely, she's not one of the Sainte-Maries? I can't believe Richard would fall for such a woman. That alone gives me reason to worry."

"Now do you finally see? That's what I've been trying to tell you."

"Why?" he asked, with a pained expression. "To cause me endless grief?"

"Yes!"

"Fiend that you are."

"Well, will you then let me go on the trip?"

Her grandfather glowered at her. "Why should I say yes?"

"Isn't it obvious? I have to see this woman for myself. I have to take up my brother's cause. I have to get to know her."

"You? What will you be able to accomplish? Do you think you can prevent some calamity from befalling Richard?"

"Yes. Certainly, much sooner and easier than a man could. Believe me, Grandpa, a woman's intuition can perceive things a man cannot, and a soft word can have more impact than the strongest word spoken by any man."

"Look at you. You act like you've become an authority on the subject."

"But I'm right, aren't I?"

He considered that for a moment, his mood recovering again. "Your flattery and persuasiveness are irrefutable. Now that I think about it, a kind word from my Margot often produced a greater effect on me than anything else could."

"So, may I go with Madelon, Grandpa?"

"Are you that committed to going?"

"Without a doubt."

Hugo mumbled into his moustache and resumed his pacing. It took a few minutes, but he finally spun on his heel like a Hussar on a parade square.

"All right. You may go," he announced. Amelia flew into his arms and kissed him repeatedly, stroking his cheek. "That's fine," he said with a smile, enjoying the attention. "You're nearly crushing me and chewing on my moustache. You really have inherited a spirited disposition from my blessed Margot. That's exactly how she used to do it when she got her way with me."

Amelia was overcome with affection for her grandfather. It was touching for her to see him still thinking of his late wife, who had meant so much to him and wielded such powerful influence in his life.

Before she could go, he put up a hand to caution her. "Now, you have to approach this in the right way. Are you going only as far as Diedenhoffen, or all the way to Ortry?" he asked.

"My plan is to wait and see, Grandpa."

"Then look after yourself. No one in Ortry can find out you're a Löwenklau."

Amelia nodded gravely, taking his warning to heart. "I know it." She cast a fleeting glance at Madelon, who was sitting back on the divan, trying to take it all in. It dawned on Amelia that her friend was now privy to sensitive information and was as likely as she to become involved in unknown and potentially dangerous situations.

"Most of all, you can't expose Richard. If you were to be recognized, it could ruin everything and place both of you in great danger. Just be careful."

"Yes, Grandpa, I'll be careful." She paused, trying to remember what else she had purposed to mention. Finally, it came to her. "One last thing. I will need traveling funds."

"Of course. When are you planning to leave?"

"Madelon's train is scheduled for a three o'clock departure."

"And you want to go with her?"

"Of course!"

Hugo rubbed his eyes tiredly. "It's all happening too fast, girl…"

"Didn't you know that since the new war deployment measures were introduced, our own mobilization has been second to none? And that goes for women, too," she teased, using a military reference to draw Hugo's favor.

"You're a little witch! Well, go on then. At least I'll be glad to avoid the usual madness that accompanies you ladies when you pack."

"Oh, I'm already set to go," she insisted. "I've barely unpacked my last suitcase. All I need are a few clothes, some undergarments. I'll just throw them on the back of the fiacre and we're off."

"Very well. Forward! Like old Blücher used to say."

True to her word, Amelia immediately went to pack. Even Madelon rushed home to complete her own preparations.

⊱✠⊰

Amelia and Madelon met each other on the platform shortly before the train's scheduled departure. They were thrilled to be able to travel together.

"Shall we ride in the ladies' carriage?" asked Madelon.

"No," Amelia replied. "Although I do prefer the non-smoking coach. It's often an advantage on such long trips to avail oneself of the experience and companionship of seasoned travelers."

Before long, their luggage was stowed, and their tickets stamped by the conductor. The old cavalry master had insisted on accompanying both ladies to the railway station and made sure they were settled in their carriage before he left. After one last kiss for his grandchild and a handshake for Madelon, he disembarked.

The train's bell rang for the second time and the already-closed door was hastily reopened. The ladies heard the conductor's voice carrying through into their compartment: "Non-smoking carriage this way, sir."

This last passenger was short and rotund. He wore a grey traveling suit, eclipsed by a large Calabrese hat. He wore pince-nez down on his nose and bore a large map folder under his left arm, with a small case in his right.

"Ladies, your humble servant," he greeted, climbing aboard. "Please, there's no need for you to move over. I don't require much room."

Amelia coughed conspiratorially, alerting her companion.

"Do you know him?" whispered Madelon from underneath her veil.

"Oh, only too well."

"Who is he?"

"The most jovial man you'll ever meet. Hieronymus Aurelius Schneffke."

"Dear God! We're doomed."

Amelia giggled softly. "I fear something will break or collapse in here, giving that unlucky fellow another opportunity to fall at my feet and prove his undying devotion."

"Maybe we should leave this carriage while we still have the time," Madelon suggested.

"Not yet. Let's wait and see what happens. Perhaps he's not traveling far."

Meanwhile, the painter stowed his belongings above him, taking his seat across from them. Just as the ladies were starting to relax, he hollered without warning, "*Sapperlot!* My umbrella," he lamented. "I must have left it on the bench. That's plain as pudding." He jumped out of his seat, reached through the open window, opened the door from the outside, and squeezed his plump body out.

"I have a feeling his encounter with bad luck is about to start," laughed Amelia.

"In any event, it looks like we're going to be rid of him," Madelon offered. "The bell just rang a third time. He won't make it back in time."

"Holy paintbrush and palette!" Schneffke's voice was heard exclaiming from outside the carriage. "Who's holding me back?"

He was being held back by his coattail, which had become entangled with the doorknob. A powerful tug set him free again, but the momentum propelled him forward faster than his short legs could carry him. He tripped and fell flat on his large stomach. He was about to head into the station lobby to retrieve his umbrella when suddenly he felt himself held back again, this time by the quick-thinking conductor.

"Hold it! Where are you going, sir?"

"To the lobby. I've left my umbrella behind."

"There is no time. It has already sounded a third time. The train is leaving."

"But I've got to fetch it."

The conductor shrugged indifferently. "Then you will miss the train."

"Tarnation! What to do?" As he looked back at the train, he spotted his severed piece of clothing. "Damn, and there hangs my coattail."

"Well, in or out?" beckoned the conductor. "Listen, the machinist is giving the signal."

"Alright, in God's name, back inside then."

"But hurry!"

Even though the conductor was willing, it didn't happen quickly. The fat fellow reached for the handrail, heaved, panted, and pulled himself upward while the conductor pushed with all his might. The wheels were starting to spin and the train would be moving at any moment. Hieronymus managed to climb aboard just in time, with the conductor slamming the door shut behind him.

In order to watch the spectacle unfold, Amelia, still seated in the coupé, had lifted her veil. The jolly painter looked about him once he regained his place and recognized the familiar face. A wide, delightful grin spread across his face.

"The honor is all mine, Fräulein Löwe. It pleases me to see that once again, I can—Heavens!" he exclaimed. Schneffke had intended on making a formal bow but found himself hindered in the attempt. Something or someone was holding him back yet again. He tried to turn around and find the culprit, but it was a difficult maneuver. After a valiant effort, he turned sufficiently to find the hindrance. To his horror, he found that the conductor, in his hurry to secure the door, had jammed his other coattail in the door.

"Well, if that doesn't take the cake," he said, annoyed. Laughing to himself, he announced, "The trip is starting in a most pleasant fashion. Are you ladies traveling far?"

Amelia and Madelon tried their hardest not to breakout laughing. Amelia decided to break it to him gently, dashing his hope of accompanying them.

"We're heading all the way to France, sir," she replied evenly.

"That's wonderful," he beamed. "Me too, me too! Naturally, we'll travel together."

Of course, he had to remain standing in place until the train reached the next station, at which time he could be freed from his temporary confinement.

CHAPTER FOUR

THE PLANT COLLECTOR

It was the dawning of a beautiful day in the countryside surrounding Castle Ortry, in the heart of France. The sun kissed the dew from the leaves and grass, leaving behind only a remnant of golden drops in the depths of a flower's chaliced blossom. The morning was progressing rapidly, the sun rising higher and higher in the sky.

Marion de Sainte-Marie spent much of her time in her brother's company, paying attention to Doctor Müller's lessons. It was unclear if she was doing it out of a sister's love or if she had merely succumbed to the interesting material in the boy's studies. She herself couldn't say for sure. Meanwhile, Nanon Köhler enjoyed occupying her time taking leisurely walks through the forest. To her, it was carefree, simple, and less confining than the stuffy room of the library. When in nature, she was surrounded by all sorts of plants and wildflowers, and if she was fortunate, prone to a visit by one who could pluck and relegate them to his large sack.

There was one particular place that she favored above all, the one where she had first met Franz Schneeberg after losing her way in the forest. Likewise, Franz never plunked himself down for a rest before reaching the same clearing. On this day, Nanon slowly made her way between the trees, singing her favorite song, neither too softly nor too loudly.

"Southward far the fair Espana

is my home, my native land,
where the shadowy castana
rushes o'er the Ebro Strand.
Where the almonds bloom so blandly,
where the grape more ardent gleams,
and the roses blush more fondly,
and the moon sheds brighter beams."

She stopped to listen, hoping to catch an echo. Unfortunately, there was no hill or rock face to return her voice. She was fond of the echo, and not hearing one, she went on her way, undaunted, singing happily.

"With my lute I wander sadly
here from house to house alone,
but no friendly eye looks gladly,
kindly on the poor unknown.
Scant the pittance that they throw me,
and they turn me from their door;
none will hear me, none will know me,
me, the gipsy brown and poor."

Again, she stopped. A slight smile spread across her joyous face. Yet the sound she heard didn't emanate from a mountain or rocky crag. Clearly not, since the sound came back a full octave deeper, and the words were different too. Were there echoes that didn't require walls to reverberate? This particular one was unique in itself:

"Ah, these fogs depress and chill me,
for they hide from me the sun;
of the songs that used to thrill me,
I remember scarcely one.
Ever firmer, ever fonder
in my strains the cry is wove:
southward home I fain would wander
to the land of light and love!"

It wasn't an alto, but rather a powerful baritone voice. Nanon listened to get a sense of the direction and, when the last syllable had resonated, she started to move, faster than before. She headed for that special place. When she reached it, she found a sack replete with material and its owner, Franz, resting comfortably in the moss. Lying there, content and seemingly without a care in the world, he looked as though he was all alone in the vast forest. He was gazing absent-mindedly up at the blue sky, as if desiring to share his happiness with those already in the heavenlies. He continued,

> *"Lately at the feast of pleasure,*
> *while the harvest dance went round,*
> *there I played my gayest measure,*
> *strung my lute to sweetest sound.*
> *But amid the mirth and gladness,*
> *as the sun set bright and gold,*
> *down my brown cheeks tears of sadness*
> *rapidly and hotly roll'd."*[1]

"Good morning, Monsieur Schneeberg!" Nanon called.

Hearing the voice behind him, Franz jumped up, looking surprised to see her. "Ah, it's you, Mademoiselle," he said, relieved. "A good morning to you as well. And here I thought I was all alone."

"Is that why you sang so beautifully?"

"Beautifully?" he asked, pretending to disagree with her assessment. "Hardly. I've never taken singing lessons."

"Still, your voice is most charming."

He cocked his head. "But only as good as a plant collector's can be."

"Like always, you are most humble. Did you know you were singing my favorite song?"

"Really? It hadn't occurred to me." And yet, he had known exactly that, as she had mentioned it on previous outings. "Ah! So that's what I heard in the distance. It reminded me of a heavenly song."

"Go on! You're joking."

Franz placed his hand over his heart. "I couldn't be more serious," he assured her. "It sounds different when you sing it. Your vocal cords are much more subtle and suited for singing." By this time, she had come closer, extending her small soft hand. "How soft and fine," he noted. "Like the finest silk. Such a dainty hand is something to behold."

"How come, Monsieur?"

"Fashioned by God's own hand, and yet it's forced to endure all varieties of earthly toil. It should serve only to entice the one who longs for it. Don't you agree?"

Nanon couldn't help but smile. "You speak in a manner which defies contradiction."

"And you show me by your kind words that I may be right."

There they stood, gazing into each other's eyes. He, the considerate, tall, and handsome man, and she, the lovely petite woman. Their eyes were fixed on each other as though meeting for the very first time. Nanon was content to gaze into his happy face, until Franz felt the need to say something.

"Aren't you tired, Mademoiselle Nanon?"

"Actually, no." Just then, she stifled a yawn. Her cheeks colored with embarrassment. "Well, maybe just a little," she admitted.

"Don't you want to take advantage of my lonely sack?"

"And crush your plants again? Surely your doctor will get annoyed."

Franz waved away her concern. "Oh, don't worry about him. He won't scold me."

"Because you're so good and accommodating to him?"

"No, not at all," he laughed. "It's because he thinks it won't do me any good. Come on! It will make you feel like you're sitting on the finest royal cushion."

Nanon gave in and sat down. "You're going to spoil me through and through."

"If only I could. I would be content to remain with you the entire year, looking after your comfort and well-being."

"Yes, that's exactly how you are, only concerned for the welfare of others. And we take advantage of you, my dear Monsieur Schneeberg."

He laughed again. "Oh, feel free to. I wish I could be of more service."

Her eyes met his, longingly. "Really? Are you serious?"

"Of course! Don't you believe me?"

"I do. I can tell that you loathe to contradict me or speak an untruth. But it's because you're so accommodating that I'm reluctant to state my plea, the one that's been on my heart."

Franz smiled at her, encouraging her to continue. "But that's exactly what I have in mind. I want to be able to fulfill your wishes."

"Still, I don't know if you would be in a position to fulfill my wish."

"Is it really so difficult? Why don't you try me?"

"No, not difficult, but timely."

He smiled and gestured all around him. "Well, I do have lots of time on my hands."

"Yes, for your wandering and gathering, but not for me."

"But of course, for you. Doctor Bertrand gives me plenty of leeway. Please, how can I help you?"

Nanon hesitated, but then decided to open up. "Well, I might as well tell you. You see, my father has just died."

"Your father?" he asked, shocked. "Dear God, but that's awful news."

"Actually, he's not my real father. He's my stepfather, my caregiver from when I was a child."

"Then you don't have your real parents anymore, Mademoiselle?"

"No, I'm an orphan."

"Just like me."

"Yes, just like you," she said, smiling.

Franz picked up her hand and gently stroked it. "I've heard it said that each child has a guardian angel; but an orphan has three, in place of an absent father and mother."

"I hope to draw some comfort from that. In any event, my caregiver, Albert Berteu, has suddenly died. The burial is the day after tomorrow, when I'll be joined by my sister."

"You have a sister?"

"Yes, a fine and lovely soul. I've already sent her a cable and expect her to arrive at the Thionville train station late tomorrow morning. Together we will travel to Metz, and then further to Etain. Think of it, all that way, just the two of us."

He frowned, clearly concerned. "That is unfortunate. Two ladies, and all alone."

"I'm not afraid, but one never knows what can happen. Just think of the last time we traveled on the Mosel."

Franz paused to reflect on the sinking of that ill-fated riverboat. "True, but who could have predicted we would experience such a calamity?"

"Since then, I've had the feeling I can only be safe when I'm in your company. Therefore, my dear Monsieur Schneeberg, I want to make a request, but it's difficult to bring up."

He smiled warmly. "Then I'll have to make it easier for you." He leaned in, so that their faces were just inches apart. "It would really make me happy if I could accompany you." Before she could express her joy, he put a finger to her lips. "But then I expect such a refined lady as yourself wouldn't want to travel in the company of a simple plant collector."

"No!" The word burst out of her like a torrent of water. "Nothing could be further from the truth. That's exactly what I had in mind, but I was reluctant to impose on you."

Franz beamed. "Really? Then our desires have intertwined themselves."

She smiled. "Will you have the time to spare?"

"As much as you'll need. All I have to do is arrange it with my employer. It shouldn't be a problem."

"Good. Will you be able to leave on the morning train?"

"Of course."

She put a hand on his cheek, stroking it affectionately. "Then we can meet at the station. I'm so excited to see my sister again. It has been several years since we've last seen each other. Did you know that I wrote to her about your lion's tooth? I thought she could make the necessary inquiries."

"Where does she live?"

"In Berlin."

At that, Franz started to pay more attention. "Berlin?" he asked. "Is she married?"

"No. She's a governess and currently employed by the Baroness von Hohenthal."

"Von Hoh—Hohenthal?" he asked, tripping over the name. He couldn't quite cover his shock at hearing it.

"Yes. Her son is with the Hussars, a cavalry master."

"Really? What is your sister's name?"

"Her name is Madelon," she said. "So, will you be able to accompany me?"

"Of course, I will."

"Then I should be going. Marion is probably waiting for me." Nanon rose and offered Franz her hand.

"Do you want to walk back alone?" he asked.

She nodded. "Yes. We will see each other tomorrow, and I don't want to take up any more of your time. Adieu."

"Adieu, Mademoiselle Nanon," he replied as they parted.

Franz remained standing in place. *Well, now what am I going to do?* he pondered. *Baroness Hohenthal's governess, Madelon, is her sister. She'll recognize me right away. And what's worse is that she'll immediately guess why we're here. What am I to do? The only thing to do is to approach my caval—I mean, Doctor Müller. He'll know what to do. This decision is too important for me to make on my own.*

CHAPTER FIVE

NEW DISCOVERIES

Franz Schneeberg hoisted the sack onto his shoulders and left the little secluded setting. As he headed back into town, he was reminded about the fortunate meeting with Doctor Bertrand in Trarbach. The good doctor had recognized both Franz and Richard (a.k.a. Doctor Andreas Müller) suspecting the purpose of their trip. Not only had Bertrand kept their confidence, but he offered Franz employment and provided him with accommodations, whereby he could be at Richard's disposal. Franz was in no way obligated to collect plants for Doctor Bertrand. Yet as often as his varied wanderings permitted, he would amass all sorts of plants and herbs and carry them home. Even on this day, he felt he should gather some specimens for a revitalizing tea or home-based remedy. It was considerably past midday when he at last returned to Thionville from his botanical excursion. After he delivered his plants, he headed for the local *Gasthaus*, the same one where he had met the boisterous performer, Eloise.

As Franz crossed the street, he spotted Doctor Müller on foot, as if he were out for a leisurely stroll. A quick nod from Franz was sufficient to tell Richard that he wished to speak with him. Franz was first to enter the tavern and headed to the backroom, so they wouldn't be disturbed. Richard was being careful as well. Rather than entering with Franz, he purposefully continued down the street, turned at the end and came in via the back alley. He crossed through the larger room and entered a smaller private room, where Franz was being served a glass of wine. Richard placed his order with the barmaid. Only after she had left the room did he approach Franz's table, taking a seat.

"Is there something you wished to tell me?" Richard asked quietly.

"Yes, *Doktor* Müller."

"Is it important?"

"Indeed," replied Franz showing a roguish face. "Well, a certain caregiver has suddenly died."

"A caregiver?" asked Richard, surprised. "Your caregiver?"

"No. I'm not aware of him having died twice," he said, grinning at his own joke. "I was referring to Mademoiselle Nanon's caregiver."

"What? I don't understand what you're getting at."

"Well, Nanon had been raised by a stepfather, a caregiver, in the vicinity of Etain. Apparently, he has recently died. She wants to attend his funeral, and I would like the pleasure of accompanying her."

"You, you…" Richard mocked, shaking his finger at Franz. "What am I supposed to think about that? I certainly hope that you're—"

"That I'm capable of escorting the lady?" interrupted Franz.

"Yes, but an old lady, a real old one. What could you possibly have in mind with a young and pretty one?"

"I only meant that a *herbossieur* accustomed to caring for plants and flowers might know a thing or two about courting a young lady."

"I see. So, you've made some progress?" Richard noted, smiling.

"I should think so. It's all because of my plant sack."

"What do you mean?"

"Because it serves as her cushion."

"Ah, now I get it. You met by accident in the woods, right?"

"Indeed."

"You plunk the sack down, have her take a seat and get her to talk."

"Naturally."

"Does she rest on that sack filled with plants?"

"Usually."

"And you sit beside her?"

"Quite often. Sometimes I even lie at her feet. My current job allows me to dispense with any form of etiquette."

"That's very convenient for you. What do you talk about?"

"Oh, the weather and the best way of wearing wooden shoes."

"Scoundrel! Don't you converse about more important things?"

"Of course, we do."

"Like what?" he prodded.

"We just look at each other. That's the most interesting conversation piece there is."

Richard looked at his servant quizzically. "Franz!" chided his master. "Don't tell me you've fallen in love."

"Heavens! Maybe that's what it is."

Richard laughed out loud. "What about Nanon? Does she feel the same?"

Franz's face lost some of that boyish bravado. "Not likely. How can such a tender little mouse get carried away by a big bear?"

"Exactly! There's nothing about your appearance that would invite a young girl's heart to open up."

"Really? You may have something there. Yes, I feel that I'm lacking the main thing that would awaken her admiration and respect."

"What would that be?"

"A hump, just like the one you're saddled with," Franz laughed.

"You're nothing but a half-wit," retorted Richard, but then joined in with laughter. "Let's leave this precarious and embarrassing topic. How long of a holiday will you need?"

"I'm not sure yet; though not more than two or three days."

"When do you plan on leaving?"

"Tomorrow, with the midday train."

"Alright. You can take a couple of days off." Richard pulled a leather satchel containing gold pieces from his pocket. "Here, take a few of these for your trip."

"Many thanks," smiled Franz, pocketing the money. "Now I can finally appear in finer circles, not having to hide from ladies. Oh, just one more thing. There's an old friend that will be travelling with us."

Richard perked up. "An acquaintance? From where?"

"From Berlin."

Richard looked puzzled. "Who could that be?"

Franz stretched out his legs and feigning importance proclaimed. "Yes, my worthy doctor, something that could prove quite unsettling for us. Who could have predicted such a thing?"

"You're making me curious. What happened?"

"Hmm. You're of course familiar with Cavalry Master Hohenthal's family?"

"Sure. I'm a good friend of the cavalry master."

"I know. No doubt you've seen his mother's governess?"

"You mean little Madelon?" Richard said, thinking back. "What about her?"

"Doesn't the name stand out?"

"Why should it stand out? Because it's French?"

"Yes. Do you remember her family name?"

"Hmm. I'm sure I've heard it before." Richard considered for a moment. "Yes, I recall how Arthur addressed her as Fräulein Köhler."

"Yes, that's her name. But that is also Nanon's last name, which leads to the obvious conclusion that—"

"That they're related?" intervened Richard.

"Yes, they're sisters."

The reality of the statement began to sink in. "Who could have predicted that? I had no idea. Are you implying that Madelon will be coming here?"

"Exactly. She too was raised by Berteu. Meanwhile, Nanon had cabled her, advising her of his death. Tomorrow, she will arrive with the noon-day train and join her sister for the trip to Etain."

"That is unfortunate."

"It could prove to be very awkward."

"Which means that you won't be able to accompany Nanon."

Franz nodded. "I've had the same thought. It would be better if she didn't come here at all. However, it still might be better if she meets me."

"How come?"

"Well, first, I've given Nanon my word. It wouldn't be easy to come up with an excuse now, and if truth be known, I want to accompany her."

Richard briefly thought back to his meeting with his superior in Simmern, where he was instructed to gather information about France's war preparations, while employed as a simple educator at Castle Ortry.

"I know, but your personal feelings have to bow to our obligations in fulfilling our assignment."

"I know that. But *Herr Doktor*, consider that the two sisters haven't seen each other in several years. After the funeral, it's quite likely Nanon will invite Madelon to spend a few days with her. Once they arrive here, it wouldn't be possible for either one of us to avoid being seen by her."

"Yes, you're quite right."

"It could prove to be quite dangerous. What if without thinking the young lady were to unconsciously blurt out your real name and title?"

"Yes, that would be disastrous. I would be unmasked."

"That's why I've thought it prudent to meet her beforehand and prepare her."

Richard thought about this. "Yes, that could work. But how can we explain our incognito presence to her?"

"We certainly can't divulge the real reason."

"Of course not. Surely you know a few details about my family's history?"

"Yes, bits and pieces that I've managed to learn over the years."

"Our old nemesis, Richemonte, has played a significant role—"

"I know," interrupted Franz. "Are you suggesting that I use him as a pretext for our presence here in Ortry?"

"Yes, I think that would be best."

"Alright. But what should I tell her?"

"I'll leave it up to you. You're clever enough to come up with the right explanation, without revealing too little or too much."

"So, Nanon can't find out that her sister knows me? That won't be easy."

"I know. I consider this Madelon to be a discreet and conscientious woman."

"Me too. I hope that she'll remain discreet, even with her own sister. Still, the moment of her arrival could prove to be an awkward one."

"Have you arranged to meet Nanon at the railway station?" asked Richard.

"Yes. Madelon is expecting to meet her there. I can picture it now: The compartment door will open, and both sisters will fly into each other's arms, while I'll look on like a klutz. Suddenly, Madelon will see me standing there, recognize me and call out, 'Heavens! It's our Fritz, the one from Blasewitz?'[5.1] I'll be recognized and unmasked in one fell swoop. Nanon will look at me dumb-founded and ask me to explain myself. An awkward scene, one that we'll have to avoid at all costs."

"You're quite right," Richard nodded thoughtfully. "There's only one way to remedy this predicament, so our presence here won't be compromised."

"What's that?" asked Franz.

Richard smiled, as if he'd just played his trump in a card game. "You'll just have to take an earlier train and meet Madelon sooner than planned."

"That's it!" exclaimed Franz, slapping his forehead. "And I should have thought of that myself."

"Don't worry about it. Now, her train arrives shortly after 12:00 pm. There are few places along the way, where the train stops. To be certain, you'll have to travel all the way to Trier, and that's only possible if you take the early morning train."

"Right. The train stops in Trier for about ten minutes. That should be enough time to discover which carriage she'll be travelling in."

"Just ask for the conductor's help," added Richard. "Once you've found her, you'll have plenty of time to advise her of the circumstances and prepare her for her meeting with her sister. I know I can depend on you."

"No worries, Doctor," Franz assured him. He glanced over his shoulder as if he'd heard something. "What brings you to town this afternoon?"

"I've come to purchase a few books from the book distributor." Richard cocked his head. "Listen. A new guest seems to have arrived."

They heard approaching footsteps next door.

"Is the barkeep around?" a manly voice addressed the barmaid.

"Yes," replied the girl.

"Then fetch me a glass of absinth and call him. You, however, can go back to your regular duties. We won't need you."

The girl turned and left on her errand.

"Ah, he desires a private meeting, or so it would seem," Richard noted. He walked up to the door and cast a glance at the newcomer through the crack in the opening. He saw a tall man, sporting a full dark beard, and even though he wore ordinary clothing there was something military-looking about him. The newcomer was leaning on the counter, slowly sipping the schnapps.

Richard and Franz remained still, resorting only to whispers. The stranger kept looking at the entranceway, growing more restless by the minute with the innkeeper's absence. At last, the barkeep showed up, wiping his hands on a towel.

"You kept me waiting for a long time," announced the stranger, none too pleased. "Lafleche, my time is short as it is."

"Ah, it's you, Cormier. I came as soon as I could. What's going on?"

"There's to be a meeting, tonight."

"Ah! No wonder you're pressed for time. Is the assembly for everyone?"

"No, just for the leaders."

"At what time?" asked Lafleche.

"Punctually, at eleven o'clock."

"Where? In the ruins?"

"No. That's no longer possible since we were spied on. I'd like to get my hands on that brazen fellow, whoever he was."

Richard and Franz looked at each other, recalling how Franz had nearly been caught. His escapade into the ruins late at night had provided useful information about the *franctireur*[5.2] organization.

"We've discussed it," Cormier continued, "and so far, we've come up with only one man."

"Really! Who do you suppose it is?"

"There's a local fellow who runs around all day through the forest, gathering plants and who knows what else. He's also been spotted among the ruins. Perhaps it was him the other night?"

"Him?" asked the barkeep, shaking his head. "He's not that bright."

"Do you know him?" asked Cormier.

"Of course. He stays with Doctor Bertrand while gathering plants and flowers for his apothecary practice. His name is Franz and drops by here all the time."

"What sort of a man is he?" asked Lafleche, his brow furrowed with skepticism.

"Oh, he's as dumb as a door post; but you know, he can drink like a fish. He rarely says anything and doesn't even play cards. He's a simpleton who only has a mind for one thing—his plant sack."

"He's lucky. If he even thought about sticking his nose into our affairs, we'd rub him out. Where does he come from?"

"From Geneva, the French speaking quarter. You don't have to worry about him."

"Alright. The old man is concerned and is thinking of having him watched. It's a good thing that I've talked to you. It'll put the captain's fears to rest."

"Good. So, we can't meet at the ruins. What about the old tower?"

"Out of the question," replied the messenger. "We can't risk it. Have you forgotten about those men who had dared to open the heathen's grave?"

"Oh, that's right," replied Lafleche. "You should have shot them."

"Pah! You're one to talk," Cormier said, irritated. "Unfortunately, the captain had misaligned the tripwire. It warned us too late of the intruders."

"Well, that only leaves us with the *trou du bois* for a meeting place."

"Yes, for the time being. So, until tonight, at eleven o'clock, in the *trou du bois*. Adieu!" He shook hands with the barkeep and left. The innkeeper saw him out and didn't return.

The two eavesdroppers looked at each other, but it was Franz looking the more pleased.

"*Bonne chance*! That went well, right?" he said, keeping his voice down.

"Very well," Richard acknowledged.

"The barkeep must not suspect that we overheard them."

"Right. We should close the door. That way he'll eventually notice our presence but won't catch on that we've overheard their conversation."

Franz walked over to the door, quietly closing it so the latch clicked into place, and returned to his seat. "So," he continued, "those fellows have become suspicious about my plant gathering activity. How fortunate that we overheard that part of their talk. Now I can prepare myself should I encounter either one."

"I'm just relieved that their suspicions didn't fall on me. Ever since the captain had seen me in the ruins, I feared he would single me out."

"They're having another meeting tonight," Franz reminded him. "If only we could overhear their plans."

"Yes. But at least we know its location …the *trou du bois*."

"That means, a hole or a depression in the woods. Are you familiar with such a place?"

"No. But I want to find out its location. This could be important."

"Your inquiries could be taken as suspicious, even intrusive," cautioned Franz.

"True. Perhaps on my way home I'll stop by at the forester's cottage."

"What if the forester is in cahoots with them?"

"I intend on speaking to his helper. He's young and inexperienced and won't become suspicious."

"So, what will you do once you find out its location? It could go badly for you, sir, if you get caught."

"I know. Still, it can't be helped. I'll have to risk it."

"But you could expose yourself to unnecessary danger, perhaps even get shot at?"

Richard looked steadily at Franz, whom he considered much more than a servant, more like a close friend or fellow officer. "I appreciate your concern, Franz. But consider what danger you had placed yourself in when you decided to infiltrate their meeting in the ruins? You didn't hesitate, did you? Just think of what could have happened if they had caught you?"

"Yes, it would have been Matthäi the Last[5.3] for me. I would have fought like a wild man. Please, send me instead to scout out the *trou du bois*."

At last Richard clued into what Franz was driving at, realizing that he was willing to place himself in danger for the sake of their mission.

"I commend you for your courage, but I still have to try myself."

"At least take me with you," pleaded Franz.

The cavalry master contemplated for a moment. "Don't you have to get some rest, in preparation for your trip with Nanon?"

"Pah! I'll survive on a few hours of sleep. I really do want to accompany you."

Richard didn't miss the sincerity of his plea. "Alright I'll allow you to come along."

"Great!" replied a relieved Franz. "Where will we meet?"

"Punctually at ten o'clock, at the place where the path from the castle leads into the forest."

"Will you be able to find out where this place is by then?"

"I hope so. Make sure that you come armed."

"Of course. Should I now quietly leave?"

"No. Let's wait for a while," Richard decided. "If we leave now, and the barkeep spots us, he may become suspicious. But if he sees us later, he may conclude that we had arrived after their meeting."

Richard took a sip of wine, savoring the nectar's taste.

"By the way, have you seen our old friend, Abu Hassan?"

"No."

"Ever since that encounter with the apparition, he's disappeared without a trace. If you see him first," instructed Richard, "come notify me right away."

"Are you intending to speak to him?"

"Yes. I have to clarify a few things. I regret that I wasn't more forthcoming with him. Now then, I want to have one final word with you about something else, Franz."

"I'm at your service, Doctor Müller."

"No, nothing to do with obligation. This is between friends. Tell me honestly. Are you in love with Mademoiselle Nanon?"

Franz turned red at the implication. He stared in front of him for a moment, and then shifted his trustworthy gaze toward Richard.

"That is a difficult question to answer. But what is love, true love?"

"Well," replied Richard laughing. "In matters of love, I'm just as ignorant as you are. I'm no closer to giving you an explanation about its magical effect."

"Is it called love, when you want to consume every part of her being from the first time you've laid eyes on her?"

"No. That's what I'd call a cannibal's appetite," he said, grinning.

"Or is it called love when that special someone has captured a piece of your heart, and you can't let her be?"

"Perhaps."

"Would you go through fire on her account and die a thousand deaths, if that were possible?"

"Hmm. I would think that it would be more expedient to live for her, rather than die for her."

"I can see that. But all in all, I believe I'm on the right track."

"Has it occurred to you what the consequences of your longing might lead to?"

"A wedding on one hand or a lonely existence on the other."

"Don't be ridiculous!"

"No, it's not what you think. If this girl doesn't want me, then I'd rather remain single."

"Is that your firm resolve?"

"Yes."

"And yet you waver. Consider who she is."

"A wonderful and chaste girl."

"Perhaps, but also a servant girl, one without a family or dowry."

"Do I have a family, or am I with means?"

"Franz," Richard sighed, "you know that I'm trying to unveil the mystery surrounding your birth."

"Perhaps it would be better to leave the veil in place," he replied stubbornly. "I'm a lucky fellow to have her and my uniform—I mean my sack. What's more, I can be content with being her protector. That's more than enough to make me happy."

"But what if it turns out that you really stem from nobility?"

"As significant as that would be, it still doesn't compare to the promise of being married to Nanon."

"Alright," conceded Richard, "let's leave it for now."

Richard's mind returned to Abu Hassan's troop. Hassan, the ringmaster had disappeared, leaving the authorities with little to go on in solving the acrobat's death. Bajazzo, the man responsible, had absconded with the circus's cashbox.

"If I manage to catch and detain that Bajazzo, I should be able to find—"

"You'll find that he was spinning tales," interrupted Franz. "Nothing more."

But before Richard could respond, the door opened with the barkeep poking his head in. When he spotted the two, his face turned a shade darker.

"Have you been here long?" he said, addressing Franz.

"You of all people should know," replied Franz in an unassuming tone.

"Me? I didn't see you come in."

"Sure, you did. When I first came in here, you were standing in the entrance."

"Really? I don't recall that."

"*Sapperlot!*" exclaimed Franz, looking puzzled. "Didn't you just ask me how long I've been here, in Thionville?"

A light went on in the barkeep's mind. "No, no, you've misunderstood me. I meant how long have you been sitting here, *today*."

"Oh! I didn't glance at the clock."

"Was someone in the other room when you came in?"

Franz made a face, as if trying to remember.

"Just the barmaid."

The innkeeper seemed to have lost some of his mistrust. Turning to face the other patron, he asked, "I've never seen you in here before, Monsieur. I'm called Lafleche. And you are?"

"Why the sudden interest?" asked Richard a little indignantly. "Does one have to identify himself simply because he wants a glass of wine?"

"No, not at all," replied the barkeep, back-pedaling. "But I like to become acquainted with my patrons. You see, it's incumbent of an innkeeper to know what goes on in his establishment as well as getting to know his customers' habits and desires."

"Perhaps," Richard said, sizing up the innkeeper. "As far as I'm concerned, I won't place demands on you. I have simple tastes. I am an educator."

"Ah! Do you teach nearby?"

"At castle Ortry," Richard confirmed.

A peculiar feeling worked its way through Lafleche's mind. He looked from one man to the other, not knowing how to proceed. At last, he ventured forth. "Then you must be the baron's new educator, Doctor Müller."

"Yes, I am," Richard replied.

"Aren't you the one who had saved our gracious mademoiselle from drowning?"

In a flash, Richard's mind raced back to that horrible day. He, along with a host of passengers, had been travelling on a steamboat on the Mosel River towards Trier. Upstream, a barge had inexplicable broken free of its moorings and later collided with the steamer. While a handful of French officers had brushed others aside and escaped in the sole lifeboat, Richard, along with Franz, had managed to save two women from drowning. He shuddered at the memory of the storm, of the raging river. All around him, the deluge impeded struggling swimmers, many of whom were struck by debris or simply succumbed to the torrent, their strength spent. By God's good grace, he had managed to elude the obstacles and swam with gargantuan effort, eventually finding safety on the river's bank, while holding a precious cargo in his arms: Baroness Marion de Sainte-Marie.

"True. I swam to shore, cradling the baroness in my arms," Richard said matter of fact, keeping to his cover of an educator, not revealing who he really was: Baron Richard von Löwenklau.

"And then the young baron, Alexandre?"

"I managed to prevent him from falling to his death, yes."

"You're a very courageous man," Lafleche uttered, as he examined him with skepticism.

"Pah! I was just doing my duty."

"Did you two meet by chance?" Lafleched asked, returning to the present.

"Yes, coincidentally," Richard said truthfully.

"Do you know each other?" continued the innkeeper.

That was a little too intrusive for Richard. He stood up and threw some coins on the table to cover his bill. "Leave your questions for schoolboys, but not for the one who's used to asking them. Adieu!"

"A rude fellow," remarked the inquisitive barkeep after the baron's educator had left.

"I agree," replied Franz.

"You saw that too, didn't you?"

"Of course. I nearly cuffed his ears."

The innkeeper looked up surprised. "How come?"

"Well, he came in the backroom just as I had taken a seat. Do you think that he bothered to greet me?"

"He didn't?"

"Far from it. I tried to start a conversation with him—"

"And he wasn't interested?" asked Lafleche, jumping in.

"No. I was being polite and brought up the weather. He didn't even bother to look my way. Then I talked about my plants, and things I had seen during my walks in the woods. Do you know what he told me?"

"No, tell me all about it," the barkeep encouraged, now drawn into the conversation.

"He told me to hold my tongue," Franz proclaimed with a hurt look.

"That was rude of him," Lafleche agreed, taking a seat.

"You bet. I was wondering why he didn't tell you the same thing. 'Hold your tongue', he said, as if I were a mouse or a dog. This fellow is supposed to be an educator, but from what I've seen, he'll make a mess of it with the young baron."

"It would seem so. But tell me, wasn't someone in the front room when you had come in earlier?"

"No," replied Franz truthfully.

"You haven't talked to anyone else?"

"No, just that rude fellow from the castle."

"That's fine then. I'm waiting for the mailman, but as you've just informed me, he hasn't shown up yet. Have you already been out in the woods collecting your plants?"

"Of course. I've been in the fields as well."

"Where are your favorite places?"

"What do you mean?"

"I mean, where do you like to stay best of all?"

"At home, in bed," replied Franz in a most unassuming tone. The barkeeper gave him a dour look.

"Monsieur, are you trying to make a fool of me?" Lafleche asked indignantly.

No, you're doing a good job all by yourself, thought Franz. "How come?" he asked instead, looking surprised. "Didn't you just ask me where I liked to spend my time?"

It dawned on the barkeep that he was dealing with a simpleton. "I meant," continued Lafleche calmer, "if there was a particular spot in the forest that appeals to you more than the rest."

Franz pretended to think about it for a moment. "Hmm, I only go to places where I can find my plants. Hard to find, out of the way places don't interest me."

"Have you been to the old tower?"

"No. It's down-right spooky there."

"Who told you that?"

"Everyone knows that."

"What about the old ruins, the ones in the middle of the forest?"

"Why would I go there? It's unlikely that I would find much growth there."

"Have you ever ventured to the *trou du bois*?"

Franz had already clued in that Lafleche wanted to sound him out. The more the barkeep inquired, the dumber Franz looked. Inwardly pleased at the mention of the place, he asked casually. *"Trou du bois?* What is that?"

"A hollow, a depression in the ground."

"You mean a place that has no trees?"

"No. It's just a large hollow in the ground, surrounded by trees."

"Hmm, there must be lots of hollows in the forest."

"This one is different."

"Perhaps I've probably already stumbled across it," offered Franz.

Could that be true? thought Lafleche. *I've got to be sure and keep him away from there.* He continued out loud. "It lies in a direct line from the large, abandoned quarry toward the next forest."

Franz made another face. "What do I know about a direct line and a quarry?"

"I meant that if you were to draw a straight line, you would reach the hollow in about half an hour's walk."

"Whatever. Why should I concern myself with measuring lines from an old quarry to who knows where and end up with nothing. That's the dumbest thing I've ever heard. That's not for me, barkeep."

The innkeeper laughed out loud, inwardly relieved. "But Monsieur," he said trying to contain himself, "I wasn't suggesting that you were to start measuring things."

"Fine. Just leave me alone with all this line business. Why did you mention it in the first place, if you didn't want me to start drawing?"

"You're priceless. So, you've never been there?"

"Never."

"Don't you find that this forest is unusually quiet?"

"Hmm, I suppose so. Still, it's much like any other."

"Oh, I've heard about places where there is much activity."

"Not that I've heard. Out here, there's no danger of anyone running head-first into a stranger."

"Surely you must have encountered some people?"

"Oh, sure."

"Who, for example?" persisted the innkeeper.

"Well, the forester for one; then there's the odd woodsman or laborer."

"No one else?"

"I couldn't imagine who else would bother going that deep into the bush."

"Still, I've heard that people have been seen at the *trou du bois* at night."

"Ridiculous! What sensible person would wander into the depths of the forest late at night?"

"Well, I've heard talk of unusual things."

"Nothing but rubbish. If it were situated close to the border, then perhaps I could see people trying to sneak across. Otherwise, I can't see it. I know better."

The barkeep listened up. *Was it possible that this dumb fellow knows something after all?* "Well, what else could it be?"

"Hmm. It's not wise to talk about it."

"No? Why not?"

"Because it's dangerous."

"Why dangerous?" asked Lafleche, becoming suspicious again.

"You have to keep quiet about it. Haven't you heard about strange things happening at night?"

"No. What do you mean by that?"

Franz looked both ways, then leaned in and whispered. "*The Wild Hunter,*" he said somberly, as if he were afraid; he quickly crossed himself three times for effect. "No one could persuade me to go into the forest late at night."

The innkeeper was convinced he was dealing with a harmless person. He pretended to agree with him and nodded thoughtfully. "Yes, I've heard much the same."

"Then you've also heard," continued Franz, "that anyone foolish enough to go poaching into the forest late at night would risk running into *The Wild Hunter*, one who'll break his neck."

"Yes, I've heard that."

"And then he'd be forced to hunt with him for all eternity. May God spare me from such a cruel end."

"Yes, that fate would be worse than death. It defies description. Well, I've talked long enough. I have to get back to my work. Adieu."

Lafleche left. But when he had entered the larger guestroom and closed the door behind him, he laughed to himself. *Oh, what a fool that I've been*, he thought. *And to think that I suspected this foolish plant collector as being a threat to our cause. Who's the dumber one?*

Back in the small room, Franz snickered to himself. *Now he'll be laughing to himself and boast about his insight and the way he fished stuff out of me. That Frenchman considers himself to be astute. Well, he was kind enough to give me just the information that I needed. Now I know how to proceed: Simply draw a straight line from the stone quarry to the edge of the forest.* He couldn't help but grin at how he played with the barkeep. *Tonight, I can surprise Richard with the good news. But now I have to go home, first, so that the barkeep won't become suspicious and second, so I can procure a weapon. One can't be too careful.*

Franz left the inn and headed next door to Doctor Bertrand's house. He found what he was looking for—a revolver. He tucked it into his waistband and left the town in a round-about way, heading in the direction of the old quarry.

⊱✠⊰

As it happens, Richard was happy to have escaped the inquisitive innkeeper. He decided not to head directly for the castle, but to go by way of the forester's cottage. As he did so, he left the street, and purposefully headed for the old quarry.

CHAPTER SIX

RALLION DEMANDS CERTAINTY

Meanwhile, a somber and somewhat unpleasant scene had unfolded at the castle. It concerned the Rallions, both of whom were still present. The injury to the Count Jules Rallion, compliments of Franz's actions while he made good his escape from the ruins, proved to be less severe than was initially thought. Although it still pained him, his son's injury was a different story. Jean-Paul Rallion's facial laceration brought with it a serious inflammation, not to mention considerable discomfort. Worse yet, it began to turn into an unsightly swollen wound, detracting from his earlier handsome appearance.

Consequently, the two Rallions were not in the best of company. Their secret business dealings were working out as expected, but in regard to Count Rallion's plans to orchestrate an engagement between Jean-Paul and the young Baroness de Sainte-Marie, there was little progress, and for all intents and purposes, it had come to an abrupt halt. While Marion chose to occupy her time at her brother's tutorial, Count Rallion decided to take up his son's cause and headed for the captain's study. He found Richemonte in, occupied with invoices and correspondence. The old man smiled and shook his hand and asked the reason for the unexpected visit.

"Here, take a look," Jules said without preamble, handing over a slip of paper. "It's a cable and came with this morning's mail."

The draft was short and to the point. Richemonte read out loud:

'To Count Jules Rallion at Ortry.

Please come at once. Your presence here is urgently requested in order to deal with countermeasures.

Duke of Gramont.'

Richemonte saw the order had come from the French Foreign Minister, a most powerful man and a member of the military inner circle.

"What do you make of that?" asked Jules.

"That you'll be on your way in a short time. Who could be responsible for this so-called resistance movement?"

"I *am* somewhat acquainted with it, but I'm not concerned with that now. You're quite right in your assessment that I will have to travel, and soon. Can you guess the nature of my visit to you this morning?"

"I think so," Albin said, nodding.

Jules coughed. "The arrangements here are not to my satisfaction."

Richemonte looked up in surprise. "I wasn't aware of that," he said, laying aside his quill. He started playing with the ends of his moustache. "Surely you have noticed that we've almost amassed our complement of *franctireurs*. Furthermore, you've toured the storage vaults, to which we continue to add daily, and—"

Rallion cut him short by the gesture of his hand. "That's not what I meant," he said, interrupting the captain. He cleared his throat before continuing. "I was referring to our private arrangement—Marion's betrothal."

"Well, don't you find it in order?"

"What would you define as being in order, my good captain?"

"The current stance of the arrangement."

"Exactly. That's what I'm unhappy about; I don't like the uncertainty."

The old man looked at Rallion with surprise.

"My dear Count," Albin said as a slight crease appeared on his forehead, "if I speak of things being in order, I trust you will give me the benefit of the doubt and leave it with me. After all, we've known each other for a long time."

"That's true. We've carried out a number of satisfactory business dealings, and yet, even the most calculating entrepreneur can fall short once in a while. Perhaps we've reached an impasse we hadn't considered."

"I see. Let's continue to work together and spur us toward a union between our children. I have already informed you that Marion will become your son's betrothed. They are both present here at this castle so they can become more acquainted with each other. Isn't that enough?"

"Not quite!" was the count's short, emphatic reply.

"Really?" asked Albin, failing to hide an amused expression. "Could it be that you're too eager, willing to forego the usual betrothal and facilitate the upcoming marriage?"

"No, that's not it. But I do want a degree of certainty."

"I've given you my word. Isn't that sufficient?" he said hoping to appease Rallion.

"No," Jules replied quietly, casting a nervous look at the other man.

"What!" exclaimed the captain, his eyes flaming. "My word isn't good enough for you?"

"Don't get all worked up, Captain. This has nothing to do with your honor. I meant to say that I respect your word and your commitments. After all, I've demonstrated my faith in your ability many times. But in this case, it deals with the word of another individual."

"What are you implying? Are you referring to the baron, or his wife, the baroness?"

Rallion was well-acquainted with the situation at the castle. The baron was weak-willed and mentally unhinged, while the baroness harassed the servants daily with her many expectations. "Pah!" Jules said contemptuously. "I know that you don't require either one's approval."

"Exactly. That leaves only one person—Marion."

"Of course. It's her will that I'm concerned about."

"Well then, you can calm yourself and not worry. Marion will come around."

"You'll permit me to voice my concerns."

"Do you have a valid reason to doubt her part?"

"I do. Just observe the lady when she is around my son. I've noticed that she's been cool and aloof, behaving in a nearly contemptuous manner toward him."

"Yes, the girl has spirit," said Albin, playing with the ends of his moustache. "But your son makes no attempt to ingratiate himself to her. Every woman longs for compatibility in a husband, and perhaps he should try to find what pleases her."

Rallion shook his head. "I don't have time for that. I've come to ask for certainty, a surety if you will, so that I can leave here without being concerned. What assurances can you offer me?"

"Ah! Are you contemplating an actual engagement?"

"Perhaps."

"Despite your son's condition? Count, he's still confined to his bed, and is in fact my patient. The inflammation still lingers."

"I am well aware of that," Jules conceded. He thought it over. "I would be satisfied in knowing that Marion will accept the proposal. This would allow me to leave without concern."

"It's not necessary, my dear Count."

"And yet, I must insist. It *is* a requirement. What if Marion has already chosen another?"

The old man's moustache curled upward, indicative of his inward displeasure. "Marion?" he asked with derision. "What does she have to say about it?"

"And if she went so far as choosing another man?"

"Then I'm still the one she has to abide by."

"Alright. Convince me."

"Count, you're incomprehensible. But as a favor to you, my lifelong friend, I will grant this request and bend to your will. I will speak to Marion myself."

"When?" Jules persisted.

"How soon will you depart?"

"I plan on leaving tomorrow morning."

"Will your son accompany you?"

"No. As you indicated, his condition requires that he remain inactive until the swelling has subsided."

"Very well. I will speak to Marion after the noon-day meal, and then you will be able to hear the confirmation from her own lips."

"I certainly hope so."

"Besides," uttered the captain, showing a more congenial face, "I have some good news to share with you from this morning's mail. Along with the usual correspondence, there came a letter that we've been expecting."

Rallion listened up. "Not the one from New Orleans?" Jules asked quickly.

"Yes, the very one."

"Finally. Is the news favorable?"

"Yes. The company is pleased to consent to our request, and their representative, a…" he referred to the letter, "Mr. Gaston Deephill, is already underway as we speak. He has the authority to conclude our arrangement and should arrive tomorrow on the midday train, bringing millions with him."

"Which train? The one coming from Trier or Luxembourg?"

"The first one."

"Then it's working out according to plan. That gives me hope that our private matter will also conclude to our satisfaction."

"You can depend on me, my friend," said Albin, grinning.

That concluded their business dealings, and they parted company.

◆❦◆

During the ensuing noon-day meal, hardly one word was said. Yes, one could even say that the mood around the table was gloomy. Baron de Sainte-Marie ate his repast like an automaton. He was pre-occupied with his inner fears and said nothing. Colonel Rallion couldn't make an appearance and his father had no desire to start a conversation. Richemonte still couldn't get over the fact that he was forced to incur Müller's presence at the dining room table. Baroness Adeline, Marion, and Nanon quietly contemplated their own thoughts and if a loud word was spoken, it came from Alexandre who was conversing with his educator.

As the participants rose from the table, the captain instructed the baroness and Marion to appear in his study. His habitual brusque and stringent manner suggested nothing pleasant was likely to follow. The baroness was first to arrive, finding the captain pre-occupied and pacing back and forth.

"Where is Marion?" Albin asked gruffly.

"I don't know," she responded evenly. "I would have thought that she would already be here."

His moustache twitched, but he didn't say anything further. The baroness took a seat, and both waited impatiently for Marion's arrival. When the latter did arrive, she found the captain leaning against his desk, frowning.

"What took you so long?" he asked, looking displeased.

Marion's face paled, but she held his gaze. She guessed the reason for being summoned and had prepared herself.

"I had to bring Papa to his room," she replied calmly.

"Pah! He doesn't need your help. It's important that you comply with my instructions without fail. I have something important to discuss with you."

"Then allow me to take a seat," she said and made a motion to head for one of the divans; but he restrained her through a dismissive hand gesture.

"That won't be necessary," Albin said curtly. "What I intend to discuss with you is important but shouldn't take long. Since I surmise that you will comply, I expect the conversation to be a short one." The captain smoothed the few remaining hairs on his bald head and turned his attention to the baroness.

"Madame," he started, addressing the baroness, "I expect you know the reason why I have summoned Marion home?"

"Indeed, Captain." A smile crossed Adeline's lips, but not one out of happiness for her stepdaughter. She of course knew the purpose of the captain's hasty summons. Adeline hated Marion, hated her with all her soul and therefore looked forward to being rid of her, all the while knowing that she would soon belong to a man whom she neither loved nor respected.

"And why Count Rallion along with his son are sequestered here at Ortry?" Albin continued.

"Yes, Captain."

"I take it that this arrangement is in accordance with your wishes?"

"Completely. I am very satisfied. Colonel Rallion is assured of a promising future and is himself a most engaging person."

"Did you hear that, Marion? My letter instructing you to return and with the presence of Count Rallion and his son, you must have drawn the obvious conclusion the count and I have resolved to see the two of you betrothed. Therefore, I am convinced that you will give the count a favorable reply when he visits you and ascertains if he can, from this day forth, consider you as his son's fiancée?"

Marion's pale yet serious-looking countenance hadn't altered in the least. She still stood near the door, having relinquished her desire to take a seat. She didn't even glance at her stepmother, but instead gazed intently into the old man's eyes.

"You mean that I should marry Colonel Rallion," she clarified, her voice sounding firm and clear.

"Of course," Albin confirmed.

"What grounds do you have for making this assertion?"

"What grounds? I have plenty of reasons, ones that I'm not going to reveal to you; in fact, they don't concern you."

She nodded thoughtfully. "But who I am and what I represent, that does concern you, right?"

"Yes, naturally."

"And you feel that you have the right to qualify or influence my decisions?"

"Certainly."

"Well, in that case, I won't draw out this meeting needlessly and will advise you that I myself have two concerns."

The captain looked steadily at his granddaughter. "Well, what could they entail?" he asked, his voice sounding patronizing.

"They are two-fold," she continued. "Apparently something you've overlooked: namely my own will and my inherent right as a human being."

"What is that supposed to mean?" Albin replied indignantly, his mustached lip curving upward.

"I thought it would be plain enough. I reject your offer of a betrothed and I will never marry Colonel Rallion."

"Really? That is amusing," he laughed derisively. "Just how do you propose to accomplish that, Marion?"

"Moreover, you should ask yourself how you plan to turn me over to a man whom I despise."

"It's quite simple," the captain said shrugging his shoulders. "I'm going to insist."

"I don't understand you at all," Marion countered. "I am not a child. The law affords me certain inherent rights and protection. If I choose to marry anyone, then the decision will certainly be up to me alone. I give you neither leave nor discretion in exercising your authority over me."

That was too much for the old man. "You dare to say that to me, your own grandfather," he thundered.

"Yes, you," she replied coolly.

"You can't begin to imagine the means I have at my disposal to force you into submission," he threatened.

"I doubt they will work."

"Your stubbornness will ruin you."

"I will find a way to bear it."

"And that includes your family too."

Marion proudly shook her head, reminiscent of a queen's displeasure. She responded with a condescending laugh. "Would you please dispense with your theatrical outbursts. On stage, or within the pages of a good novel, there you may see a daughter, who for her family's sake, accedes to the act of offering herself to a man whom she doesn't love. But we're not in a play, you're not the director and I have no desire to make myself the sacrificial lamb."

"Impertinent girl!" he objected. "Don't you realize that I have the authority to send you packing?"

"Well, go ahead!" Marion challenged. "Then I'll be free of you at last. That's what I desire above all."

"Really!" Albin replied irritated. "You desire to be free? Well, I'll find a way to tame you. I'm going to confine you until you recant."

"You wouldn't dare! The law will punish you for overstepping your bounds."

"What business do I have with the law? Here," he motioned around the room, implying the vast estate, "it is *my* will that counts, nothing else. Trust me, I will find a way to break yours."

The baroness had expected some reluctance on Marion's part, but not outright defiance. She rose to her feet, mesmerized by the scene unfolding in front of her. As the captain stepped closer toward Marion, Adeline inwardly winced remembering the captain's brutality against her. Yet Marion didn't show the least bit of fear, instead replying without any sign of timidity.

"I stand by what I've said. I will *never* marry Rallion."

"Then you'll face the consequences. Come here, girl." Richemonte was about to grab her but recoiled with an outcry as if he'd seen a ghost. Even the baroness had jumped back, hugging the wall behind her. What they saw was nearly as improbable as a ghost. Marion had stood there calmly, keeping her right hand out of view, concealed in her large purse. Just as the captain was about to grab her arm, she quickly withdrew her hand, clutching a spectacled cobra. The reptile, freed from its captivity, rose up and hissed at him from its open throat.

"*Sacre bleu*! What is that thing?" Albin called out shocked. "Where did you get that beast?"

"Never mind. Consider it a greeting from Algiers," she replied. "Just try and touch me."

The captain was beside himself. He longed to grab her, but he couldn't approach her. Then a thought struck him. "Ah! Now I get it. Have you been with that charlatan, Abu Hassan?"

"Yes, I have," Marion admitted, not seeing a reason for denying it.

"Well, where is he?"

"Go and look for him. See if you can force me to marry that haughty colonel." She tucked the snake back into her purse, turned around and left the room.

Baroness Adeline, still standing against the wall took a deep breath. "Dear God! What a scene. What an affront. How could this girl risk handling such a poisonous creature?"

"Don't despair, Madame," the old man cautioned as he turned to face her. "Marion managed to catch me off guard, that's all. This is the first time that has ever happened. I should have caught on sooner. That snake couldn't have been poisonous. Didn't you notice that the larger fangs were missing? Had they been there, the creature might have bitten her first."

"Then why did you back down?"

Only now did Richemonte realize he had committed a blunder. "How does that concern you?" he snapped at her. "Leave me alone. Better yet, go see that stubborn girl and tell her that I'm going to give her until sundown to change her mind. If she fails to comply, I will impose harsh consequences on her for rebuffing my plans."

He pushed the baroness out the door and locked it behind her. It wasn't clear what he purposed to do.

※

After some time had elapsed, Count Rallion came to seek out Richemonte in his study, but he wasn't in the mood to admit visitors.

"Who's out there?" was the captain's curt response.

"It's me, Count Rallion."

"What do you want?"

"I need an answer."

"Wait until tonight," Albin said, evading the question. "I don't have any time right now."

Reluctantly, the count withdrew, forced to bide his time until the evening.

CHAPTER SEVEN

MARION'S ALLY

When Marion returned to her room, she found Nanon seated on the divan, waiting for her. Nanon had of course witnessed the captain's summons and intuitively felt her friend would need consoling after the meeting.

"Dear God! You look so pale," she lamented. "What happened to you?"

Marion composed herself, not wanting the confrontation with Richemonte to dictate her mood.

"Something that I've been expecting for a while," Marion said, facing her friend.

"Was it concerning Colonel Rallion?"

"Yes, my dear Nanon."

"Did your grandfather demand that you give your consent?"

"Yes, he did."

"What did you tell him?"

"That which I've already decided: I will *never* become Countess de Rallion," replied Marion, taking a seat beside her friend. Nanon was eager to find out what had happened yet chose a different approach.

"Marion," she began, "do you remember what you remarked about Jean-Paul Rallion the first time you laid eyes on him?"

"Go on."

"You said he wasn't half-bad looking."

"Nothing else?"

Nanon considered for a moment. "Well, that he seemed gallant, yes, even chivalrous. And now?"

"That wasn't my verdict, rather the initial impression he left on me."

"And you've changed your opinion?"

"Completely. The colonel strikes me as a braggart. Not only that, but he seems to be an unscrupulous man. His father doesn't leave a favorable impression on me either; instead, I feel I should be afraid of him. Just consider the colonel's conduct toward that poor and brave Doctor Müller."

Nanon nodded. "Yes, to throw his infirmity in his face, something he can't do anything about."

"I didn't realize it at the time, but Monsieur Müller put up with the insult only because of my presence. In many ways he's an extraordinary man. Even though he's only an educator, I find myself holding him in the highest regard."

"You're quite taken with him," commented Nanon, smiling.

"I suppose so."

"I think I might know the real reason," Nanon offered.

"Really? What do you mean?"

"Well, it's his uncanny likeness to your ideal of a man."

"It's true that this trick of nature left a profound impression on me. Still, appearances aside, Doctor Müller is a man whom I can trust, perhaps even love, if he weren't—"

"Well, weren't what?"

"If he weren't—ah!"

"You mean if he weren't just an educator, particularly one with a handicap?"

"Of course. He left a most singular impression on me. It's as if I needed to embrace him. I know I can confide in you, my close friend. I somehow feel that I could trust him with my life, my everything."

"Oh dear. And what about your ideal?"

Marion looked pensively in front of her. "He's unattainable," she sighed, "and will probably remain that way. Where is he? Is he a real man, or just another egotist, like Rallion? It's foolish to hang your heart and hopes on a phantom. It's as if I'm two people trapped within one body. Reality will ferret out my true self. Nanon, I feel that I'm headed for a dark period in my life."

Nanon put her arm around her friend's shoulder. "I'm not going to leave you," she said. "I'll be right here."

"Yes, my faithful friend. I believe you. Yet, I fear my grandfather is planning something awful. He's inconsiderate at the best of times and capable of almost anything." She looked up. "He even tried to lock me up."

"Lock you up? Dear God! How did you manage to get away?"

"I threatened him."

"With what?"

"With the law." Marion was being truthful, but not completely forthright. She didn't want to disclose the existence of the viper just yet.

"The law will protect you," Nanon said convincingly.

"Only if I'm able to call for its aid. But what if the captain suddenly overpowers me? How can I then claim a judge's protection?"

"I would report it."

"Who knows what good it would accomplish," she said despondently. "A short time ago we were so happy. And now…" she sighed. "Do you remember how Monsieur Müller had intervened on the steamship, by jumping into the deluge with me?"

"And the other man with me," Nanon added quickly.

"It seems to me as if another danger is about to engulf me. When I sit with my brother and listen to the educator's lesson, I feel his eyes resting on me and sense that I can depend on him to carry me through whatever danger lurks ahead."

"Isn't that a little too dramatic, dear Marion?"

"What do you call dramatic? Do feelings belong to the realm of reality or fantasy? Will you make fun of me, if I claim that an ordinary house teacher has left such a profound impression on me, to the extent that I'm constantly thinking about him?"

"Not at all. He saved your life, as well as your brother's."

"And then, when I see him seated across from me at the supper table, or when he walks down the hall, it strikes me that he's the one who's really in charge, and even grandfather fears him. I simply don't understand it—I, a baroness, attracted to a simple educator."

In a moment of tenderness, Nanon laid her head on Marion's shoulder. "If you don't understand it," she whispered, more bashful than certain, "then perhaps I do, Marion."

"You? Since when have you become such an authority?"

"Just recently," she added, smiling. "My own situation might help explain your feelings."

Marion gently pushed Nanon from her shoulder and looked into her glowing face. "Nanon, are you in love?" she asked in an endearing tone.

"I don't know," replied Nanon, looking down. "He's…"

"But you think about him, don't you?"

"Yes, often."

"Are they happy thoughts?"

"Very happy. And then when I meet him and start to talk—"

"Ah, so you meet, and you even converse with him?"

"Yes, occasionally."

"Think of it, Marion, we regularly meet out in the forest."

"In the forest? How romantic. You have an admirer, and I didn't even know."

"But Marion, I don't know how I really feel about him."

"Surely you know."

"I only know that I'm pleasing to him. I can see it in his eyes."

"Well, that sounds like love to me. May I know who he is? Or does it have to remain a secret?"

"Perhaps it would be better that way."

"But why?"

"Maybe you would be surprised, perhaps you would admonish me, even laugh at me."

"Don't even say such a thing. Why would I embarrass my best friend?"

"Because he's not refined, not even a gentleman."

"You're wrong about that. Nanon, consider the man that I'm interested in. He's only a tutor."

"But my friend is only—"

"Only what?"

"He's much less than a tutor."

Marion was becoming exasperated. "Please tell me, Nanon."

Nanon came closer and buried her face in her friend's bosom. "Think of it, he's only a plant gatherer."

Marion motioned with her hand, clearly surprised.

"A plant collector?" she asked. "The man from the Mosel, the one who saved your life?"

"Yes, the same one."

"And you've met him in the forest?"

"Yes, by sheer coincidence."

"How wonderful. Still, it's easily explained," she mused. "The one to whom we owe our very lives often occupy our waking thoughts. Does he suspect that you love him?"

"I'm sure he's noticed that I'm fond of his company. There's one more thing, dear Marion, something that I need to confess."

"What?"

"Please, don't laugh at me."

"No, my dear, surely not. You look so serious that I wouldn't even contemplate it."

"Well, then I'll reveal it, but only to you, that … that I have already kissed him."

"Really? So soon?"

"I'll have to start at the beginning. Coincidentally, we had met in the forest. You see, I had lost my way, and out of fear, I started calling loudly for help. That's when he appeared."

"And rescued you for the second time?" laughed Marion.

"Yes. I was overjoyed, tired from stumbling around. He told me to sit down on his plant sack, and then he sat down beside me in the moss. Have you ever looked at him closely?"

"No."

"Well, as he lay there in front of me resting on the moss, it struck me how strong and agile, yet well-proportioned he looked. What surprised me though were his hands; they weren't big and rough like you would expect a farm worker's hands to be, but fine and smooth like a gentleman's."

"You looked at him that closely?"

"Yes, go on now," Nanon said, embarrassed. "You're laughing at me. And then there's his face, so good-natured and honest… and his eyes, they speak of faithfulness and integrity. We talked and laughed, and eventually came to the subject of the river rescue. I told him that I considered myself to be forever in his debt, and that I felt beholden to him. That's when he told me that I could cancel that debt with one simple act."

"Ah! Now, I can guess the rest. Did he ask you for a kiss?"

"No, at least not in the way you think. He's too modest. He asked for my permission, so he could just kiss my hand."

"Which you naturally allowed."

"No. To this day, I still can't explain what came over me. I sensed a deep inner stirring within me. I could have cried, whether out of pain or joy, I'm not sure. It seemed as if it would have been an insult just to let him kiss my hand, and then—"

"And then?" asked Marion, completely captivated by the story.

"And then I let him kiss my lips."

"I see it differently. It was impulse. You couldn't help yourself, Nanon."

"Yes, that's how it was. Have you ever experienced anything like it?"

"Yes."

"Really? When?"

"It's happened a few times, but I've never followed through."

"Why not?"

"It's this… this… oh, please, leave it be. When I look into his face or admire his dexterity, it's like I could kiss him right then and there."

"I understand you. You're speaking about Doctor Müller, right?"

"Yes," she whispered, collecting her thoughts. "So, he kissed you on the lips?"

"You see, his kiss was so subtle and so tender. He confided in me that he wouldn't kiss another with his lips, since they had touched mine.

It sounded so sincere, and I noticed how moist his eyes had become. I saw how he kept his distance, almost out of reverence and that he was reluctant to declare his love for me."

"How noble of him."

"That's when it happened again—that peculiar urge. I don't know what came over me, but all of a sudden, I took hold of his face and kissed him passionately on the lips—three times, I think."

"Nanon," said Marion clasping her hands, "that has to be love, real love."

"Do you really think so?"

"Yes! And then you've met him again?"

"Yes, quite coincidentally. It's as if an inner voice had urged me to head into the forest, saying: Now you must go, or else you'll miss him."

"And you really came across him?"

"Every time."

"I envy you. But dear Nanon, let's be serious for a moment. Where can this lead?"

"How can I know what the future holds for us?"

"He's only a plant gatherer."

"Oh, is that what you're thinking, that I'm too good for him? That I'm too elevated on the social ladder? You're wrong. For the time being, he's just an ordinary sort, but then—oh no, I've nearly broken my word."

"What word?"

"To keep quiet. I'm not supposed to reveal anything."

"What about? It sounds quite secretive."

"And it is. I'm not supposed to talk to anyone about it, not even you. I wrote about it to my sister, and he was upset. It was so touching to see how he tried to be angry, but he couldn't bring himself to do it."

"So, it really deals with a secret?"

"A most extraordinary one. As soon as I see him again, I intend to get his permission so I can fill you in."

"Yes, do it! When will you see him again?"

"Tomorrow at noon."

"But I thought you were leaving on a trip?"

"Of course, I am. But he's coming with me."

Marion looked at her in amazement. "Look at you now. Our crafty Nanon. She conveniently arranges for her admirer to accompany her on her trip."

"Go on!" laughed Nanon. "It's not what you think. He's not like other men. I know I can trust him."

Yet before Marion could reply, there was a knock at the door.

The baroness was waiting outside. "There is something I need to tell you," Adeline said, walking in. "The captain has sent me to convey a message."

Marion rose from her seat to acknowledge her yet appraised her with cool resolve. "The messenger is worthy of the same respect as the one who sent her."

The baroness either didn't catch the slant or acted as if she didn't hear it.

"The captain has decided to give you until sundown to reconsider."

"Thank you for the gratifying news," Marion replied sarcastically.

"If you should fail to abide by his wishes, then you yourself will reap the consequences."

"No, stepmother, it won't be me," she rebuffed her, "but it will be the both of you who will face the consequences. I trust that this concludes the matter."

"Yes, but only until tonight."

"No, as far as I'm concerned—forever."

The baroness shrugged her shoulders and left the room.

Marion walked up to the window and gazed out at the distant forest. Nanon couldn't tell what inner thoughts she was struggling with. She had after all, just a few minutes ago declared to her that she struggled inwardly, unable to differentiate between two people that vied for control of her destiny.

"They've given you a few hours reprieve," Nanon noted.

"An unnecessary extension, since I have no plans of changing my mind."

"But what will happen then?"

"That's up to God. I need to get clarity and sort out my thoughts. I think I'll go for a stroll."

"Where to? May I accompany you?"

Marion thought about it. "Nowhere in particular. Please, allow me to go by myself. There are times when one needs to be alone."

"Alright. But please, let me know the instant you've returned." Nanon kissed Marion on the cheek and left her room.

Only after the door had closed did Marion reach into her bag and extract the snake. Ordinarily, most women have an aversion toward reptiles. But it was remarkable to see how she had no pangs about handling one with her bare hands.

"Hassan was right. You've protected me," she said to the animal. "Come, I'm going to hide you again." She stepped up to the bookcase and hid the snake behind some books, placing it in a cotton lair she had fashioned beforehand. Then she changed into apparel suitable for a lengthy walk and left the castle without being hindered.

CHAPTER EIGHT

A FOREST ENCOUNTER

Marion de Sainte-Marie wandered into the forest, heading toward the old tower and eventually ending up at her mother's grave. It was here that she had met Doctor Müller on that stormy day. *But why do my thoughts keep returning to the educator? Is it his accomplishments as tutor that draw me to him? Is there an emotional connection?* She contemplated these thoughts without coming to a resolve. Marion knelt at the grave and prayed, unaware that it had recently been opened. As she prayed, she glanced at the broken tower, half expecting the same mysterious apparition to re-appear, speaking the Islamic prayer and sending the words into the wind. She remembered how at the conclusion the clouds had parted and sunshine had replaced the dreary day. *Are there prayers which can calm the storms of life?* she thought. It nearly seemed that way, because as she rose from the grave, she felt calmness come over her.

Encouraged, the young baroness walked out of the forest and across the open meadow. The path sloped downward until she came to the base of the quarry, whose walls rose majestically upward. She examined the rock face with her eyes, following it to the point where she could discern the edge, probably where the wagon had careened over and plunged into the abyss. Alexandre would have perished along with the careless groom, had it not been for Müller's timely intervention. An involuntary shudder went through her. Marion found a suitable place and sat down on a boulder.

Marion was holding her ornate purse, the same one she had carried on the ill-fated steamship. She opened it and reached inside. Was it on purpose or merely by coincidence that she pulled out a small picture—the one she had pilfered from the photographer's studio in Berlin? Remarkably, it hadn't been damaged, thanks to the purse's watertight seal. She was examining the photograph in her hand, the one depicting a uniformed Prussian officer. However, she wasn't thinking about the consummate rider, the one she had encountered on the road to Blasewitz, rather her thoughts drifted to Müller, the plain-looking educator.

Just then she heard approaching footsteps. She quickly replaced the picture in her purse and turned to face the newcomer coming around the corner. Marion stood up, a slight redness spreading over her beautiful face as she recognized Andreas Müller, the young baron's educator.

Richard showed surprise, but not embarrassment upon seeing the baroness. He quickly removed his hat in greeting. "I didn't expect to find you here, Mademoiselle," he said bowing. "Please, forgive the intrusion. I will leave at once."

Almost imperceptibly, Marion shook her head. "No, Monsieur. You're not intruding."

"Still, Mademoiselle, solitude can be a form of refuge which one should exercise from time to time."

"Were you perhaps seeking the same, Monsieur?"

"No," he smiled. "My walk coincidentally led me this way, and I wanted to see—"

"The place where you had performed your noble deed," she said, interrupting him. "It's only now that I realize how indebted we are to you for rescuing Alexandre. Did you know, Monsieur Müller, that you are a courageous man?"

"One acts in the urgency of the moment," he replied modestly.

"Yes, each one acts according to his convictions. One fights, while another flees. It just occurred to me that I need to ask for your forgiveness."

Surprised, Richard looked at Marion, prompting her to qualify her remark.

"Do you recall my surprise at the manner in which you handled yourself after being insulted by Colonel Rallion?"

"I remember it."

"That which I mistook for a lack of courage on your part was actually a demonstration of self-control; you triumphed over yourself, Monsieur."

A feeling of pride swept over him as his eyes shone at the compliment.

"My thanks to you, Mademoiselle," Richard replied gratefully. "You offer me a gift that is most precious."

"And you presented me with a sacrifice, one that cost you much but gave me little satisfaction."

"Pardon me," Richard replied bewildered. "Would you have preferred that I had struck the colonel?"

"I wouldn't have rebuked you if you had."

Richard appraised her speculatively. Deep within his blue penetrating eyes, something shimmered, as if the bright sun tried to penetrate a dark and cloudy sky but couldn't. "There was no way for me to have known that," he finally acknowledged. "I had been informed that Colonel Rallion stood on the verge of being included in your family's circle, hoping to proclaim you as his—"

"That won't happen!" she snapped, cutting him off. Then in a milder tone, continued. "Please, won't you take a seat beside me, Monsieur? I want to discuss a few things with you."

Richard complied, and since the stone wasn't particularly large ended up sitting close to the young baroness. She reached into her purse and retrieved a few loose papers, but in doing so also brought out a photograph that ended up falling to the ground. She hadn't noticed it drop, but he did and as he bent down to pick it up, he coincidentally glanced at the subject.

Richard looked perplexed for a moment as he stared at his own picture. He looked away, as a sudden and powerful tremor worked itself through his innermost being, yet not borne out of fear or pain, but from heavenly bliss. He was at a loss to explain how she had acquired his photograph.

Just then she noticed the photograph in his hand. Marion blushed, though not to the point of embarrassment.

"Ah, this photograph must have become entangled in my papers," she commented, reaching for it. "Thank you. Please, won't you examine it?"

Richard pretended he hadn't looked at it, then glanced at his own portrait. It took all his composure to look nonchalant, as he carried out her wish and perused his own image.

"What do you think?" she asked.

"Hmm. A Prussian officer," he offered, hoping it sounded noncommittal.

"Curiously, I don't even know him. Do you find such a thing possible?"

"If you say so, Mademoiselle. I won't doubt your word."

"I was in Berlin, a short time ago" she explained. "I had an appointment with a photographer to get my picture taken. Then a few days later I came back to pick up the finished work and the clerk must have accidentally included this one with my own."

A smile twitched on Richard's lips. A photograph, especially that of a stranger, wouldn't typically be carried around in a lady's purse.

"Do you notice anything unusual about it? Anything that stands out?" she prompted.

Richard looked at it again, trying to come up with something 'unusual', but then shook his head. "I must confess that I don't," he apologized.

"That is curious. Don't you find a close resemblance?"

"With the subject? How could I possibly know the officer?"

"No, not with him—with yourself! Don't you see the similarity?"

Richard was forced to examine his own portrait again, seemingly paying more attention than the first time. "I would agree," he confirmed reluctantly, "that some of the lines and features do have a resemblance. Nature often plays its tricks on us."

"Some of the lines?" Marion questioned. "Far from it! It matches your face exactly. Only your hair color is different, and your skin has a darker tone. Also, you don't have any facial hair, while the officer sports a goatee." She looked away briefly and continued. "However, it wasn't my intent to single out the photograph. It was this letter. Please, would you be so kind as to look at it."

Richard took the scroll from Marion's hand and examined it.

"Are you familiar with this strange script?" she inquired.

"Yes, it's written in Arabic," he confirmed, unable to hide his surprise.

"Really? Can you read it?"

"Insofar that I'm able to read these few lines, yes."

Marion's eyes rested on him, her demeanor clearly showing approval.

"Monsieur Müller, I *am* impressed," she admitted. "I have yet to come across something that you're not familiar with nor competent in. How did you come to understand this language?"

"My father had previously travelled to the Sahara Desert. As his son, I was fortunate in being able to draw from his experiences, and that included learning some Arabic."

"That is interesting. I want to disclose to you that these lines contain a secret that in some way pertains to me. Yet, I am unable to find out on my own. I can only do it through you. Will you keep this in confidence?"

"Mademoiselle," Richard responded, a little offended. "I ask that you not question my loyalty or discretion."

"Alright. I do trust you. Please, would you read it out loud?"

"Of course. Just allow me to scan the lines, so I can grasp the overall meaning."

She nodded her assent, and he began to read, all the while her eyes resting on him. If he hadn't earlier reapplied the walnut solution, the one that gave his face that darker shade, she would have detected how his face paled. Even so, she noticed that it made a deep impact on him.

"Do you understand the words?" she asked.

"Only too well, Mademoiselle," he replied taking a deep breath.

"And what do they say? Please, translate for me."

Richard slowly shook his head, read it through to the end, and only then rolled it together. "Do you have any idea of this document's significance, Baroness?"

"That it is important, that much I do know, but to what extent, that I don't."

"Where did you obtain it?"

Marion made a dismissive hand gesture. "I'm not sure if I'm permitted to reveal it."

"Then in that case, I'm not sure if I'm permitted to divulge its contents."

"What? How can you suddenly become reluctant?"

"You force me to," he replied simply.

"But how?"

"If you don't place your trust in me, then I can't place any in you."

Instantly Marion's brows furrowed, transforming her angelic appearance to that of an exacting disciplinarian.

"Monsieur, what am I supposed to think?" she said none too pleased. "Is this your idea of co-operation? I feel that I've misjudged you. Please, return my letter."

Richard stood up and bowed. "As you wish, Mademoiselle," he replied quietly handing it over. "On the contrary, you haven't misjudged me. You see, the contents of this letter could prove to be more vital to my interests than yours. By returning this edict, I have sacrificed much more than you can imagine. Adieu."

Richard turned and started to walk away. Marion looked at his departing form with dismay. "Monsieur, please wait," she uttered. It was more a plea than a commanded.

"What can I do for you?" he asked, coming to a stop.

"Please, won't you come back?" When he complied, she continued. "Is it really possible that this foreign letter is of such importance to you?"

"Of course!"

"In what way?"

"I'm not at liberty to disclose it since you've shown reluctance in your faith for me."

"Dear God! Is it that difficult for you to believe in me?" Marion stood in front of him, exasperated, yet displaying the essence of beauty and charm.

"I'm quite prepared to reveal all to you, Mademoiselle, but I'm not permitted to do so."

"You believe in me, you trust me, but you can't disclose those things? I don't understand you."

"And yet, it's quite simple," he said, showing the beginning of a smile. "Those secrets aren't mine to share. That is the only reason. I have to respect the other party's confidentiality."

Marion considered that for a moment. "I suppose I can accept that."

"Further, my full disclosure would only cause you grief, gracious lady."

"Well, then I will reiterate my earlier request. I do want to know. I'm not unaccustomed to hearing painful news."

Richard took her by the hand and led her back to the stone.

"Mademoiselle, please resume your seat," he pleaded. "Would you be so kind as to answer a few questions?"

"Go ahead and ask," she said sitting down. "I will supply you with any and all answers, if possible."

"Yet, before I commence, I have to get something off my chest."

Marion looked at him expectantly.

"Mademoiselle, would you be alarmed if I were to tell you that I care deeply about you, me a simple educator? I would be willing to endure all sorts of hardship just to please you. Ever since that calamity on the Mosel, I've been drawn to you."

Richard stopped speaking. Marion had turned pale and stared at him with large, incredulous eyes, failing to say even one word. He took this as permission to continue.

"I had to divulge that to you, Mademoiselle," he clarified. "You see, a man who is concerned with your well-being can be trusted. The questions that I wish to bring before you are important, even though I'm not able to reveal to you the reasons."

While Marion considered what they might be, Richard's thoughts had shifted, turning to recent events: the chance meeting with the circus ringmaster, Abu Hassan, on the grounds of Castle Ortry and their subsequent partnership in unearthing a heathen's grave.

He vividly remembered the unexpected appearance of the apparition during the storm and how Hassan had fled in terror from the gravesite, screaming that a devil was on the loose. A chill went through Richard's body, signifying just how much the event had affected him. It stood to reason that Hassan still had a vital role to play in solving the mysterious disappearance of Sheik Menalek's daughter, Liama. That peculiar midnight escapade was bound to remain embedded deep in Richard's memory.

"Doctor Müller?" Marion asked, bringing him back to the present. She looked at him expectantly.

Richard smiled at her reassuringly. "Please, Mademoiselle," he continued, "from whom did you obtain this parchment? Was it from Abu Hassan, the magician?"

"Yes," she said, surprised at his insight.

"When did you speak to him?"

"On the eve of the second day, after the ill-fated performance in Thionville."

"Where did you meet him?"

"In the garden, here at the castle. He must have been waiting for me."

"May I know a few details of your conversation with him."

"I came to the garden alone, seeking some solitude," she said. "All of a sudden there he was, standing in front of me. I was initially afraid, but I didn't cry out because he spoke to me in a reassuring voice."

"Did he mention Liama, your mother?"

"Yes. He told me that her spirit had sent him to seek me out, to protect me."

"He means well. He's an honest yet driven man. Please, go on."

"He also told me that I should expect nothing but grief from my grandfather, the captain."

"He's absolutely right there. Anything else?"

"Yes. To circumvent the captain's plots, he gave me two talismans."[8.1]

"What might they be?" Richard asked with growing interest.

"This letter and a live snake."

"Really? One of his spectackled cobras?"

"Yes. Hassan told me, that should my grandfather threaten me in any way, I should defend myself with it. One menacing hiss should be sufficient enough for him to back off. Although she's no longer poisonous, one bite from those fangs can still cause a great deal of pain."

Richard looked at Marion with new-found respect. "Did you really accept the reptile from him?"

"Yes."

"Without being afraid of it?"

Marion smiled fleetingly. "He has a way of convincing you that he means well and there's something about his manner that is reassuring."

"You were wise to trust him. Do you still have the snake?"

"Yes. I've fashioned a little nest for it, in a cavity behind my books. She's quite used to me already."

"Were your fears warranted?"

"Unfortunately, yes. With my stepmother looking on, the captain tried to force me into an engagement with Colonel Rallion. I resisted him and refused outright. Then he tried to resort to another tactic, by declaring that he would rob me of my freedom. As he reached his hand out to grab me, I pulled the snake from my purse and held her out in front. She hissed at him, and he recoiled in horror."

Richard let out a low whistle. He appreciated the level of trust she had shown him. "I'm grateful for your faith in me. Won't you require further protection?"

"I suspect so since my stepmother let me know that my grandfather expects my consent no later than this evening."

"I see. It's still possible that the captain will come to the conclusion that the viper isn't poisonous. That way, it won't have the same effect as before."

"Then I'll avail myself of the second talisman."

"How can it help you?"

"Abu Hassan told me to turn it over to the local police if I felt I was in danger."

"He stems from the Orient and is widely respected as a magician, but he's not familiar with French law. These lines," Richard said, pointing to the edict in her hand, "are not sufficient proof to act as your *Deus ex Machina*."[8.2]

"But he swore it to be the truth and that it would protect me."

"I have no reason to doubt his sincerity, Mademoiselle. But what if the captain should succeed in confining you? How would you then be able to show it to a magistrate? What if he simply destroyed the parchment?"

Marion's face paled at the implication. "I hadn't considered that possibility."

"I know. Abu Hassan has also failed to take it into account. Even if this document were to make it so far as to actually be examined by a magistrate, consider that it is written in Arabic. Would the official bother to get it translated? And if he went to all that trouble, what would he end up with? A tragic tale out of the mysterious reaches of the Orient; one that is certainly gripping and revealing yet fails to provide any real burden of proof. If I may be so bold, my advice could prove to be far more expedient than either of your talismans." He paused to let his words sink in. "Are you expecting another meeting with him tonight?"

"Without question."

"Then I have a surer way, a more powerful means, one that will repel your adversary on the spot. But first, Mademoiselle, please answer me this one important question. Do you love your grandfather, the unscrupulous captain?"

"No, not in the least."

"Do you hate him?"

"No, actually I don't. I'm not even afraid of him," she said, smiling awkwardly.

"Do you have any fondness for the Baroness?"

"Adeline? No, I despise her."

"Then you have no reason to show them any consideration. Here is my advice. If the captain should press you to comply with his demands, then look him straight in the eye and ask him if he's acquainted with the following people: Hajji Omanah, his faithful son, then the fruit merchant, Malek Omar, and his accomplice, Ben Ali. Shall I repeat the names?"

"No. I will remember them. Hajji Omanah and his son, then Malek Omar, a fruit merchant and Ben Ali, his accomplice."

Richard was surprised at the ease with which the names rolled off her tongue but decided not to mention it.

"Good," he continued. "A long time ago, the devout Hajji and his son had been murdered by Malek Omar and Ben Ali in order to come into possession of important documents."

"Dear God! Is my grandfather connected to this murder in some way?"

Richard contemplated how much he should reveal. "Do you find him capable of committing such an act?"

"I honestly can't say."

"Then allow me to leave that question unanswered for the time being. Are you acquainted with the captain's past?"

"Yes, but only in part. He's a pensioned officer, having served in the emperor's Old Guard."

"Hmm. Are you familiar with the names Goldberg or Löwenklau?"

"Yes. I seem to have heard them once or twice, the last time through Count Rallion."

"Just one more thing, where did Hassan go?"

"Back into the Sahara, or so he claimed."

"Will he return to France?"

"I think so. He spoke of proof, of evidence that he's going to collect and return with."

"Do you know what kind of proof?"

"No, he kept it to himself."

"Then it's up to me to reveal a secret, one that the captain would like to keep buried. Do you recall the day when the sudden rainstorm forced us to seek shelter in the ruins of the old tower?"

"Quite clearly," she replied, recalling her recent visit to her mother's grave site.

"Both of us saw the apparition which passed by and climbed the tower's steps."

"My mother's ghost," said Marion, the memory passing like a shadow across her face.

"That's what you thought. But I wasn't as convinced as you were. I wanted to follow it, remember, but you held me back."

"I know. The town's people are convinced that her ghost roams the ruins because she's not a believer in the Almighty, the Christian God."

"And yet, for all their gossip and speculation, they've been mistaken. Your poor mother has never died. And if somehow, she had passed away, her resting place will be found elsewhere. But I'm inclined to believe in the first instance. If I were a betting man, I would wager that Liama, the daughter of the Beni Hassan, is still alive."

"Dear God!" Marion exclaimed, her large, expressive eyes locked on his. "Do you have any basis for this assumption?"

"Yes, a very valid one. I might as well admit to you that I'm Hassan's friend, an ally in fact. He came all the way from North Africa, from Algiers actually, hoping to find a trace of Sheik Menalek's daughter. He learned that Liama had died and was buried near Ortry. He wasn't content with that and purposed to unearth her remains. He convinced me to help him in the act, and one night, aided by a third man, we opened the grave to settle the matter.

Marion stood there stiffly, her face masked with apprehension and disbelief.

"That... that's what you ended up doing?" she managed to say after a lengthy pause. What did you discover?"

"A coffin... one filled with stones, sawdust and sticks. Yet a body had never occupied that confined space."

"My God! That's awful. Is it possible that her body has been moved?"

"I don't believe it. What possible reason could there have been to move it?"

Marion looked absent-mindedly in front of her. "Yes, I was there when it happened," she said quietly. "I was only a child, but I still remember when they brought the coffin to the grave site. Strangely, it was lowered without any song or lamentation. There wasn't even a ceremony or accompanying prayers. I suppose, because they all considered her to be a heathen. I know she wasn't buried anywhere else."

"That leads us to the one conclusion—she has never died."

"She's alive? But where? Where could my mother be, Monsieur Müller?" Marion found herself in an indescribable excited state.

Richard placed his hand on her shoulder to comfort her. "I suspect that Liama willingly gave her consent to the deception. I hope to discover the reason she may have had for enduring the agonizing separation from you."

"And my father was a party to it?"

"Perhaps. It's more than just conjecture on my part to believe that his current mental state is directly attributed to whatever part he played in subjugating this poor woman. Someone had concocted a clever scheme to remove your mother, replacing her with the current baroness. I intend on ferreting out the truth."

"I seem to be enveloped in secrets and surrounded… by criminals."

"Yes, I believe you've finally stumbled onto the truth."

"Dear God! Who can I trust? Who can I turn to now?"

"You can find comfort in our gracious God. And if possible, place a little more trust in me."

"I thank you with all of my heart," Marion said relieved. "I've often felt like a stranger here, even though I was born in France. I've felt like I have no place that I can call home. I have often struggled with a misgiving notion that everything around me is based on one massive, twisted lie. And now, you've finally given me hope. Monsieur, you yourself strike me as a mystery, one that I feel will be revealed to me in good time."

"You're quite right in your suppositions," Richard confirmed. "But even though I may come across as a puzzle, allow me to convince you of one thing—that you can trust me."

She smiled at him. "I don't need convincing."

"I have dared to reveal how precious you are to me. I know that my love for you is unrealistic, even hopeless. Still, I want to remain your friend, your protector."

Marion hesitated for a moment. "As you please, Doctor Müller. But such a pact should be solemnized, with… a handshake."

Richard agreed wholeheartedly. "Here is my hand. Please, don't hesitate to reach out to me at any time."

Marion smiled at her new collaborator. "First of all, I have to prepare myself for tonight. Do you really think that those names you had mentioned earlier will be sufficient in repelling the captain?"

"I'm convinced of it. However, what schemes that evil man can conjure up, no one can predict."

"I intend on being courageous."

"Discretion is the better part of valor," he said, smiling. "Besides, you can take comfort in knowing that I will watch over you. Now then, may I safeguard this scroll?"

"Yes," she nodded. "Keep it. I will trust you just as I did when we faced the deluge on the Mosel River. Farewell, my friend."

Marion reached out her hand, which Richard pulled to his lips. She then turned around and departed leaving him gazing after her.

CHAPTER NINE

RICHEMONTE'S ULTIMATUM

"She loves me! She really loves me," Richard exclaimed jubilantly. "And she has my photograph. But where did she get it from?"

"She likely pilfered it from the photographer," a manly voice answered, the intrusive sound coming from behind him.

Stunned by the unwelcome interruption, Richard spun around and looked none too pleased to see—Franz, his meddling servant. The plant collector had just emerged from behind the rock out-cropping and was standing there grinning.

"Zounds!" Richard exclaimed more displeased than he intended. "Were you listening?"

"I must confess that I was."

"Scoundrel!"

"Thank you for the honor."

"Why did you come sneaking after me like that?"

"Sneaking after you? Not in the least, sir."

"Then why did you come to the quarry?"

"I was looking for that dubious straight line."

"Don't speak in riddles," Richard said, still annoyed. "What are you talking about?"

"A line that leads from the forest's edge directly to the *trou du bois*."

"Ah! So, you've managed to find something out?"

"Indeed."

"Who told you?"

"It was that pompous barkeep," replied Franz, grinning again. "Doctor Müller, that man is a scoundrel through and through. I'm convinced that he plays a significant role within the *franctireur* organization. He intended to sound me out, but I played along pretending to be dumb and naïve so that he couldn't help but run at the mouth, eventually telling me all I needed to know."

"That's good news," Richard noted, his face relaxing a fraction. "I haven't yet had the opportunity to make my inquiries. So, where is it?"

"Like I said, in a straight line from here to the forest's edge. It requires only a forty-five-minute walk to get there."

"Were you going to scout it out ahead of time?"

"Yes. That way I would be *au fait*.[21] I was just on my way, and was about to circumvent this old quarry, when a lady approached from the other side. I thought it best not to reveal myself, so I quickly ducked behind this large boulder. Then all of a sudden you showed up and I was forced to remain where I was, a witness to all that was said."

"I hope you'll approach this differently the next time."

"I certainly intend to," Franz replied with conviction.

"What!?"

"I'll arrange it so that I will be talking to the lady, while you're looking on."

"You! I should—"

"*Herr Doktor*," interrupted Franz, "I meant my girl, not yours. But if I may say so, Mademoiselle Marion is an exceptional lady. There's something mysterious, something foreign about her. I think you could have a great future with a lady like that."

"And less with you… you meddler. Come on, let's climb to the top."

They scaled the side of the quarry, ending up exactly where Richard had rescued Alexandre that fateful day. They spotted the forest's edge and headed toward it. They entered the forest and slowly made their way through the dense undergrowth.

"We should be close by now," Richard commented after half an hour of walking.

"I would think so. I'm sure we haven't deviated from the direction."

"Then let's be more cautious. A place that is being used for secret meetings could easily be watched, even during the day. We should assume that someone could already be there, keeping a lookout. We must take every precaution not to be spotted."

"Shouldn't we forage ahead separately?"

"You mean split up? Yes, that's a good idea. But we have to keep track of each other. The one who finds the hollow first can notify the other, perhaps through a sign."

"What kind of sign?"

Richard thought about it for a moment. "Are you familiar with bird calls? Can you imitate any of them?"

"Only the rooster."

"I suppose it'll have to do. So, the first one to spot it will give the rooster's call."

They split up, cautiously moving forward. Here, the trees were bunched closer together, with signs of new growth in between the trunks. After a few minutes, Richard heard their pre-arranged signal and headed toward the area he thought it came from. He spotted Franz standing near a large birch tree.

"Did you find it?" asked Richard.

"Yes, this has to be it, the *trou du bois*."

They found themselves at the edge of a deep, crater-like depression, which had a diameter of at least sixty meters. The edge was augmented with dense brush, and as they gazed down to the bottom, they could see the trees were just as dense down there as near the top. Blackberry bushes and ferns had cropped up between the trees over time. Here and there was a moss-covered stone. The entire scene looked surreal, like a wide shaft that had been filled in hundreds of years prior and had sunken in over the years.

"We've found it alright," confirmed the educator, pleased with their efforts. "Not a bad spot for holding secret assemblies."

"Indeed. There's ample room for hundreds of people. Anyone walking around up here would have no idea that a secret meeting was taking place below."

"Even better for us to crawl into a bush and listen in."

"Hmm. And get caught and end up with a sound thrashing," complained Franz.

"Only if you approach it in the wrong way."

"And what about a quiet descent to the bottom? These people will no doubt place sentries."

"My thoughts as well. We'll just have to leave before they have a chance to post guards."

"Hmm. It strikes me that we should just remain here."

"Of course. Unfortunately, I'm not able to stay. I can't afford to let anyone know I'm planning a late-night excursion."

"That's true, Doctor. Yet no one is keeping track of me. I can stay."

"Right. It's certainly more expedient to stay on site, that way you'll be on your guard so nothing will escape you. But first, let's check out this strange meeting place. I want to be sure that we're the only ones here."

Both men carefully searched the perimeter, unable to find anything suspicious. Only then did they venture climbing down into the hollow, relieved to find no sign of recent human activity.

"Do you think the *franctireurs* use this place more than just once in a while?" asked Franz.

"Probably not."

"Why not?"

"Otherwise, the moss and surrounding foliage would show more signs of being trampled," replied Richard, looking around. "Look closer. Do you see how everything on this side seems to grow more uniformly, and how all the leaves are spread out?"

"Indeed. It's as if every plant and wild grass has been groomed by hand."

"Well, probably not by hand, more likely with a rake."

"I see what you mean, Doctor. Look here. I can still make out marks where an implement has been used to smooth things over."

"This discovery is very timely. First, it allows us to conclude that the meetings occur with regular frequency, and second, that those involved are being careful to conceal their activity by raking the downtrodden growth."

Franz glanced around, considering the educator's words. "But why only here," he asked, "and nowhere else? The marks start over there and stop abruptly near the edge of the hole."

"That leads me to believe there's only one path that's being used, making it easier to conceal. That fact should help you out in the evening. Look Franz!" he said pointing up at the western embankment. "It's starting to get dark. Nightfall is approaching and I have to get back."

"Where should we meet tonight?" asked Franz once they had climbed back up.

"It's too difficult to predict now. If you conceal yourself, say here at the edge and keep watch by that beech tree," he said pointing it out, "I should be able to make it back before midnight. If I don't find you, I'll take it as a sign that you've moved closer to the hidden path. I'll make my way after you, until I find you."

"Should we use another bird call to signal each other?"

"It won't be necessary; in fact, it's probably too dangerous. Do you have any weapons on you?"

"Plenty."

"Did you bring any food?"

"I hadn't thought of it."

"Don't worry. I'll bring something with me. Now, keep a good lookout, and don't let them see you. Adieu."

The two friends parted company.

⚜

While Franz looked around for a good hiding place, Richard hastened his way back to the castle. Dusk was just spreading its shadow as he crossed the threshold of the entrance, spotting Marion coming out of her room.

"I've been summoned to the captain's study," she whispered to him in passing.

"Have courage," he said, hoping his words would provide the needed encouragement. Then he climbed the steps to his room, leaving the door slightly ajar so he could discern when she had left the captain's room.

As Marion entered her grandfather's study, she found her stepmother waiting on the divan. The captain's face was grim, showing his displeasure.

"Do you remember," Albin began angrily, "what you said to the baroness in your room?"

"Quite well, actually."

"While in the presence of your friend?"

"Nanon certainly was there."

"You said that we both deserve the same respect."

"That's what I said."

"What did you mean by that?"

"Exactly what it sounded like."

"You're hiding behind your words. If I were to learn that it was a slant on me, I won't hesitate to punish you."

"I'll leave it to you then to come up with an interpretation."

Tired of the verbal jousting, Richemonte continued. "You know that I have given you more time, so you could give this important matter careful thought."

She nodded. "It wasn't necessary."

"I beg to differ and will prove to you the opposite. So, what have you decided?"

"Decided? You mean recanted, don't you," she said, throwing her head back proudly. "I haven't changed my mind."

"Damn it! Then I'll find a way, so you *will* reconsider."

"Is that all you have to tell me?" asked Marion, turning around to leave.

"No!" he thundered. "I'm informing you, that effective this evening, I intend to proclaim your engagement to Colonel Rallion quite openly and publicly."

"I'd like to see how you plan to accomplish that."

"You'll find out soon enough."

"Indeed," she said dismissively. "Even so, I don't wish to embarrass you. All I would have to do is to say no, and then I'd like to see that impertinent Rallion squirm out of it."

"I'm going to force you to comply," he said attempting to stare her down. "You're going to wait right here until I bring you into the dining hall. Now, sit down."

Deprecating laughter was Marion's response. "Don't be ridiculous," she replied. "Just earlier today, I was denied the privilege of taking a seat, and now you insist that I comply. When will you finally realize that I've moved past the point of learning my simple ABC's and that I am perfectly capable of making my own decisions? You would be wise to dispense with comments that are bound to lead to your embarrassment."

"That's strong! That's too strong," Adeline exclaimed, puffed up.

The old man stood there stiffly, seemingly in shock. Nothing of the sort had ever happened to him before. No one had dared to affront him in such a way, least of all in his study. His mustached lip curved upward like a hyena's bristles, and his teeth grated against each other.

"You dare to say that to me, to my face," Albin erupted. "Listen here, you impertinent girl. Kneel before me this instant and beg for my forgiveness." Richemonte was beyond anger. He pointed to the floor in front of him, shaking with rage.

"I only kneel before God," Marion replied coolly. "Certainly not before man, and least of all before you."

"Very well, not here then!" he yelled incensed. "But downstairs, in front of our guests and the servants. That's when I'll force you to tell all—"

"Forced to tell all?" Marion interrupted. "I don't need anyone to force me to speak. I will do so openly and willingly, just like you demanded of me, so that all will hear about the fruit merchant, Malek Omar…" She paused deliberately, allowing her words to sink in. The baroness couldn't hide her surprised look while the captain stepped back a pace, clearly shocked and unprepared. "And about Ben Ali, his accomplice."

"What do you know about Malek Omar?" Albin demanded.

"Just as much as I do about Hajji Omanah, who was murdered... along with his son."

The captain swayed as he grabbed his head. His head was spinning, and his ears were throbbing. He grasped the edge of the table in front of him to steady himself. Slowly, his hard-practiced constitution brought him back to a semblance of his normal self.

Richemonte faced the baroness. "Please, leave us for the time being," he said unexpectedly. "It's not necessary for you to become a witness to the chastising."

That was sufficient for the smug baroness. Marion was to be disciplined, perhaps physically, which was more than satisfactory to a woman who was beside herself out of jealousy for her stepdaughter.

"She certainly deserves stringent punishment," she uttered, as she rose from the divan. "Any leniency would be a sin." She left the room and cast a malicious smile at Marion. The old man waited until she had closed the door behind her. Then he crossed his arms in front of him and asked almost timidly.

"What do you know about Hajji Omanah?"

"That he was murdered; both he and his son."

"By whom? Who murdered him?"

"Malek Omar and Ben Ali."

"That's a lie! It's a damn lie!"

"No, it's the truth, God's plain truth."

"What possible reason could they have to murder them?"

"Because they were in possession of important documents."

"How do you know that?" he asked, taking a deep breath.

"That's *my* secret."

"Damn it! I have to know," he exploded.

"You? You know more than you let on. Don't you ever mention my engagement or my chastening to anyone again. If you do, I won't hesitate to inform a magistrate about all that I know concerning your past. You've never shown anyone pity, so don't expect any from me."

Marion turned around, opened the door and left without taking another look at her grandfather's pale face. She walked past the partially open door, the one leading into the baroness' chambers. Adeline had wanted to witness what sort of discipline Marion was going to be subjected to, and so had stationed herself at the threshold. Consequently, she had no opportunity to evade Marion's disapproving look as she walked by.

But Marion didn't bother to glance her way. It was her proud look that caused the baroness to speculate the old man had failed in his attempt to put Marion in her place. Marion returned to her room and found Nanon waiting for her. Clearly, Nanon had suffered just as much anguish as the young baroness.

"How did it go?" asked Nanon out of concern.

"Very well. I'm quite satisfied," replied Marion.

"And I feared the opposite would happen, knowing you had decided to stand your ground."

"I didn't give in," replied Marion, her eyes shimmering, "and still won."

"A direct result of the providential idea from your afternoon walk?"

"Yes."

"How did you come up with it?"

"It wasn't my idea. It was Doctor Müller's."

"Really! Did you meet up with him?"

"Yes, at the old quarry."

"And he came up with a plan?"

"Yes. He proposed a unique plan, I followed it, and I'm thrilled with the effect it had on my grandfather."

Nanon, no fool, pieced things together in her mind. "If he supplied you with a plan, then you must have asked him for advice."

"Of course."

"Did you discuss the unwelcome engagement with him?"

"Yes."

"I find that a most intimate topic to confide in another man."

"Perhaps. Yet he strikes me as a trustworthy man, one whom many could confide in. I'm going to say it again: I find myself not just respecting him, but capable of loving him."

"Yes, to love and to cherish, like you intimated earlier."

"I know. I could kiss him just now, in a real passionate way, for rescuing me yet again from a real predicament."

❧✠☙

In the meantime, the old captain paced back and forth in his study, fuming and clenching his teeth. He balled up his fists, cursing quietly to himself.

"Damn! She managed to get away this time, but only for today, maybe for tomorrow, but certainly not longer than that." He stopped abruptly in his tracks. *Who could possibly know about that night so long ago in the Atlas Mountains?* he thought. *Not a single soul. Aside from Henri, no one else was there. Could he, the half-crazed baron, have spilled some of the story? I don't believe it. He's kept it to himself, even in his darkest moments. But Marion's going to pay for her insolence. And how! I'm still going to lock her up and render her harmless, and she'll only regain her freedom as the Colonel's wife. Basta!*

CHAPTER TEN

AN UNDERGROUND PASSAGE

In the meantime, Franz, hidden by the foliage of the trees, made himself as comfortable as possible anticipating the arrival of the band of *franctireurs*. The approaching darkness, a welcome relief and ally to his concealment also brought with it its own sense of the passage of time—it dragged by at a snail's pace. Then, at about ten o'clock, his growing boredom instantly vanished at the sound of approaching footsteps. Two men walked around a birch tree and came to a stop near the edge of the ravine. One of them let out a low whistle, waiting for a response.

"Hmm, we've come a little too early," Franz heard the other proclaim, not ten paces away.

"That's good, Caron," said the first. "Then we have time to settle our business arrangement. So then, are you with us?"

"How much will each man get?"

"Five thousand francs."

"That's damned little, Poirier," replied Caron sounding disappointed. "I've heard that he's carrying millions."

"But we're all going to benefit by it."

"Still, it's too dangerous."

"Don't be a simpleton," chided Poirier. "What danger can there be in plundering a wounded, likely an unconscious man?"

"Not much. How many men have you chosen?"

"Only three; that should be enough."

"Yes, that should do it. That reminds me, do you know which train he's travelling on?"

"He'll be on the noon-day train from Trier. He's coming all the way from New Orleans. He's an American and goes by the name Deephill."

"Hmm, unusual name," mused the other man.

"So, are you in or out?" persisted Poirier. "Or should I look for another?"

"Well, five thousand francs is a nice little sum."

"Of course, it is! There's quite a difference between having it and doing without. Now, make up your mind before the others show up."

"So, the old man wants it done at any cost?"

"Yes, he devised the plan and now wants us to carry it out."

"In that case, I'll risk it. Alright, you can count me in."

"At last, you're coming to your senses and I—" Poirier stopped speaking, alerted by distant voices. "Someone's coming. Let's go."

The two men left the ridge and headed down the embankment. Other men arrived in quick succession. Franz had already counted more than twenty, when something or someone tugged at his sleeve.

"Franz?" a voice whispered.

"Is that you, Doctor Müller?"

"Of course. How many are there?"

"Twenty-four."

"Really? How come I can't hear them?"

"I'm not sure. As soon as they had climbed down, I wasn't able to hear them either. Maybe they're keeping still until they're all assembled."

Richard thought about it. "But we should be able to hear something. Which side were they coming from?"

"From over there," said Franz, pointing. "They all came this way and continued past me."

"Ah, I see. Down this carefully groomed path. Thunder and Doria![10.1] Did you just see that?"

"See what?"

"A flash of light."

"Maybe they've lit a lantern."

"No," replied Richard shaking his head. "I saw it clearly. It came out of the ground. The more I think about it, the more I'm convinced that there has to be an underground hide-out."

"You might have something there. While we supposed they were sitting near the trees, they've retreated into some sort of hiding place."

"Of course. We'll have to risk it and have a look for ourselves. I'm going to make my way down."

"Can I come?" asked Franz.

"Yes. Come on, but quietly so they won't notice us. The smallest errant rock could betray our presence."

"And if they were to spot us, then what?"

"We'll make a run for it. I'm not going to let them catch me. I'd rather shoot a few."

"Right. I won't hold back either."

They crawled out of their hiding spot, down the side of the embankment stopping often to listen for anything unusual. They had nearly reached the bottom, when they stopped abruptly. A momentary, penetrating flash spread out over them.

"*Sapperlot!* Where did that come from?" whispered Franz.

"From over there, in front of us. Let's move to the left, so it won't reveal us. Look!"

Suddenly a glaring light swept over the area they had just vacated.

"Do you think we've been spotted, Doctor?" asked Franz.

"No. The light that swept over us earlier was pure coincidence. But now we know that it originated from a confined space, a narrow opening, probably wide enough to allow entry for one man at a time. Look at this stone. That has to be the key."

"But how does it move?"

"It has to be via mechanical means. There's probably a wedge or fulcrum for easy opening. I'll have to come back tomorrow during the day and have a closer look."

"Too bad I won't be able to accompany you. Besides, I might experience an adventure myself."

"Really, where?"

"At the Diedenhofen railway station. Apparently, a foreigner, one who's in possession of millions is to be deprived of his money."

"By whom?"

"By three of those vagabonds that are sequestered down there. I overheard two of them earlier. Each man was to receive five thousand francs for his part in the robbery. The unsuspecting man is called Deephill, and comes from New Orleans, in the United States."

"And you actually heard that?"

"Yes, every word. The old man had ordered it."

"The old man?" asked Richard, with a thousand thoughts going through his head. "They must have been referring to the old captain. I was about to instruct you to notify the local police, but since the captain has a hand in it, we'll have to hold off. At best, you can keep an eye out for this American and privately warn him. Listen! I hear voices. They seem to have assembled themselves. No one else is coming and they've begun."

Both Franz and Richard could make out muffled sounds of human voices from within. Then suddenly the light went out and there was nothing more to hear.

"They've sealed the entrance," whispered Richard. They heard a sound, as if one stone scraped against another.

"There's no one outside," replied Franz. "They haven't bothered posting a guard."

"That gives us an opportunity to examine this entryway."

"Do you think they can hear us out here?"

"How can they? We'll avoid every noise. Besides, they were quite loud. Come on."

The two eavesdroppers moved to the spot where they perceived the light had escaped from the ground. They found a moss-covered stone, one they had noticed during the day.

"This stone seems to double as the door," commented Richard, while carefully probing the edges with his fingers. It looked ordinary enough, much like the others. He tried moving it, though without success. The stone, and several others, seemed to be connected. It stood to reason that they were movable and not firmly grounded.

"If is moveable, then it must recede to the inside," Richard said.

"Exactly! Had it opened to the outside then there would be a sign of its movement in the moss. But how does it move?"

"Let's give it a try," Richard said. "Put your shoulder against it."

They both knelt and heaved against it; yet the stone refused to budge.

"There must be a locking mechanism," Richard offered. "There's nothing else to do but wait until their meeting has concluded. Perhaps we'll observe something that will give us a clue."

"Yes. We should conceal ourselves close to the entrance," said Franz looking behind him. "What about these bushes?"

"Yes. That might work. They're close together and the branches are dense enough to hide us."

"I never imagined how dumb these Frenchmen could be?"

"Why dumb?"

"Well, the fact they haven't bothered to post a sentry. When conducting secret meetings, it's imperative to have a measure of confidence in not being found out. They didn't even bring a dog along."

"True. But a dog could prove to be more of a hindrance and end up disclosing their presence to passersby."

"Sure, but I was thinking of a well-trained dog, not just a barking hound. They could keep him inside, and at the conclusion of their meeting, it would have sensed our presence."

"Hmm. We can only hope that when the time comes for war with this great nation, they won't develop any significant acumen. Come on!"

They crawled into the thicket and found a passable place, one that wouldn't reveal their presence even on a less dark night. One hour passed, then another half, when they heard a distant scraping noise.

"Now, pay attention," Richard urged his companion. The same light source appeared again, revealing the absence of the stone, which had presumably disappeared within. Then began a sortie of men who came crawling out, one after another, disappearing through the trees. Richard and Franz were able to get a good look at each face but didn't recognize a single one. The last two men stopped near the entrance, apparently waiting for someone. At last, another man crawled out, stood up and approached them.

"Well," he said distinctly, "you can see that everything is in place."

"It's the old man, the captain," Richard whispered.

"Of course," replied one of the men. "Our people won't require much preparation, and weapons and ammunition are in plentiful supply."

"As soon as I have news and have need of you Poirier, I'll alert you in the usual way. We'll only assemble here."

"I wish it would start soon."

"There's no reason to declare war just yet."

"Could it be that difficult?"

"Hmm," considered the old man. "I wouldn't think it unlikely that the emperor will come up with a suitable reason sooner rather than later. He desires a war and the empress even more so. Gramont is at the forefront of current negotiations. As a confirmed enemy of Germany, he's doing everything he can to stoke the political fires. That's why I'm optimistic things will happen quickly."

"*Sacre bleu!*" exclaimed Poirier. "And then, we'll march toward Germany."

"It won't be us first. The glorious army will advance, and we'll follow. They have to abide by the international laws of war, while the *franctireur* is a free man, and will do what pleases him."

"Great! We'll get rich."

"Let's hope it will be favorable for us," Albin offered. "Up until now, we've had nothing but expenses, and significant ones at that. Germany will have to pay and pay dearly. I wish that after we're through with them, there won't remain one stone upon another. I have plenty of reasons to hate anything German."

"But I've heard that Prussia is quite strong, and they have decent artillery," Poirier objected.

"Pah! A single *Mitrailleuse* will silence three or four of their batteries."

"What about that rifle, the *Zündnadel?*"[10.2]

"It's quite amusing, isn't it? Have you ever heard of someone using a needle-gun in warfare?"

"That's true."

"And then there is our *Chassepot*. None of their rifles can match its accuracy."

"Yet I've read in the newspapers that their king prides himself in having formidable generals."

"Who, for example?" Albin asked in a condescending tone.

"Well, Steinmetz for one, and there's Seidlitz," Poirier said.

"And don't forget about Zieten," added Caron, "the famous Hussar general."

"Although he stands in good stead with the Prussian king," Albin admitted, "he's supposed to be quite old. Besides, you've probably heard that the Prussian officers are permitted to sleep at the table.[10.3] That should give you an idea what I think about their whole army."

"What about the commander-in-chief of their army?"

"Moltke? He's nothing more than an idealist and a dreamer. Let's leave all this speculation. We're assured of victory and can leave all the worries to the diplomats. Let's stick to the present. Both of you have an assignment to carry out, which is far more pressing than all these unfounded concerns. Do you understand my instructions?"

"Completely, Captain."

"Then make sure that you get underway on time, so you won't miss the train."

"Don't worry, we've worked it out."

"Lefleur will be there ahead of you and do his part. The chief thing is that he will quickly pull back and that you ensure no suspicion befalls you."

"Leave that to us, Captain. We're going to search out the railway attendant and distract him with conversation, so that Lefleur will be able to work unmolested. Then we'll head straight for Ortry."

"Good. I'll be waiting for you. If you can carry it out according to plan, you can expect a bonus. You know that I can be generous when it comes to a job well done." Richemonte, feeling fatigued, yawned. "I'm heading back. Oh, just make sure you position the wedge correctly so that the stone closes properly," Albin cautioned.

"Good night, Captain," Poirier said, nodding.

CHAPTER ELEVEN

TWO CONSPIRATORS

Richemonte got down on his knees and crawled back inside the opening, with the stone closing behind him. Caron bent down to ensure it had closed properly. Satisfied, he stood up and stretched.

"So, we're due for a bonus," said Poirier barely above a whisper.

"Yes. The old man does have his good moments."

"Pah! He can well afford it. But what do we get in return? Just a meager portion. Think about it. We're taking the chestnuts out of the fire for him."

"And risking our freedom and honor."

"Right, while he relaxes on his plush sofa, patiently waiting for us to bring him millions."

"Dammit! Now I see what you're driving at."

"Can you?" said Poirier, grinning. "I'm happy knowing that you're no slouch."

"Have I ever given you reason to hold me for one?"

"Of course not. That's why I think I can include you in my plans."

"That sounds like you're about to make me an offer."

"An offer, and what a grand one it is."

"Well, out with it."

"Hmm. It's risky to speak one's mind."

"Don't you trust me?"

"You know all too well that I trust you more than anyone else."

"Should we be discussing it here, out in the open?"

"Don't fret, we're perfectly safe here, far from prying ears."

"One of the men could have stayed back," suggested Caron.

"Who would dare do that? They all have too much regard for the captain."

"You mean like us? One of the others could have had much the same idea."

"I'm telling you that they wouldn't. It's different with us. Once in a while he lets us look over his shoulder, catching a glimpse into his cards."

"Alright then. So, what do you have in mind?"

"For now, nothing. I'm only thinking about the fact that the old man will get everything and give us virtually nothing."

"Next to nothing," nodded his companion.

"Wouldn't it be splendid if he ended up with nothing?"

"Hmm! Who would get it then?"

Poirier looked at him surprised. "Who else, but us!"

"*Sapperlot*! What a thought."

"Isn't it fabulous? So, what do you say?"

"I'll have to give it some thought."

"Well, don't take too long. Remember, there are millions at stake," encouraged Poirier.

"And here we are, two poor devils, only promised to get a mere handful."

"But that can quickly change."

"Perhaps, but whether we keep the money for ourselves or hand it over to the old man, it still carries the same risk."

"That's true. And then there are undeniable consequences."

"The only result, undeniable or not, is that I'll become rich and finally enjoy life. Tell me, why did you enlist with the *franctireurs*?"

"For the booty, of course."

"Exactly. Then why wait if you can have it now?"

"I agree with you whole-heartedly. But the old man…"

"Well, what about him?" asked Poirier, rolling his eyes.

"He'll find us… and kill us."

"Pah! Once we have all that money, and all that money can buy, who could possibly catch us?"

"Richemonte. If anyone is capable of pursuing his quarry, it's him. I wouldn't put it past him."

"We'll just have to stand our ground."

Caron looked at Poirier in disbelief. "He won't accept any entreaties or settle this reasonably; he'll be ruthless."

"I know. But we can play the same game."

"It's not a game. He wouldn't hesitate in putting a bullet through your head."

"You're nothing but a coward!" exclaimed Poirier, pretending to be upset. "I can see that you shake in your boots at the thought of him. Go ahead then and leave all those millions to the old man."

"Hold it!" exclaimed Caron quickly grabbing him by the arm. "I haven't changed my mind. I just needed to be sure."

"Look, it wasn't my intention to draw out a detailed plan just yet. I only wanted to know if you were prepared to go along with my plan."

"Well, I'm not opposed to it."

"That's what I wanted to hear. The rest we can discuss later, even tomorrow. There will be plenty of time once we get our hands on all that money."

"One more thing. How do we recognize the American?"

"It shouldn't be too difficult. He'll probably be dressed like a foreigner, certainly talk like one."

"And if he's still alive when we catch up to him?"

Poirier suppressed an oath. "Then a quick thrust of my blade, or a tight grip around his throat should finish him off. Enough with all these unnecessary questions. Once it's time to act, everything will fall into place. Let's go."

They departed, taking the same path as the others and headed up the embankment. Only after several minutes had elapsed, did Richard whisper to Franz.

"Come on. It should be safe to move now."

They crawled out from underneath the cover of the bushes, happy to be free of the confining space.

"You couldn't meet two nicer fellows," commented Franz, stretching.

"They're both fit for the gallows."

"Actually, wasn't it our duty to stop them?"

"How would you have carried it out without revealing our presence?"

"I would have struck them down."

"True, but end up revealing that eavesdroppers had been present. No, Franz. We had to let them go."

"Perhaps it's not too late. What did they have in mind?"

"As far as I could make out, an attempt on an American's life."

"Yes, of course. But where and how is it supposed to be carried out?"

"Hmm. That's the question, isn't it? From what we've heard, he's supposed to arrive on the midday train."

"Yes, I caught that as well."

"I shouldn't think that they would carry it out in the open, at the railway station."

"My thoughts exactly. Perhaps they intend to do it underway."

"It strikes me that he has an appointment with the captain at the castle."

"We'll have to find a way to circumvent their plans."

"Of course," agreed Richard. "You will see to it."

"It could prove to be difficult. I'm travelling further on the same train and may not have the opportunity."

"It's easier than you think. You're travelling to Trier on the early train, remember? That way you can advise the railway police upon your arrival. They'll watch for the American and notify him in time. Besides, you may have an opportunity to warn him yourself, during the trip."

Franz nodded. "It's all arranged then. Shall we head back?"

"No. I hate to leave without being at least a little familiar with the layout. Who knows what we can learn by a little skulking around. But first, let's have a closer look at the entrance."

"Ah, do you mean the lever the captain had mentioned?"

"Yes. I surmise from his words that the opening can only be accessed through a lever or hinge. Let's have a look."

They approached the rock face, one on the left and the other on the right, and carefully felt around the edge.

"*Sapperlot!* I think I have it," exclaimed Franz. "Down here in the corner. I pressed down and it gave way."

"Let me have a look."

With Franz guiding his hand, he too found that something gave way after he depressed it with his fingers.

"This has to be it," Richard confirmed. "It's some sort of wedge that can be pushed back. There's a cord attached to it, presumably so you can retrieve it. Let's see if I can now move that stone."

Richard pushed against the stone, and it moved back with relative ease.

"Open sesame," he said. "Now, let's have a closer look."

"Be careful, Doctor," cautioned Franz. "Take a revolver with you just in case."

"I already have one in my hand. I'll crawl through first, and then you can follow."

The opening was just wide enough to permit entry for one. The hole was at most one meter deep, and Richard felt space above him. He stood up, reaching above his head, but was unable to touch the ceiling. A few seconds later, Franz stood beside him.

"Do you have your lantern with you?" he whispered.

"Yes. But first, we'll have to make sure that it's safe to use it."

"There doesn't seem to be anyone here."

"Still, we don't know what's ahead," Richard cautioned. "It could be a deep cavernous room or a long passageway. If we light up prematurely, it could be detected from the other end. We'll have to examine the space in the darkness. I'll go right and you head left; but quietly and use caution. I don't want anything to happen to you and then have to answer for it to Nanon," he said with a grin.

Richard felt his way along the stone wall until he came to a corner. He continued to his left, meeting Franz in the middle. "Already here?" he asked surprised. "We seem to be in a square room, possibly a cellar."

"It would seem so. Did you come across a door?"

"No."

"Me neither."

"But there has to be one. The captain couldn't have disappeared through the stone wall. I'm going to light the wick."

Once they had light, their suspicions were confirmed. They were standing in a square room, enclosed by walls of cemented stones. There was no sign of a door.

"Where could it be?"

"We can rule out the ceiling."

"Right," laughed Franz. "Perhaps there's one in the floor?"

"Not likely. There has to be an entrance way. If we follow the way back from the entry door, it should lead to the back wall."

"We should be able to find it then."

"Hopefully. But first we should push that stone back in place, so we won't give ourselves away from the outside."

They accomplished this quite easily and set about finding the other door. They examined the floor using their boots and then probed with their hands.

"It really is uniformly firm," noted Franz. "I can't find any sign of a trapdoor. That leaves only the back wall."

He approached it and started to tap.

"Hold it!" cautioned Richard. "Don't knock. We don't know what's situated behind this wall."

"But how else will we discover a hollow place, Doctor?"

"Think about it, Franz. Here we have nothing but stone upon stone. Hence, there can't be a conventional door. More likely it's the same as the entrance way."

"Hmm. You mean another stone plate that will recede into a cavity?"

He considered. "Yes, and probably fashioned in similar manner."

Richard shone the light at the far wall, aiming the beam near the bottom.

"What did I tell you?" he said happily. "Here's the wedge and there's the stone plate that forms the door. Let's give it a try."

It moved back nearly noiselessly. They stood before an opening much like the previous one.

Richard closed the lamp's aperture but allowed the wick to keep burning. He crawled ahead, with Franz close behind him. They sensed that they were in a narrow passageway.

"Interesting. But where does it lead?" whispered Franz.

Both men kept perfectly still, straining their ears for anything unusual or alarming. Only after Richard was reasonably satisfied that there was no one to hinder them, did he produce his small lamp and allowed the light to escape.

"There's no end in sight," whispered Franz.

"The passageway goes straight ahead. We'll simply follow it."

Franz replaced the stone plate and followed Richard, who made every effort to make the least amount of noise. After a few minutes had elapsed, they came across a large wooden door on their right. A few paces further, they found a second one on the left, followed by a third and a fourth in close proximity. All the doors were reinforced with metal strapping and appeared to have solid locks.

"What might these rooms contain?" whispered Franz.

"I'd like to find out, even if we can't today. But for now, the chief thing is to find out where this passageway leads."

They continued on. Even though there was no indication of others in the passage, Richard was prudent enough to allow only a momentary flash of light to escape from time to time. They covered a considerable distance when Richard suddenly stopped, holding Franz back. They encountered another door, but unlike those beforehand, it was slightly ajar. The educator quickly concealed his lamp and carefully peered through the crack, but all he could make out was darkness. He pushed the door open wider and stepped inside, with Franz following closely behind.

"Quiet!" Richard whispered, straining to hear.

"I hear it too," replied Franz equally quiet. "I hear someone talking back there."

"Yes, now I can make out the voices as well," he said, inching forward. "Wait a minute. There's something here." He reached out, gingerly probing the object with his fingers. "Crates. There are a whole bunch, and they seem to be stacked."

Richard pulled out his pocket-lamp, allowing a momentary flash to escape. What he saw made him take a step back. He was gazing into a massive storage cellar. Crates seemed to be stacked all the way to the ceiling. In the dim light he could make out a pathway between them. It bore to the left, in the direction where the voices were coming from.

Careful not to make any noise, both men followed the pathway. When they reached the bend, they made out a glimmer of light in the distance.

"I have to find out what's going on back there," Richard whispered. He extinguished his own light and slowly approached the illuminated area, with Franz close behind. The voices became clearer, but he couldn't see anyone because of the stacked crates. Richard paused and addressed Franz.

"I recognize the voices. It's the old captain and Count Rallion. Wait here."

"For God's sake," warned Franz. "You're not thinking of going closer?"

"Yes. I have to risk it. But if I should I call out, don't hesitate to follow."

Richard advanced cautiously. He saw an opening ahead where a square space had been cleared. In its center, the two familiar men sat on a trunk, and in front of them, on a plain wooden crate was an open bottle of wine next to a lit lantern. They were engaged in loud conversation with each other and smoking cigars. Judging from their relaxed demeanor, they clearly felt they were alone.

"That's how you intend to force the girl to comply?" Richard heard Rallion's nasal voice.

"Of course."

"I fear it may only drive her more toward obstinacy."

"And I intend to drive it out of her. Darkness, thirst and hunger can break the strongest will. It's only a matter of time before she bends to my will."

"Perhaps she will do so, only to break her word later."

Richemonte gloated. "You don't know her character, dear Count. Once she's given her word, she's loathe to break it, even if the end result doesn't favor her."

"So, when are you proposing to carry it out?"

"When it suits me. Today, tomorrow, the day after; it doesn't matter."

"What if she still resists, and refuses to change her mind?"

"What?! Not change her mind?" laughed the old man, motioning over his shoulder. Rest assured my friend, just a few days of solitary confinement and she'll beg to be released. Let's leave all this speculation for now. I *am* certain our plan will succeed, and you can depart with confidence."

"Unfortunately, I must travel. Who knows when we'll see each other again. Each day brings with it unexpected events."

"Well, we're thoroughly prepared. All these underground vaults are filled to the brim with weapons and ammunition. I wish it would start tomorrow."

"Yes, those in authority are doing their best to speed it along. No one plans on starting a war in December, and summer is on the doorstep."

"Well, in that case, you can advise the war minister that at least here, at Ortry, we're prepared. I'm more than ready to settle the account with Germany, the one which has remained outstanding for so long. Let's drink up and head back. There was much to do today, resulting in frustration and vexation. All of a sudden, I feel tired."

"Yes, let's go. Aren't you going to put away the ledger and the wine?"

"Of course," replied Albin as he looked about him. "Damn, where did I leave my keys?"

Richard had heard enough. He retreated as fast as he could, without giving himself away. Once he reached Franz, he pulled him along.

"Quickly. They're leaving." Once they turned the corner and approached the door, the educator felt it was worth the risk to light their way, so they wouldn't run into any obstacles.

"*Sapperlot!* Two keys," exclaimed Franz, pointing to a crate that was jutting out from the rest.

"I'll take those," Richard decided in the moment. He scooped them up and headed out into the passage with Franz close behind. "Now, let's quickly head back," he instructed, allowing the lantern to light their way. They hurried down the passageway until they reached the nearest door they had passed earlier. Franz wanted to hurry past, but Richard held him back.

"You're not planning on going in there, are you?" asked Franz, surprised.

"Why not? As long as I can open this door."

He pulled out the newly appropriated keys and feverishly tried them in the lock. The second one did the trick. Richard quickly pushed the door open, while extracting the key. They entered the dark room, only concerned with closing the door behind them.

"Why did we come in here?" asked Franz perplexed.

"The captain will probably look for his keys, which I now have," Richard clarified. "It's possible he believes he has mislaid them. In any event, it's likely he'll come back here looking for them. It would be to our advantage to find out if he's become suspicious, which is why we've concealed ourselves in here."

"Still, we're risking quite a bit."

"Not as much as you think. He can't enter here, and besides we're armed."

"Alright, I'm not afraid of them either. But the manner in which you rushed back left me concerned, thinking you had been spotted and they were hard on your heels. I don't hear them at all."

"They're probably looking for the keys. Listen!"

Richard unlocked the door and opened it a crack. He took a peek down the passage, spotting the captain and the count slowly walking down the corridor. They were talking loudly, a good sign for the two listeners. If they had become suspicious, they likely would have spoken in whispers. The two doors were about twenty meters apart, a fortunate circumstance that allowed Richard to hear every word.

"No," said the captain, "I didn't leave them here. I must have left them back there somewhere. How else could I have opened the cell and then the trunk?"

"True. But didn't we go back later to count the crates?"

"Hmm. Did I bring them with me?"

"As I recall, you placed them on a crate."

"Then they should still be there."

"Hmm," considered the count. "Are you sure we're all alone down here?"

"Without question."

"Well, you must know if anyone else has access to these storage rooms. I still think I'm right about the keys."

The captain shook his head stubbornly. "No, I must have had them with me by the trunk. Maybe they dropped in between two crates. I'm not happy with it, but I don't have the time right now to go looking for them."

"What will you do about the door?"

"I'll leave it closed, though unlocked. I'll have to return later to properly lockup."

"Do you have another set of keys?"

"Of course. Keys can easily be misplaced or go missing, as we've just found out. That's why I'm in possession of another set of master keys."

"*Parbleu*! They were master keys. Wasn't that a little careless of you?"

Rallion's rebuke struck a nerve. "Keep those comments to yourself," Albin replied irritated. "I'm not some schoolboy, and I'm certainly old enough to know what I'm doing. Once we've moved those crates and shipped them out, we'll be sure to find them. Basta!"

The captain abruptly turned and left the cellar, with the count in tow.

※

Franz had also overheard the conversation.

"Congratulations, *Herr Doktor*! Master keys yet. Of all the luck."

"Yes, coincidence or providence; either way I have a feeling that the keys will prove invaluable to our cause. How fortunate that you spotted them."

"It's a good thing you chose that spot to open the lantern," replied Franz modestly. "I would have thought the old man would have been smarter. He's become careless."

"I don't agree with you in that respect. More likely he just can't conceive the idea that anyone would be bold enough to venture into these underground passages and steal the keys from under his nose."

"Well, we have a fabulous opportunity to have a good look around right now."

"Unfortunately, we'll have to dispense with that."

"How come?"

"Have you forgotten that the captain plans on returning tonight? I'm not going to risk being surprised by him."

"We'll just have to be careful."

"Perhaps, but we don't know if caution alone will be sufficient. The best course of action is to postpone any exploration until a better opportunity presents itself. We're not familiar with the layout. It's possible that we could stumble onto something unforeseen, or a trap, having absolutely no warning of it."

"Shall we head out then?"

"No, I want to stay behind for a little while longer."

"*Sapperlot*! But those two have just left."

"Quite right, Franz. Still, I want to wait until the old man returns. I want to be here and see him for myself when he comes back to lock up. It's important for me to find out if he's become uneasy or even suspicious."

"Fine. Then we can have a quick look around."

Richard closed the door and fully opened his lamp. As he suspected, they found themselves in another large storage room, stacked to the ceiling with crates and barrels.

"Probably full of weapons and gun powder," suggested Franz. "Heavens! A single spark in one of these kegs and your future would go up in smoke. Still, I'd like to deprive the captain of these kegs."

"And blow yourself up with the works."

"Not at all. I know how to set it up. All you have to do is supply a long enough fuse, so you can set it and still be a safe distance away when it blows up."

"It would be a shame to destroy these vast supplies."

"Indeed. What booty if we could get our hands on it."

"Still, even if our side is victorious, this could all be lost," Richard mused.

"How come? I would rather blow it all up than to let it fall into the hands of the *franctireurs*."

"That's what I was getting at."

"So, you were serious about destroying it? I suppose we should evaluate the contents of these store vaults."

"Yes, we'll have to explore these passages carefully and inspect each vault. Unfortunately, it will be very time consuming."

"And run the risk of being surprised by the old captain," Franz cautioned.

"I've considered that. We need to come up with a means of keeping him occupied, so he won't come down here."

"What do you have in mind?"

"I'll have to give it some thought."

"Why all this unnecessary contemplation? It should be relatively easy."

"Are you that astute, Franz?"

"Yes. I've already thought of a way."

"That was inordinately quick of you."

"To think quickly and on one's feet, that is a requisite of a good soldier."

"Alright. So, what's your idea?"

"All we have to do is ensure the old man gets sick; then he'll be confined to his bed and unable to leave his room."

"That's not a bad idea. But how do you propose in carrying it out?"

"You're forgetting that I'm a competent *harbossieur*."

"Yes, a *botanicas* extraordinaire. I still don't know if I can totally rely on your skills. Have your studies gone past that of broadleaves and progressed to stinging nettles?"

"Oho! I know my stuff. I'll give the old man a dose of *datura stramonium*."

"You mean the stuff us laymen call biting apple? Not a bad idea."

"Or an apron full of fermented cherries."

"That might work."

"Or a basket full of belladonna."

"Even better."

"Perhaps a sack full of fly mushroom? You know, *agaricus muscarius*?"

Richard laughed out loud. "Stop! I'll admit, you know your plants. Then we would be rid of the captain once and for all. I don't believe we want to get that drastic."

"Then I know of something better."

"What? More potions?"

"Sort of —Doctor Bertrand."

"Him? What about him?"

"I could turn to him for advice and ask for a remedy that will compel a person to remain home, confined to his bed."

"That's too dangerous."

"Not at all. The potion shouldn't be lethal yet be sufficiently strong enough to put him out of commission for a day or two."

"I wouldn't shy away from such a solution. But I maintain that such a proposal could still prove to be dangerous."

"We wouldn't expose ourselves to it."

"That's not what I meant. I don't know how far I can trust the good doctor."

"Oh, he's discreet enough. I feel that we can trust him implicitly."

"Perhaps. But now he works for the local populace, and it might be prudent if we didn't appeal to him for help, so—Richard stopped speaking. They both heard the distinct sound of approaching footsteps.

"Listen! Someone's coming."

Richard cracked open the wooden door. Sure enough, it was the captain returning. He was carrying a lantern in one hand and a ring of keys in the other. He locked the door in question and headed back the other way.

"Do you suppose he was still suspicious?" asked Franz.

"Not at all. He had the look of a man who doesn't have a care in the world."

"Well, may God further your insight. We'll do our utmost to mislead him. Can we go now?"

"Not yet. A few minutes either way won't make much of a difference, but we have to make sure that he's actually gone."

"When do you want to examine the passages?"

"As soon as possible."

"I was hoping to help you with that task, but unfortunately I'll be away tomorrow and the day after as well."

"Well, if it's any consolation to you, I would prefer to have you with me. If there's nothing pressing, I'll wait until your return."

Franz's face beamed at the news. "I've been thinking about that passageway, the one the old man came from?"

"And?"

"Well, it heads straight toward the castle."

"Right. The castle and the *trou du bois* lie in a direct line, coinciding with this passage. Can you deduce anything else?"

"That it leads beyond the castle?" asked Franz.

"No, not beyond it. I think that it connects with two side-passages."

"Really? Which ones?"

"One that leads right, toward the old tower, and the other one left, toward the monastery ruins where you were nearly caught."

"*Sapperlot*! That makes sense. This castle stems from medieval times, and the inhabitants likely made good use of these storage rooms and passageways. How fortunate, that we're now in possession of the keys."

The educator looked pensively in front of him. "If I'm right, these keys will be of great help, but won't solve all of our problems."

Franz nodded. "They're master keys, which should give us access to all."

"True, but only to the doors."

"Well, that's what I meant."

"But I suspect that other passages may be secured in the same way as the entrance at the bottom of the hollow—by means of a stone plate."

"Yes, that may be the case. Actually, that's secondary since we now know how to open it."

"Furthermore, I intend on making good use of it. Just don't prolong your time at the funeral. One never knows what can happen in the meantime, and in our present situation each minute counts."

"I know. If it weren't for Nanon's request, I wouldn't be going at all. I would much rather sit with her in the forest than at a funeral service."

"On your plant sack?"

"Of course, *Herr Doktor*. Clearly, it's more appealing than swimming with her through that deluge on the Mosel."

"I believe you, Franz." Richard took another look down the dark corridor. "It seems that the old man has left after all. Let's go."

After Richard had carefully locked up and pocketed the keys, they left the confines of the vault and headed down the corridor. He had no qualms about using his lamp on the way back. He was convinced there was no further need for their earlier caution. They retraced their way back to the original entrance, being careful to replace the stone plate in the exact position they had found it.

Once out in the open, they quickened their pace and parted company at the pre-arranged spot at the edge of the forest. Richard scaled the lightning-rod support to reach his room unobserved. Everything went well, and he gained entry without detection. He quickly undressed and lay down for a few hours of much needed rest.

CHAPTER TWELVE

DOCTOR BERTRAND

Franz, who had further to go, thought about his recent conversation with Richard as he walked back into town. Finding a way of incapacitating the captain was of considerable importance. When he spotted a light still on in Dr. Bertrand's study, he made up his mind to pursue his idea. He knocked softly and entered.

Philippe Bertrand was perusing a book and a little surprised to receive a visitor at such a late hour.

"Ah, Franz, it's you," he said upon recognizing his plant gatherer. He laid his book aside. "Something important must have occurred for you to be coming this late. Is someone ill?"

"Good evening, Philippe," Franz greeted. He looked around to make sure they were alone. "One is already dead," Franz quipped, "but another may succumb to a malady."

"What? Already dead?" asked the physician perplexed. "Ah, I presume you're referring to a viewing. But I don't understand the second part."

"I'll have to make myself clearer."

Philippe eyed him. "Here, take a seat and light up a cigar."

"With pleasure. You carry nothing but the best."

Franz knew exactly where he stood with the doctor. Philippe had given him plenty of opportunity to get acquainted and so he felt comfortable enough to trust him. Franz accepted the offered cigar and took a seat in a nearby chair.

"I'm your servant," he started, "your plant collector as it were, and as such I find it necessary—"

"No, not at all, my good man," Philippe voiced. "You're starting off with the wrong premise. I'm not your master or your employer, but your friend, and I remain at your disposal."

"Very well. I came to ask for a favor, that you grant me a short holiday, no more than two days at most."

"Of course. As long as you want. You know as well as I do that you're not answerable to me. So, you're planning a trip?"

Franz nodded. "I need to pay my respects to the dead man's family. Fortunately, he wasn't one of your patients and his passing doesn't concern you. Actually, he's a distant relative of Mademoiselle Nanon, her former caregiver. She wants to be present at the burial, and has therefore asked me—"

"To accompany her?" interjected the astute doctor.

"Yes, that's it."

"Congratulations," quipped Philippe, a smile forming on his lips.

"On behalf of the corpse?"

"No," laughed the doctor. "On your conquest."

"Hmm. That is a peculiar story. You see it wasn't I who wooed her, but the other way around."

"It's one and the same. As far as Mademoiselle Nanon goes, I would escort the young woman myself, if…"

"If you weren't already married, dear Doctor?" Franz quipped. "I trust we understand each other."

"Completely," Philippe said, smiling. "Well, we're clear about one thing; now, what about the other?"

"The one who's supposed to become ill?"

"Exactly."

"Yes, well, that story is even more unusual. I still find myself in a quandary. It's a little awkward to explain properly."

"Don't beat around the bush, just come out with it."

"Alright. I know of a man, a particularly bad sort, one we don't have to feel sorry for if he stumbled, died, and ended up in hell."

"That's a very unchristian thing to say."

"Oh, it's very appropriate, since the Good Book speaks of a personal devil, one who goes around devouring people. Actually, my remark about going to hell wasn't meant literally. I meant that he should die and find his place among his earthly relatives."

"Really?" Philippe replied dryly. "Go on."

"Still, my intention is not to bring him to the brink of death, only to give the appearance of having done so."

"How very noble of you."

"Don't you think?" said Franz, his pearly whites adding credence to his intentions. "He's supposed to be sick for only a short time."

"That's a most peculiar request, my dear fellow."

"I have my reasons."

"Furthermore, I believe I know why you've chosen to disclose it to me."

"I don't want to come across as unfair and I don't propose to do anything which might be construed as illegal. The man whom I have in mind purposes to carry out things that I can't allow to take place. I can only prevent their outcome if I succeed in confining him to his bed for a day or two."

"Hmm. So, he's the one who's supposed to become ill?"

"Yes."

"I don't want to ask to whom you're referring," Philippe said, leaning in. "I've gotten to know and to trust you." He considered for a moment. "But I do need to ask you a few questions. Is Doctor Müller aware of your plan?"

Franz nodded.

"Did he instruct you to seek out another's help, perhaps me?"

"No. I myself have taken it on."

"And he gave you, his blessing?"

"He didn't exactly forbid it; but then he may pursue another course of action."

"I understand you now. He realizes, that at least openly, I'm not permitted to accommodate such a request." Bertrand said this matter of fact, yet his face conveyed something else. Franz would have had to be a simpleton not to have caught his hidden meaning.

143

"I'm well aware of that," Franz said. "It wasn't my intention to make a formal request. Yet the matter interested me, and when I saw the light on in your study, I felt I could impose on you a little. Are there ways of feigning an illness?"

"Of course."

"Surely, those means could prove to be dangerous?"

"In the hands of a layman, yes. However, a physician is much more likely to succeed, thus averting tragedy."

"*Sapperlot*! Shouldn't a doctor make his patients well?"

Bertrand smiled. "Ordinarily yes, but sometimes one must prevent something more serious. Let me illustrate by way of an example. When I vaccinate a patient, it may cause temporary and unsightly pimples, yet prevent something considerably more dangerous, like smallpox."

"That's understandable. I've done much the same. As a soldier in battle, I've had to wield my saber, sometimes inflicting a serious gash in the arm, but avoiding a far more serious injury such as a head wound. As you've pointed out, my means could prove to be dangerous in the hands of a novice. But getting back to my dilemma, is the drug I'm looking for only available in an apothecary?"

"Usually. Still, some doctors prefer to have smaller doses in their home for the sake of practicality."

"That is convenient."

"And at times quite necessary. There are instances when a doctor wants to spare his patient a costly trip to the apothecary. If one should come to me with a toothache, why should I send him away, especially if I have the remedy to provide immediate relief for the pain?"

"I'm glad to hear of it."

"How come?"

"Because I have an awful toothache," Franz replied, hoping to sound convincing.

"Since when?"

"Oh, for the past three days."

"Where? Which tooth troubles you?"

"On the left side, one of the back teeth."

"You should have come to me sooner. Do you want to show me?"

"Sure, if it's no trouble."

Franz rose and walked up to the doctor, his face looking serious. With equal seriousness, Bertrand picked up a lamp and asked him to open his mouth. He then lit up the indicated area and started to probe with his finger.

"Is that the offending tooth?" he asked.

"Yes, indeed."

"Would you wait here for just a moment? I'll see to it right away. A toothache is nothing pleasant. One can't be free of the pain soon enough."

"That's true. I'll be happy once it's gone."

"It shouldn't take more than a couple of minutes."

During his initial examination, Doctor Bertrand had observed two shiny rows of the healthiest teeth he had yet seen in his practice. He suspected a ruse but decided to play along and fetched a chest from his examination room. As he opened it, Franz spotted a collection of all sorts of instruments, with his eyes settling on a device that suspiciously resembled pliers.

"What are those?" asked Franz with reservation, his teeth admittedly feeling exposed.

"These are my new forceps."

"Heavens! Are they really necessary?"

"I'm afraid so."

"Oh no! I was hoping to avoid such drastic measures." Suddenly, it seemed to Franz that his perfect teeth were feeling tender.

"There's no way around it," replied Philippe. "The back teeth have decayed and are beyond repair. They'll have to come out."

"Is that necessary? I mean since I've kept them for so long."

"Yes, they're being attacked by disease."

"That's curious. What could have foiled them? Isn't there a less invasive means, a less painful procedure?"

"Certainly."

"Then let's hear it."

"But I have to caution you that it won't serve you well."

"Why?"

"This remedy is temporary at best. The root nerve can be pacified for a while with a few drops of medication, but once it has worn off the pain will return again."

"But it's a more humane way. I mean, by not deadening the nerve right away and forestalling the agony through the use of a few drops."

"I don't share the same opinion. Now then, shall we?" asked Bertrand while holding a set of forceps of gigantic proportions.

"No, thank you," Franz declined quickly. "Leave your jawbreakers where they are and let's see if a few drops will do the trick. Do you have an analgesic or painkillers?"

"I have both on hand, but neither one is sufficient to stem the pain. I, however, have acquired new medication which will attack the painful nerve and stop the pain immediately; but I can only dispense this remedy to a patient I'm familiar with."

"How come?"

"It could have serious consequences. One drop on the affected tooth and it dulls the pain; but administering a larger dosage, as in a drink, would ensure that the patient won't leave his bed for several days."

"That is dangerous."

"Indeed. Especially when it could easily be confused for other medicine."

"You mean putting it in a drink, instead of on the affected tooth?" Franz prompted conspiratorially.

"And forty drops instead of a few."

"Yes, I can see how one could lose track. One would have to exercise great caution. Does it have an odor?"

"Not at all."

"Does it taste bad?"

"No, it has no taste and is undetectable."

"What color is the liquid?"

"Clear, like water."

"What about cramps or side-effects?"

"There are none. That is its good side."

"Then I'd rather have it than all your instruments. May I try some?"

"Yes. Here is the flask. So then, only one drop and not forty."

"*Sapperlot*! What if I miscount and end up with eighty?"

"That's not possible. The vial contains no more than forty."

"How convenient. I'm relieved. And the bill?"

"I'm not going to give you one, on the condition that should the remedy not work, I can remove those burdensome teeth."

"I'm sure it will work as predicted. Good night, Doctor."

"Good night, Franz, and have a pleasant trip."

Once Franz was alone in his room, he examined the little vial containing the colorless liquid. *That worked out perfectly*, he thought. *One has to stoke the iron while it's hot. That doctor is a good sort, and his intervention will put the captain in his place. While I'm still up, I'll lay out my travelling suit and grab a little rest.*

As a soldier, Franz was accustomed to rising early and wasn't concerned about over-sleeping. He rose on time and as he got dressed, pondered the day that lay ahead. *I'm supposed to make a report to the police. Perhaps it would be better if I dispensed with doing so. I fear that they'll detain me unnecessarily. It's possible that I'll meet up with the American while underway. And if that's not the case, I can still deliver a note to the conductor once I've returned to Thionville. By the time they realize its significance, I'll be on my way again. Yes, that's the best way to handle it. I'm sure the cavalry master will forgive my little deviation from his orders.*

Clad in his new suit, Franz headed for the railway station and purchased a second-class ticket, an extravagance he allowed himself on this one occasion.

CHAPTER THIRTEEN

AN AMERICAN BUSINESSMAN

Franz Schneeberg arrived in Trier, a city dating back to the time of the Celts. Situated on the banks of the Mosel River and nestled within low-lying hills, it was an important city for the Moselle wine region.

Franz disembarked quickly and decided not to waste his time waiting at the railway station. Instead, he strolled through the city and headed for the closest inn where he hoped to get a little refreshment. It was still early, and he saw there was only one other guest in the tavern. It struck Franz that there was something foreign about his appearance.

The man's face was tanned, and he had black curly hair. A large moustache adorned his upper lip. Clearly, he was a handsome man, leaving an aristocratic impression. There was life in his eyes, and his graceful movements hinted at strength and agility. The cut and style of his clothes suggested that he was a man of means. He was perhaps forty years old and if it came to capturing a young lady's heart, he would have given a younger man a run for his money.

The stranger read his newspaper, yet repeatedly laid it aside clearly bored, as evidenced by his impatient gazing out the window. During one of these pauses, he looked over at Franz, appraising him. He rose and started to pace, eventually coming to a halt in front of Franz.

"Excuse me, Monsieur," he started. "It strikes me that neither one of us stems from this part of Germany."

"You're quite right. I too am a stranger in these parts," Franz agreed.

"Do you come from the south or the north?"

"From the south, Monsieur."

"Far from here?"

"No, not too far."

"Then I envy you. Quite often a journey can be more taxing on the mind than on the physical body. The monotony of train travel and the endless familiarity of hotels can sometimes be too much to endure. Here I sit and wait for the train bound for Metz. What utter boredom. What can one do to pass the time?"

Franz looked up at the imposing stranger hovering over him. His quick speech, impatient mannerisms, the lively movement of his facial muscles, all pointed to one obvious conclusion; the man was a Southerner.

"You're travelling as far as Metz?" inquired Franz.

"Not quite. I'm only going as far as Thionville."

"That's where I'm heading as well. You see, I reside in Thionville but on this occasion I'm travelling further."

"Thionville you say? Please, allow me to join you."

"Of course. That way we can pass the time together."

"Which train are you taking?"

"The eleven thirty."

"Me too. Are you acquainted with the town and its vicinity?"

"Somewhat."

"Are you familiar with a place called Ortry?"

"Yes. There's a castle close by that goes by that name."

"Whom does the castle belong to?"

"The Baron de Sainte-Marie."

"Doesn't an old gentleman, one who served during the old Emperor's first realm, reside there?"

"You're probably referring to Captain Richemonte."

"Yes, none other."

Franz nodded. "He lives at the castle."

"Do you know if he's currently on the estate?"

"Yes. I saw him just yesterday," remarked Franz, thinking back to his subterranean adventure.

"That is reassuring to know. I have business to conduct with the captain. Are you personally acquainted with him?"

"No, although we've seen each other several times in passing."

"But you must be familiar with his circumstances."

Franz didn't know what the stranger was driving at, so he decided to proceed cautiously. "Only from hearsay."

"Can you tell me if he's a rich man?" probed the stranger.

"I wouldn't dare to venture an opinion on another man's finances."

"I've heard that he's supposed to be a patriot."

"That's certainly true. He's a man who has shown himself to be in contention with Germany."

"There's a rumor that he's well-acquainted with members of the emperor's court."

"Do you have a particular individual in mind?"

"Indeed, Count Rallion."

"Yes, they know each other. In fact, the count was there for several days, though I believe he has since left."

"That's too bad."

"His son, Colonel Rallion, however, is still at the castle."

"That is comforting. I've heard the old captain plays a significant role in stirring up the local people," the stranger said with a penetrating glance.

"Yes, I've heard. He gathers all those who desire to be at war with Germany."

"Do you include yourself in those circles?"

"No, I'm afraid not."

"Why not?"

"Because I'm not enamored with the prospect of an imminent war."

"Surely, you're a patriot?" questioned the Southerner.

"A patriot? I have no wish to become the recipient of a sound thrashing."

"Pah! What's there to worry about? France is assured of victory."

"Perhaps," Franz said, shrugging his shoulders as if the whole thing didn't concern him in the least.

"Perhaps? Only possibly?" continued the stranger. "Quite likely, yes, most probably France will prevail. He who claims the opposite doesn't know the capability of the French military."

"And perhaps Germany's prowess even less."

"*Sacre bleu!*" the stranger exclaimed. "Are you suggesting that Prussia is superior to France?"

"Who can say? They haven't tangled yet. Prussia has fought the Danes, the Austrians, the Bayern, Würtemberg and Baden states, and prevailed over them. Likewise, France has fought with the Austrians, Russians, Moors, Chinese and the Mexicans and come out on top. But pit one against the other and we'll see who will prevail in the end."

"Monsieur," the stranger replied with disdain, "you're not much of a patriot."

Franz looked around the room. "Monsieur, we're currently on German soil. One has to be careful."

"Pah! This is just between you and me," he gestured. "There's no one else here. I am convinced of an imminent war between the two and that France will triumph. I've come from afar to offer my country unconditional support."

"Perhaps you're bringing an offering, one which you may end up regretting."

"I'm not going to regret it. I'm proud of my country, even though my time here has been an unhappy one. How I detest those Germans."

His appealing dark eyes had transformed themselves into a fiery darkness that would have made many uncomfortable at the sight. "You probably sympathize with them," the Southerner remarked unkindly.

"I'm generally not opposed to anyone," Franz countered while stretching out his legs. "Every individual and each race have the inherent right to exist. Any man who considers himself to be cultured, should behave in accordance with his upbringing; likewise, nations should also conform to this simple etiquette."

"What you speak of sounds fine, even commendable. But such a man probably has blood as slow as molasses flowing through his veins.

We Southerners love passionately and condemn with flaming zeal." He paused for an instant, looking Franz squarely in the eye. "Have you ever loved?"

"Well... of course I have."

"Were you engaged, perhaps contemplating marriage?"

"No."

"Then you've never had the pleasure of raising precious loving children, ones who love you and bear your likeness?"

"I'm afraid not."

"Then I ask that you keep your opinions to yourself. You're in no position to differentiate between France and Germany."

The stranger had nearly jumped out of his seat and was now pacing anew. Surprised, Franz looked at him as an endearing smile spread across his face. This stranger was the genuine article, the true embodiment of a Southerner: handsome, impulsive, passionate, courageous, but also honest, direct, and not afraid to speak his mind.

"What difference can there be between the two?" Franz ventured to ask. "Is one married and the other single? Does the former have loving, adorable children, whom he loves with passion, while the latter has dumb, ugly cretins, not worthy of a second glance?"

"Don't get carried away. You misunderstand me. This has nothing to do with rearing children. Let me be plain. I was married once—to a German woman. Doesn't that say it all?"

"Sure," replied Franz, ignoring the underlying tone. "I've heard it said that a German wife is a model of faithfulness, thriftiness and domesticity. Furthermore, they're known to be warm, hospitable and well-suited for raising children."

"Monsieur, how dare you!" the stranger reacted. "I see that you've ploughed with inferior horses.[13.1] This woman, who became my wife, carried a French name, yet she was German. I treated her like a goddess—"

"Ah, you idolized her?"

"Yes, she was my ideal, my everything. I was supposed to marry another, according to my father's wishes. But I was young and impulsive. I didn't want to listen to him. I was madly in love with a German fräulein, whom I eventually married, only to be disowned by my own father."

"All this because she was of German descent?"

"Yes, for that sole reason," the Southerner stated.

"I would have liked to have a word or two with your father, but in private."

"Although I refused to see it at first, he was right all along."

"What do you mean?"

"She had blessed me with two daughters, the girls a picture of loveliness, daughters who—"

"That was considerate of her."

"Let me finish. Business, being what it is, called me away, and I was absent for several months, nearly an entire year."

"That's regretful. To be removed from your loved ones for such a long time."

"And when I finally returned, I found out my wife had left."

"Heavens!"

"Not only that, but my children had gone with her."

"*Sacre bleu!* Where did she go to?"

"How should I know?"

"Didn't you search for your family?"

"For days on end, with weeks turning into months."

"Did you find out anything?"

"Not a trace, nothing."

Franz shook his head. "Then you must have employed less than competent agents. A woman with two children simply doesn't vanish without a trace."

"She had every reason to cover her tracks."

Franz couldn't hide his surprise. "What are you implying?"

"She left me for another man," the stranger admitted.

"Hang it all!"

"It's what I've been trying to tell you. It all makes sense. She was German."

"Now listen here, Monsieur," Franz objected. "Are you suggesting that all German women are prone to being unfaithful?"

"More or less, yes," the stranger admitted, standing his ground.

"Then you yourself are worthy of the consequences, should you be confronted over your prejudiced views."

"Monsieur!" exclaimed the stranger threateningly.

"What! Now you're offended? You ramble on without regard for another's feelings. Surely, I can do the same. I believe we're now even. Do you even have the slightest proof of her infidelity?"

"Of course. My father and another witness assured me of it."

"Your father?" A light seemed to go on in Franz's head. "The one who disowned you because of her in the first place? How peculiar. Who was the reprobate who led her astray?"

"He's unknown to me."

"I see it all now. The infamous unknown culprit. The one who's been blamed for countless calamities. What happened to the children?"

"They absconded with both of my girls."

"Listen, Monsieur. I have a feeling that your southerly genial nature has departed with your common sense. Did you really take the time to verify what you were told?"

"Yes, completely."

"Then who can make any sense out of this. I find it curious, even suspicious, that your own father, the one who was opposed to the marriage in the first place, is now the chief witness against your wife. I wonder if she really was as unfaithful as you claim. A careless woman bent on leaving her marriage wouldn't burden herself by taking young children along."

"I suppose she must have loved them."

"Finally, some clarity. Certainly, she loved them. A caring mother wouldn't leave her husband, depriving him of his children, even if she were German. If she does leave, there have to be tangible reasons. Likely, she ends up leaving with a broken heart. Wasn't there something, anything that she had left behind?"

"Yes. She left a letter. A cold, worthless letter."

"Hopefully you kept it."

"What for? There was nothing to be gained by keeping it. I left the letter as well as her portrait with my father so he could destroy them. Then I left in search of my children."

"Without finding a trace?"

He nodded solemnly. "As I've already told you."

"Forgive me for being intrusive. How old were you when you married?"

"Twenty years old."

"And when your wife left you?"

"Twenty-two."

"Was your wife younger than you?"

"By two years."

"Yes, I can see how such an arrangement could be convenient to a Southerner," continued Franz. "The man falls in love at eighteen, mesmerizes the girl with who knows what, and marries her at twenty completely against his father's wishes, then departs on a long trip at twenty-one and leaves the poor woman alone and defenseless looking after two young children, subject to all sorts of offences and schemes, finds her gone, believes the lie that is fed him, and lastly blames all of Germany for his misfortune. Listen to me, Monsieur, I'm certainly not the man you were then, but I can't imagine committing such reckless folly."

"Monsieur!" exclaimed the stranger indignantly.

"Hear me out. Where did you go then, in the hopes of finding your children?"

"I crisscrossed all of France, headed to England, and ventured as far as America."

"Without finding any trace of the seducer?"

"How could I possibly find him?"

"Hmm. It seems to me you approached this from the wrong side. You laid too much credence in your father's version of events." Franz stared absent-mindedly in front of him, deep in thought.

"Well, are you really interested?" asked the stranger, uncomfortable with the way Franz had illuminated his motives.

"Have I compelled you to reveal the secrets of your heart? You did so of your own accord. You've asked me about all sorts of things, and now that I've acceded to being a participant, you've become brash and claim to be offended."

"Monsieur, spare me your platitudes," the Southerner refuted.

"Very well. There's no need to prolong this pointless conversation. Please, go back to your newspaper and leave me alone."

"Alright, have it your way. Let's leave it. It's obvious that you're not familiar with the rules of etiquette and lack common courtesy."

Franz turned away, irritated by the foreigner's tactlessness. Yet the stranger couldn't overcome his own reservations as quickly. His chest heaved as he labored to expound his frustration; and his eyes spoke volumes. Finally, he slowed his pacing and sat down, once again picking up his discarded paper.

Franz, lost in his own thoughts, slowly drained his glass. He called the waiter, paid for the bill and left the inn without a farewell parting. He headed for the railway station to await the train's arrival. A few minutes later, the Southerner entered the waiting room, taking a seat on the opposite bench. Both men ignored each other. At last, they heard the signal from the approaching train. The locomotive came to a stop and the bell sounded for the first time, with all passengers hurrying to the platform.

⚜

"Five-minute stop!" yelled the conductor, as the compartment doors opened.

Franz was about to step out onto the platform, when another man came bursting through the entry door. He was short, portly and wore a large Calabrese hat. The man was in such a hurry that he failed to notice Franz. They collided with such force that the portly fellow stumbled backwards and fell to the ground, flattening his glasses that had slipped from his nose.

"Tarnation!" the stranger cursed. "Why are you standing there like a statue? Can't you make a little room for disembarking passengers?"

"Indeed," Franz replied laughing. "Now get up, go home and sin no more, or something far worse will befall you; only your pince-nez fared the worse."

The portly man looked about him, spying the spectacles as they protruded from under his posterior. "Heavens!" he exclaimed, clearly annoyed. "Both lenses have broken. This is all your fault, you... you inconsiderate Urian."[13.2]

"That's true," Franz acknowledged. "Because if I hadn't stood there, then you would have had the misfortune of running into someone else. Now then, may I inquire your name, as a reminder of this unexpected encounter?"

The rotund fellow straightened up. "My name is Hieronymus Aurelius Schneffke," he uttered in a huff. "That's plain as pudding. I can—Heavens! I'm supposed to place an order for the ladies, and it just sounded for the second time."

Hieronymus collected his hat and rushed toward the closest door. He opened it and called the occupant. "Two buttered ham sandwiches with the fixings. But make it quick. I'm in a hurry."

"Is that what you wish to telegraph, my good man?" Franz heard an amused voice in front of him.

Hieronymus looked up and to his horror saw he had mistakenly ventured into the telegraph office. "Of all the luck. I've got to get a move on," he yelled and threw open the door. He looked around for the appropriate sign.

"Re—re," he read squinting. "Yes, that has to be it. And I've wasted four minutes already." He threw open the second door and proclaimed his order as he stepped inside.

"Two buttered ham sandwiches with fixings. But quickly. I'm in a rush." He pulled out his purse with one hand, while he wiped sweat from his brow with the other.

"Well, how much are they?" There was no response. "What do they cost?" Still no answer. At last, Hieronymus squinted for a better look. To his chagrin, he found himself all alone in the room. Once again, he left empty-handed and tried to decipher the sign outside the door.

"Re—re—reservations," he stammered. "Well, if that doesn't take the last straw. How could I have been so blind? Now I really have to hurry."

❧✠☙

In the meantime, Franz had ventured out onto the platform and looked around for the first and second-class carriages. Walking past the second-class coupé, he spotted an open door. On impulse he climbed aboard and immediately recognized Madelon, seated next to a veiled lady.

"Your humble servant, Fräulein Köhler," he greeted bowing.

"Is that you, Sergeant?" she asked surprised. "What are you doing here in Trier?"

"Franz, Franz!" exclaimed the other woman, removing her veil.

"Fräulein Amelia!" he said surprised. "You're here as well? What a coincidence. "And as I can see, you're not travelling alone," he commented, pointing to a peculiar looking suitcase.

Amelia smiled at her brother's trusty valet. "A funny painter is travelling with us. He wants to spoil us by purchasing some ham sandwiches."

It was Franz's turn to grin. "Do you mean that portly fellow who ran into me and fell to the ground, cursing at me for his self-inflicted calamity?"

"What, he fell again?"

"Yes. He landed solidly on the platform, crushing his glasses."

"If we take Berlin into account, then this makes it the eighth time. Tell me, Franz, is it by sheer coincidence that we meet?"

"No. I have instructions from Mademoiselle Nanon to meet up with Fräulein Madelon and—hmm, here comes another passenger. I'll fill you in once we're underway. Please, allow me to take a seat opposite you."

The passenger who entered the coupé was none other than the stranger whom Franz had encountered at the inn. He greeted politely and took his seat.

❧✠☙

Meanwhile, the portly painter had at last found what he was searching for. A sign that read: 2nd Class Waiting Room. He was about to open the door, when it rang for the third time, followed by the locomotive's shrill whistle.

"*Donner und Doria!*" he shouted as he opened the door and stormed inside. In his haste to reach the buffet table, he knocked over a chair, nearly losing his balance. "Two ham sandwiches with fixings. But hurry. I don't have a minute to spare."

"Warm or cold?" asked the waiter.

"Cold, naturally. How much are they?"

"Twelve groschen for both."

"Here, take it," he said, throwing the required amount on the table.

"That's not enough, my good man."

"No, why not?"

"That's not an eight-groschen piece; it's only a three-piece," he said holding it up.

Schneffke exchanged the coins and scooped up the plates. "Adieu!" he called over his shoulder, as he hurried away.

"Hold it!" called out the waiter, holding him back. "Are you taking the sandwiches with you?"

"Yes!" yelled the painter, his voice a mixture of annoyance and fear.

"Then would you be so kind as to leave the plates and cutlery behind, sir."

"For God's sake, man, there's no time!" And with that parting comment he was out the door.

The waiter had no choice but to go after him.

❧✠☙

All the coupé doors had been shut and the wheels started to turn. The two ladies had advised the conductor that one of the passengers was missing. He waited as long as he could, but then was forced to signal the machinist for departure. The women felt sorry for their portly companion and stood at the window, watching for him.

"There he is!" Amelia announced, pointing him out as he came bounding out the station door, a plate of sandwiches in each hand.

"Hold it! I'm coming—the sandwiches. I have to get on board," Hieronymus barked at the conductor.

The passengers, alerted by the commotion, pressed their faces to the windows for a better look.

"Get back!" the conductor warned. "It's too late."

"Don't be ridiculous. I've paid my fare," he blurted out, pressing ahead.

"The plates, give me the plates," the overzealous waiter called out, trying to catch up to him.

Hieronymus looked back at the irritating waiter, and in doing so sealed his own fate. The clever conductor had, when he realized that Schneffke wouldn't be resuming the trip, grabbed his suitcase at the last second and left it behind on the platform. Hieronymus had just reached the coupé he had disembarked five minutes earlier, when he was distracted by the pursuing waiter. He looked back, missed the suitcase and tripped over it. His hat, plates, cutlery, pickles, mustard dish and ham sandwiches scattered in various directions. The unlucky painter tumbled head over heels, coming to rest on his stomach. As on previous occasions, he had the presence of mind to look up at the departing train.

"My dear ladies, once again I have the pleasure to—"

They couldn't hear the rest. His words were drowned out by the screeching of the wheels and accompanied by the laughter of countless onlookers who witnessed the amusing spectacle.

"Well, that must be the ninth time," Amelia announced, resuming her seat.

The newcomer had taken a seat across from her, while Franz sat down opposite Madelon. While she considered his unexpected appearance, Franz pondered the reason for Amelia's presence.

"Didn't you tell me earlier that Nanon had sent you?" Madelon inquired in a subdued voice.

"Yes, that's what happened, Fräulein," he whispered.

"Were you at Ortry?"

"Yes, I passed by there. Are you planning on going there?"

"On the way back, yes."

"Then I'm forced to reveal a secret to you. Will you give me your word that you'll keep it to yourself?"

"Of course."

"Cavalry Master von Löwenklau is there now."

Madelon couldn't hide her smile. "I already know."

"Really? Who told you that?"

"Fräulein Amelia."

"Do you know why he's there?" She nodded. "For God's sake!" he whispered, nearly blurting it out.

"Don't worry. I'm on your side, Sergeant."

"Psst! I'm known as a plant collector in these parts, not as a sergeant. The main thing is that Mademoiselle Nanon has no idea that we're acquainted."

"Does that mean I can't tell her that we already know each other?"

"Please, under no circumstances."

Madelon nodded and said, "I've arranged to meet her at the Thionville railway station."

"Yes, she's expecting to meet with you there."

"And travel with me from that point on?"

Franz nodded. "I have the honor of accompanying her."

"Really? How did that come about?"

It was Franz's turn to smile. "Mademoiselle Nanon was kind enough to ask for my protection."

"I can't wait to hear her explanation."

"I trust you won't have to wait too long. But please, tell me, what is the significance for the gracious lady's presence?"

"That's also mystery, and like us, you'll have to patiently wait for the explanation."

"I have no choice but to bow to your feminine intuition. Does Fräulein Amelia intend on going to Ortry?"

"I believe so."

"*Sapperment!* That could prove to be a little awkward. Does my master have any idea that she's coming?"

"No, not in the least."

"Forgive my saying so, but that was a little careless of her." Just then, Franz glanced over at Amelia and noticed the stranger's interest in her. "Ah, the fellow is admiring her."

"Who is he?"

"A Southerner, one who despises Germans because his German wife had left him taking both their children with her."

"Oh dear, that poor man," Madelon sighed, casting a sympathetic look his way, one that Franz didn't agree with.

Up until now, the stranger had remained quiet, content with looking at the beauty seated across from him. Her appearance left a profound effect on him. She was beautiful and her Germanic features hadn't escaped his notice. Sitting opposite him, her easy-going, yet confident manner had an unusual effect on him, inviting him to look at her again and again, so that he struggled from staring.

It was clearly the same with Amelia. There was something melancholy and at the same time inviting about him. Although he was older, she didn't pay any attention to their age difference, being drawn to his handsome face.

A man will often contemplate a woman's age, but a lady will seldom reciprocate, at least not initially. She allows his character rather than his age to influence her. Still, a young woman can easily succumb to the entreaty of a silver-haired suitor. They exchanged glances without either one opting to break the silence. Finally, Amelia turned to Madelon with a question. "What is the next station?"

"Wellen, gracious Fräulein," answered the stranger in her stead.

"Thank you, sir," Amelia replied, nodding slightly.

He pulled a business card from his vest pocket and handed it to her, revealing the name of Gaston Deephill from New Orleans.

Following his lead, Amelia reached into her purse. But could she disclose her real name? It was possible that this gentleman was somehow connected to Thionville, even Ortry. She hesitated for a moment, and then with resolve fished out a friend's card that she still carried in her purse. She reasoned it might be prudent to pass herself off as an Englishwoman: Miss Harriet de Lissa, London.

"So, you're English, Mademoiselle?" Gaston commented, clearly enjoying his discovery.

"Yes," she replied, blushing slightly.

"Ah, London. The city brings back fond memories for me. As often as I needed to travel to London, I've always enjoyed the hospitality of your countrymen. It was such a refreshing experience, considering I'm a stranger all over."

His words sounded sad, his eyes glistening with a misty look. Amelia guessed that he must have suffered much.

"Did you lose your home, Monsieur?" she ventured to ask.

"Unfortunately, both home and family."

"I feel sorry for you. The one who has lost both has missed out on the best and noblest in life. Yet, that which was lost can be found and that which has fallen can be resurrected."

"Perhaps. But who would want to rebuild on top of rubble? Luck has clearly passed me by."

He turned away, looking out the window. In this way she could admire his profile. What was it that drew her to him, that left such a deep impression on her? Amelia noticed that Madelon too kept looking at the American. As Amelia absentmindedly played with his card, it fell out of her hand without him noticing. But the astute Franz saw it fall and bent over quickly to retrieve it. In doing so, his eyes fell on the name, and he wasn't able to suppress his surprise. As he handed the card to Amelia, Deephill caught the movement and the surprised look on Franz's face, prompting a slight facial twitch, one which Franz couldn't ignore.

"Excuse me, Monsieur," he started, "but is that your card?"

"Who else would it belong to?" the American replied a little brash.

"Monsieur Deephill from New Orleans?"

"Yes," Gaston replied, a little annoyed. "What brings you to broach this topic again?"

"Pardon me, but would you allow me a little leeway. You see, I've been looking for you, and it's very fortunate that I've finally found you."

"That is most curious. Now that you've seen my card, may I see yours as well, Monsieur?"

"I'm afraid I don't have one. My current financial circumstances would consider it an extravagance. However, I can tell you that I'm employed as a *harbossieur* with Doctor Bertrand in Thionville."

The American's astonishment grew. His southern nature, often teetering on his inconsiderate side, couldn't hold back.

"What a fascinating country, where plant collectors can travel about in either first or second-class carriages," Gaston noted condescendingly.

"I agree with you," Franz replied. "In other lands, bank directors on the run and ruined oil barons avail themselves of first-class travel as well. Besides, there's not that much difference between a lowly plant collector and a gentleman who amasses money for a living. Each person reserves his or her own right to pursue their own pleasures in life. My passion is for gathering plants, which turns out to be most fortunate for you."

"You'll pardon me if I tell you that I'm not following your line of thought."

"I can well understand your consternation, and only ask that you be patient for a little longer. Now then, you're expected at Ortry, correct?"

"Yes, indeed."

"And meet with Captain Richemonte?"

"Naturally, as I've told you earlier."

"Your main reason for coming is in regard to your support of France, right?"

"Monsieur, I wouldn't have expected such a question from you, considering you're not a patriot yourself."

"I sympathize with all honorable Frenchmen, sir. Are you per chance carrying millions of francs with you?"

The American looked at him in surprise. "Who told you that?"

"I'll come to that shortly. Are you denying it?"

"I can certainly admit to it, but I choose the right in how I qualify it. Why are you so concerned with this matter?"

"It could turn out disastrously for you, even cost you your life."

Deephill wasn't impressed and his face showed it. "Monsieur, you're joking."

"On the contrary, I am very serious."

"How did you come to that assertion?"

"I know for a fact that someone is bent on killing you to relieve you of your money."

"Ah! They'll have difficulty in doing that."

"Even if you end up facing three men?"

"Monsieur, I'm armed," Gaston retorted.

"Still, what recourse can a weapon have against a sudden and unexpected robbery?"

"That's true," Gaston admitted. "But who is after me?"

"Perhaps I should elaborate, but I prefer in allowing circumstances to speak for themselves. I fear that you wouldn't have reached Ortry alive if you hadn't met me. You see, I took it upon myself to seek you out and warn you of the danger."

The two ladies were shocked by the direction the conversation was taking but remained quiet. The American, initially exhibiting doubt about Franz's disclosure, was becoming more apprehensive.

"But how did you find out about this planned attack?" Gaston asked.

"I was walking in the forest last night," Franz elaborated. "I had misjudged my time and it was already getting dark by the time I headed home. Quite by accident, I came across two men who were engrossed in conversation. They failed to notice me and continued speaking about a businessman, 'Master Deephill' from New Orleans, who was due to arrive in Thionville on the noon-day train, carrying millions with him. They spoke about subduing the unsuspecting American, and if necessary, using a knife. They had already decided to split their reward and mentioned a third man, one who was already in place."

"In place... in place where?" asked Gaston, becoming deeply concerned.

"They didn't reveal that. They made scant references to parts of their plan, leading me to believe that it had been well-thought out and only needed to be implemented."

"Didn't you report this to the police?"

"No."

"Why not?"

"Considering the vague information, I felt this was the best course of action open to me, warning you directly of the planned robbery."

"But the police could have intercepted them," suggested Gaston.

"We can still do that."

"It's a mystery to me how these vagabonds could have learned that I'm carrying millions. Only two people knew about the details of my proposed trip."

"I know who you mean," Franz stated.

"Really? You know of them?"

"Of course: the old captain and Count Rallion."

"Monsieur, if you know that much then you must be in league with us."

"I have yet to express my views," evaded Franz.

"And perhaps you're more involved than the captain himself."

"This is not the time to confirm or contradict your suspicions. What is important is that I've taken it upon myself to warn you."

"Thank you. I still don't understand how those scoundrels could have found out about my business dealings. I was assured that both Richemonte and Rallion were discreet men."

"Perhaps they were spied upon?" Franz suggested, not wishing to disclose everything that he and Richard had overheard.

"Yes, in the absence of more information that's likely what occurred."

"It's the only logical conclusion."

"But the place… the place where all of this is supposed to happen? Have you no idea, didn't you glean anything from their talk?"

"Well," Franz considered, "there was talk of a railway worker."

"Alright. You would expect to find railway employees at or near the tracks, not at the station. Do you suppose there could be workers between Thionville and Ortry?"

"No. There are no tracks between the two places."

"That is most curious. In what context did those two mention the third man?"

"The two wanted to seek him out, even speak to him, so as to be able to later prove that they had nothing to do with the plot."

"And yet, they planned on robbing me."

Franz thought back to the conversation. "In a way, it seemed that something was supposed to occur before the robbery. They spoke of finding things in such a way as to make their job easier. In the event that you were still alive, they planned on strangling you, even using a knife."

Even though Deephill was composed, he still paled at the revelation. "Dear God!" he exclaimed. "I'm beginning to piece together what they're up to."

"What?" all three uttered in unison.

"Could the third man, the one they talked about, be planning to stop…?" The American stopped speaking, as an ominous thought worked its way into his brain, a plan so devious that he couldn't readily dismiss it.

"What, what could they be planning?" Franz prompted him.

"Could the third man be planning to derail the train?"

"That's it! That has to be it," exclaimed Franz, jumping out of his seat and hitting his head on the upper berth. "He's planning on removing a section of the rail, or simply cover the tracks with an obstruction. The train will derail in either case and the coupés will break apart. Countless people will be injured, and some will undoubtedly die. All those two will have to do in the ensuing confusion is to find you, the unconscious American, and relieve you of your wallet. If you're dead, they'll have an easy time of it. If you're only incapacitated, they've devised a plan of finishing you off: A quick thrust of a blade or a strangling hold."

The ladies had been following the rapidly unfolding conversation, shocked and speechless at the robbers' audacity and frightened at what may yet occur.

"There's no time to lose," Amelia cried out, composing herself. "We must act. Where are we now?"

Franz opened his window and the American did the same on his side.

"We've already passed Königsmarchen," announced Franz.

"How many more stations until we reach Thionville?" inquired Gaston.

"We just passed the last one. Thionville is next. If something is about to happen, it will be very soon. Where is the emergency cable? We have to alert the engineer."

Both men looked about the interior of the coupé but couldn't find one.

"Let's open the compartment door," Franz said. "I'm going to climb onto the running board for a better look."

He reached out the window and opened the door from the outside, with the American following suit on his side. Just as each man stepped onto the running board, they all heard the locomotive's shrill warning signal. The train was just entering a bend. Franz found himself on the inner side of the curvature and could make out the section of the railway tracks ahead of the machine.

"Dear God! Rocks on the rails ahead," yelled Franz. "There's no way for the train to stop in time. I fear it will derail. Monsieur", he yelled while turning to face Deephill. "We have to get the ladies out. Our only hope is to jump off and take our chances."

Franz reached back inside, grabbing Madelon's arm. In one swift motion, he picked her up and jumped off. He half-ran and half-slid down the embankment, all the while holding onto her.

CHAPTER FOURTEEN

A HORRIBLE DEED

The American possessed no less presence of mind than the fearless Franz.

"Come on, Miss!" Gaston yelled, determined in his resolve not to leave the English lady behind. Amelia recognized there was no other way and fell into his arms. Although he wasn't as powerfully built as Franz, Gaston was no weakling, summoning every ounce of strength.

The locomotive strained against the screeching brakes. The manifold clamor of the fear-laden passengers nearly drowned out the squealing wheels. He scooped up Amelia with his left arm, gripped the handle and took a calculated jump. He landed on his feet, which buckled momentarily under their combined weight, but managed to straighten up and, like Franz, slid down the other side of the embankment. And not a moment too soon.

A crash, a horrible, dreadful crash resounded as if half a mountain had exploded, followed by shrill, droning, stamping, rolling groaning sounds. The American's prophecy was fulfilling itself in an unimaginable way. The train derailed and rapidly headed down the steep embankment. The carriages had separated, and sliding down the embankment, they twisted, flipped and crashed into each other, coming to rest in all sorts of unnatural positions. It had the appearance of a junk yard, a mountain of rubble, that covered the unfortunate place.

Then suddenly, everything was deathly quiet. After what seemed like an excruciating long moment, sounds gradually drifted up. They were unpleasant sounds, human sounds: whimpering, pleading, crying, and yelling, defying all description. Not far from the accident site, two couples were resting from their ordeal. One, on the left side of the embankment, and the other on its right. Amelia lay unconscious on the grass, as Gaston knelt beside her, concern written on his face. He hoped she had only passed out from the ordeal and was otherwise unscathed. He opened her bodice so she could breathe easier and in so doing came to appreciate her beauty.

Nearly speechless, he whispered to himself. "How perfect, so well-proportioned, like only a woman of English breeding should be. What was my Amély, my little kolibri compared to this woman? Can I possibly win the love of this goddess-like beauty?"

On the other side of the embankment, Franz was kneeling beside Madelon. She was awake, having fared a little better than her friend. She dared to open her eyes, looking dazed and bewildered.

"Am I still alive?" she whispered.

"Yes, you're still alive, Fräulein," Franz replied gently. "Thank God that we managed to evade that horrible collision at the last moment."

"Where is my friend, Amelia?"

"On the other side, I should think."

"Is she safe, did she make it?"

"I don't know. I hope so."

"You only hope so? Haven't you checked?"

"No. My place is with you. I couldn't get across. The train tumbled down that side. Dear God! I hope they managed to get out as well."

"We'll have to see for ourselves. Come on, Franz!"

Just in that moment, her concern for her friend gave her renewed strength. She climbed up the slope as if she hadn't experienced the slide at all. Franz was barely able to keep up. They scampered across the tracks and down the other side. To his relief, Franz spotted their companions down the slope on the grass and out of harm's way. Deephill was sitting up, but Amelia wasn't moving, still lying on the grass.

"Dear God! Is she dead?" called out Madelon frightened.

"Not at all," Gaston replied reassuringly. "Come down and see for yourself."

Franz and Madelon worked their way down. Madelon kneeled at her friend's side and began to examine her. "She fainted, that's all," she said with relief. "Please, Messieurs, leave us alone. I'm sure your help can be put to better use elsewhere."

"That's true. Come on," acknowledged Franz, beckoning Gaston to follow him.

The two men, uninjured and willing to help, rushed toward the accident site. They faced an awful view, a horrific picture of destruction. The locomotive had buried itself deep in the earth. It hissed, churned and ached, like a dying dragon that had spent its energy. The mutilated bodies of the machinist and stoker lay nearby, nearly unrecognizable. It wasn't much better in the coupés and other carriages. Franz saw that those who were either unhurt or had sustained only minor injuries, had managed to crawl or extricate themselves from the wreckage.

Franz and Gaston rallied the uninjured in a rescue effort. Off in the distance, they noticed three men walking toward them, one in the uniform of a railway worker and the other two in regular clothes.

"Monsieur," Franz whispered to his new-found accomplice. "Those two must be the perpetrators."

"Yes, you're probably right," he agreed, sizing them up. "Let's apprehend them right now."

"Sure, but what if we could catch them red-handed?"

"How can we? They've committed their heinous act, but we can't pin it on them since you didn't recognize them."

"I wasn't able to distinguish their facial features the other night, that much is true. But nevertheless, we will outsmart them."

"How?" Gaston asked skeptically.

"Are you inclined to play a dead man, Monsieur?"

"I have no objection, but what about their planned knife attack?"

"I'll make sure I'm nearby and keep a close watch."

"Alright. I'll risk it."

"Just remove the money from your billfold."

"It's not necessary. Those vagabonds have underestimated me. There are no actual banknotes. I'm only carrying papers, instructions to banks. They're worthless in someone else's hands. Even if their coup had succeeded, they wouldn't have been able to cash in one franc."

"Then let's move quickly. I spotted them up front by the locomotive. But they shouldn't see you walking about."

"Where should I go?"

"Here," Franz said, pointing to a coupé. "Crawl into this first-class carriage. It's quite demolished. I'll cover you up with loose debris. That way they won't realize you're unhurt. I'll keep an eye on them from that opening up there. If one of them so much as looks like he might try something, I'll finish him off with my revolver."

Satisfied with the plan, Gaston crawled inside the damaged car and Franz covered him with debris, leaving only his head and upper body exposed.

"Now then," continued Franz. "All we need is a reliable witness."

By coincidence, Franz spotted the conductor walking about. Uninjured, he was orchestrating the rescue effort, while they waited for much needed help to arrive. Franz approached him circumspectly and motioned him to accompany him behind an overturned coupé, where they would be out of the perpetrators' view.

"What do you want?" inquired the railway man. "Can't you see I'm busy?"

"Are you interested in apprehending those responsible for this mayhem?"

"Monsieur, if that were only possible."

"It's quite possible. They're still on site."

"Here? Out of the question," replied the conductor with skepticism. "Who would be so stupid to remain behind?"

"No, it's true. Look, there's no time to go into a lengthy explanation. Here is what happened. Only last night, I overheard a conversation between two men in a nearby forest. They spoke of an American who would be travelling by train and carrying millions. They planned to murder him—after his arrival in Thionville, or so I surmised. I headed out to intercept the foreigner and warn him of the plot. I was able to meet him half-way, but the vagabonds had devised something devious with the help of another. As you now know, they forced the train to derail and have returned under the guise of lending assistance to the injured, but in reality, came to find the American and abscond with his money."

The conductor was speechless, trying to absorb it all. "Really?" he finally managed to say. "Well, we will certainly accommodate them with a reception they won't soon forget. Where is this foreign gentleman now?"

"I've concealed him in the first-class carriage, where he's intending to play the part of the corpse."

"Excellent. But I need to speak to him first."

Franz led the conductor to the prescribed spot. The man looked into the damaged coupé and spotted the American. "My name is Chaisson," he began. "Is what this man says about the plot really true?"

Deephill nodded vigorously and corroborated the entire story. Lastly, the conductor asked to see the billfold. Gaston produced it, showing him the documents.

"I'm satisfied," Chaisson nodded sternly. "Now let's see if those two are brazen enough to follow through with their plan."

"Just a minute, Monsieur," pleaded Franz. "I have to climb up and watch over him, so they won't kill him."

"I commend you for your prudence," Chaisson acknowledged. "There's some canvass over in the corner. I'll throw it up and you can cover yourself with it. I'll arrange it so those reprobates make their way over here. The rest will work itself out."

The conductor left. Franz climbed on top of the carriage and concealed himself under the canvass. He was in perfect position to observe everything below him. The American businessman really did resemble a corpse. His coat was open at the front, making it child's play to remove the billfold.

In the meantime, the conductor had returned to his former post and continued to oversee the rescue effort. He noticed two men working alongside the other volunteers, seemingly eager in their efforts. Yet after observing them for a few minutes, Chaisson saw that they only spent a few moments at each place before moving on to the next casualty, seemingly looking for something. He approached them and commended them for their assistance.

"Good work, men. More help is required back there," he said pointing over his shoulder. "Several wine merchants occupied the second-class carriage and as I recall, there was an American businessman in first-class. Perhaps you can go check on them."

It was clear by the looks on their faces that this was welcome news. This would bring them directly to the man they were searching for. They didn't need further prodding. Chaisson turned away, pretending to occupy himself with another matter.

"That turned out as if we'd planned it," whispered Caron to his accomplice. "So, we can look for him in the first-class carriage. I can hardly contain my excitement. Do you think he has the money with him?"

"We'll find out right away. Come on," urged Poirier. They approached the coupé and peered inside.

"*Sacre bleu!* He must have been crushed," Caron said pointing out the pinned body.

"Good. Then he's already dead."

Franz's handiwork in rearranging the debris was enough to fool them.

"Let's not waste any more time," Poirier said, crawling forward and reaching inside the American's coat. He retrieved the thick billfold and eagerly opened it. "The devil!" he exclaimed a little too loud. "Look at this wad of money; nothing but large denominations," he said, assuming the papers were actual banknotes.

"Great! Let's get out of here."

"Not too hasty, my friend. We don't want to stand out. Let's pretend to help out in the other coupé. I saw them wire to Thionville and Königsmarchen for help. It should arrive soon, and when it does that will be our opportunity to slip through unnoticed."

"Are we sticking to our plan?" asked Caron.

"Of course. The old man can choke on it."

"And Lefleur?"

"He can complain all he likes. We'll just tell him we came up empty-handed."

"Then lead the way."

They crawled out of the wagon and headed for the 2nd class carriage.

❧✠☙

Franz used the opportunity to slide down from his vantage point and sought out the conductor without being spotted by the two vagabonds.

"Did they make off with the wallet?" Chaisson asked.

"Yes," Franz said, nodding grimly.

"Well done. Wait, do you hear that noise?" the conductor said, turning on his heel. "That must be the relief train coming from Thionville. Let's wait for reinforcements to arrive. Then we can arrest those devils."

"Their plan was to wait for the train's arrival and then abscond at the first opportunity."

"Hmm. Then it's prudent to keep an eye on them. Can you manage that?"

"Of course."

"As I've noticed, you have a revolver on you, Monsieur."

"Yes, as a precaution."

"Then make good use of it if one of those fellows tries to escape. Ah, here comes a locomotive with wagons. Thank God!" He rushed away.

Franz walked over to where the two men were occupied and indicated that he wished to support them in their effort.

Upon receiving the news of the train's derailment, the authority in Thionville immediately made preparations for assistance. A locomotive pulling two carriages was dispatched, equipped with a military contingent, railway workers and two doctors. No sooner had the train come to a stop, than the officer in charge, a captain, started issuing orders to his men.

The conductor recognized the officer and rushed toward him. "Thank God for your speedy arrival, Captain Savoie," Chaisson proclaimed nearly out of breath. "I implore you to ensure that none of the personnel currently engaged here are allowed to leave without your express permission."

"Why the precaution?" asked Savoie puzzled.

"Because those who caused the derailment are still on site."

"*Sacre bleu!*" the captain said, taking a step back. "Then this was no accident? It was deliberate?"

"Yes," nodded the conductor. "The perpetrators had placed rocks on the rails."

"Do you know who's responsible?"

"Yes. They were identified to me. I'll point them out to you shortly."

"Good. I will see to it that they get what's coming to them."

Workers disengaged the locomotive from the two carriages. It steamed back to Thionville for more supplies and additional wagons that had been requested from Metz. The captain didn't waste any time in taking charge of the scene. He issued his instructions loudly and with authority, including the directive for all to remain at the scene. Further, he warned that should anyone leave without his permission, that offender would risk arrest, even being shot. He then distributed his soldiers about the place in such a way that they were able to cover the entire area.

The two villains, now in possession of the American's billfold, were in the process of extricating a corpse from under the sides of a broken-up carriage. Franz, though nearby, was holding up some debris and couldn't overhear their subdued conversation.

"Hang it all!" Poirier swore. "Did you hear that?"

"You mean the captain's last order?"

"Of course, what else."

"That idiot yelled loud enough to be heard in the next county. What do you think?"

"It's damned awkward."

"They must suspect something."

"Pah! They're guessing, that's all."

"But what if they start searching and find the wallet on us?"

"How could they come up with the idea of singling us out? Highly unlikely."

"I disagree with you there. Take a look around. With all these personal things strewn about, some might be tempted to take them. What if the soldiers were ordered to search everyone who took part in the rescue effort?"

"They won't do that," Poirier persisted. "It would be perceived as a disgrace, even an insult to those who've helped out."

"Perhaps. It's still smarter to sneak away. But how can we?"

"Simple. We'll pick up one of the injured men and carry him to the rescue wagon for treatment. It's up there, and away from the soldiers. When no one is looking our way, we'll scurry down the other side and disappear."

"Good idea. I don't see any guards there yet."

"Alright then," Poirier proclaimed. Then, for Franz's benefit, he continued a little louder. "This man is dead. We're wasting our time. Hey there, friend!"

Even though Franz hadn't caught their earlier conversation, he had maintained his surveillance on them being careful to watch their every movement.

"What's going on?" Franz asked. "Just pull him out."

"No, he's dead," replied Poirier. "Let's move on, where we're actually needed."

They left, thinking of leaving him behind. But in the next instant, there he was beside them. "Right you are," Franz said. "They need us over there. Come on."

"Damned irritating fellow!" cursed Caron, forced to keep up appearances.

❧✠☙

In the meantime, Amelia had regained consciousness. It truly was miraculous that both men had been able to jump from their respective running board without either man or their charge sustaining injury. This was partially due to the fact that the alert machinist had already applied the brakes, with the end result that the train was moving at reduced speed when they jumped.

With Madelon kneeling beside her, Amelia slowly opened her eyes. Her second glance was at the carnage not far from her, instantly bringing her back to the present.

"I'm so glad you're safe," she said, fixing her gaze on Madelon.

"And you, too. Praise God! Can you stand up?"

Amelia managed to sit up. Gingerly, she rose to her feet and tested her joints, all apparently working normally. She felt minor aches and some discomfort because of the slide but was thankful to have escaped serious injury.

"Yes, I can manage, thanks to my rescuer," she announced. "Where is he?"

"Who?"

"The stranger, the one who jumped with me from the coupé. Is he alright?"

Madelon detected a concern in her friend's voice, more than one would normally attribute to a stranger.

"Yes, he's fine," Madelon replied.

"And Franz?"

"That brave man. Yes, he too escaped without injury."

Amelia looked around her. "But all those poor people. It looks so horrible down there."

"They could certainly benefit from a woman's help."

"Then we should go. Come, dear Madelon."

"Of course. But first, I have to come to an understanding about something vital."

"About what?"

"About you," she smiled. "I noticed how you didn't give the American businessman your own card."

"You're right. I followed an inner prompting that I should be careful about my identity."

"So, which name did you use? Who are you supposed to be?"

"What it said on the card: Harriet de Lissa, London."

"Alright. So, you're an Englishwoman and we coincidentally met in the carriage. Does Franz know?"

"No. Would you please let him know if you see him first?"

The two women quickly brushed the dirt from their clothes and headed to the staging area where their help was most welcome. It was not a pleasant sight and required their composure in facing the difficult task before them.

❦✠❧

Nanon had arranged for a ride to the train station in Thionville, where she planned on waiting for her sister's arrival, intending to join her in her coupé. The train was expected any minute but failed to show up as scheduled. Something wasn't quite right. All of a sudden, she heard a commotion in the waiting area, the news spreading like wildfire.

"The train derailed!" Nanon heard one man shout. "It happened somewhere between here and Königsmarchen," she heard from another source, and shuddered. She felt light-headed and sat down on a nearby bench. When she regained her composure, she found a porter looking at her with concern.

"Are you expecting relatives, Mademoiselle?" asked the porter.

"Yes, my sister, Madelon," she whispered.

"Was she on the Trier train?"

"Yes. I just overheard that there was an accident."

"That's true. It's supposed to be an awful scene."

"Dear God!" she whimpered. "I have to go there and see for myself." Nanon tried to get up, but a tremor went through her body, so that she sank back onto the bench.

"Get a hold of yourself, Mademoiselle," the porter urged with a calming voice. "Not everyone was injured, and there's a good chance your sister was among the more fortunate ones."

His reassuring words gave her comfort and renewed strength to carry on.

"Thank you, Monsieur," she replied. "But I can't just wait here. I have to go and see for myself." She rose from her seat, but he gently held her back.

"Just a moment," he said. "They've already sent for help. A military troop train is being assembled and doctors are being sought. Fortunately, there is a stoked locomotive ready to get under way. In just a few minutes we'll depart for the accident site."

"But can't I come along? I could help."

"Don't worry," he said, a slight smile forming on his lips. "I will arrange it so that you'll be able to accompany us."

As it turned out, the man had some influence and was able to keep his word. He escorted Nanon himself to the waiting carriage, allowing her to arrive so early. But when she spotted the carnage and heard the whimpering and cries of the injured, she sank back into her seat. It took a few minutes before she could muster enough courage to climb from the wagon. As she made her way down the embankment, she spotted someone she hadn't expected to see here—Franz, *her* Franz, the unassuming plant collector. She was shocked since she had been looking for him in vain in Thionville. The sight of him gave her new strength and boldness. She hurried toward Franz and in no time stood beside him. Franz was in the company of two men and kneeling beside an injured man.

"Monsieur Schneeberg," she called, taking him by the arm. "I didn't expect to find you here. Have you seen my sister?"

Franz rose from his kneeling position, smiling from ear to ear. He pointed along the embankment. "Don't worry, Mademoiselle Nanon. Here she comes."

Nanon shouted for joy and rushed with open arms toward her sister, who was walking toward them and accompanied by Amelia.

"Madelon! Madelon, my dear sister. How glad I am to see you unhurt."

Her sister cast a probing glance at the one who approached in such a hurry, and then in a moment of recognition, opened her arms in welcome.

"Nanon!" she cried, overjoyed. "Finding you here, my God what a reunion." A moment later they were in each other's arms, laughing, hugging and kissing.

"I feared you were dead," Nanon managed.

"No. God, in his mercy, chose to spare my life."

"You could have been crushed. It's nothing short of a miracle."

"Yes, it was a miracle, but one borne out of daring."

"Out of daring? So, it's not by chance that you're standing here?"

"No. The train was still in motion and just as the machinist gave the emergency signal, one of the passengers grabbed me, stepped out onto the running board, and we jumped off at the last second."

"What boldness and presence of mind. Is your savior also uninjured?"

"Yes, thank God."

"I want to thank him for his timely intervention. Where is he?"

A happy, yet mischievous look spread across Madelon's face. "He's that tall, muscular fellow, the one who's engaged in helping the wounded over there," she said pointing him out.

Nanon followed her outstretched arm, her gaze settling on Franz. "Him?" she asked puzzled. "That man?"

"Yes, him."

Nanon clasped her hands together, not believing her eyes. "But that's Franz Schneeberg, my friend and protector."

"Evidently, my dear Nanon."

"But how could he have rescued you? He wasn't even on the train."

"Sure, he was. He joined us in Trier."

"I don't understand it," Nanon said, puzzled. "I specifically asked him to meet me at the railway station in Thionville." Then shrugging off her confusion, she said. "I have to see him right away and thank him."

"Of course, but first, allow me to introduce you to this lady," she said pointing out Amelia. "My sister Nanon—Miss de Lissa from London, who was rescued in exactly the same way I was."

Nanon's surprised meeting with Madelon had played out so quickly that she hadn't paid the lady any attention. Now that they had been introduced to each other, Nanon bowed politely.

"Were you also rescued by Monsieur Schneeberg's actions, Miss?"

"If not directly, certainly through his prompt intervention," replied Amelia. "If he hadn't climbed into our coupé, we both would have ended up badly wounded or even dead in that first-class carriage."

"That is incredible. I must see him." She rushed to meet Franz, with Amelia and Madelon following behind her. Franz was applying a dressing to a wounded passenger when Nanon approached him, putting her hand on his shoulder.

"Monsieur," she started, "was it really you who rescued my sister Madelon? I will never forget your bravery."

"Mademoiselle," he replied, smiling at her flushed face, "it was pure coincidence that I met her on the train. Let's talk about it later. These poor, injured people require our full attention."

"Yes, you're quite right. I've gotten over my initial shock and I'm now ready to help out."

The three women turned their attention to the two doctors who had arrived with the train. Meanwhile, the two criminals were still with Franz, or more accurately, he was with them, not deviating from their side. Just then, they picked up the injured man whom Franz had bandaged and were prepared to carry him to the waiting carriage, up above on the tracks. Franz intended to accompany them, but Poirier tried to dismiss him.

"It's not necessary. We can carry him by ourselves."

"Up this steep incline?"

"Yes. We're not weaklings."

"Maybe not; but it will still take all three of us to get him into the carriage."

Without waiting for a response, Franz took hold of the stretcher. He wasn't going to let them out of his sight, much less stay back. They had no choice even though they inwardly cursed his interference. As they labored up the slope, the two vagabonds traded knowing glances, intimating this was their best opportunity to make their getaway. They erroneously assumed that Franz wasn't aware of their involvement, presuming him to be just an eager helper. But he caught their wordless exchange and felt man enough to hinder their flight.

While the three men slowly made their way up the embankment, the conductor at last found an opportunity to speak to the officer in charge of the detail.

"Captain," he said, pointing at the three men, "those are the two rogues I had mentioned earlier."

"Really? What about that tall, muscular fellow?"

"No. It's on his account that we've been able to unmask the real perpetrators. He's staying close by to keep an eye on them until you can intervene."

"Good. I see they're transporting that wounded man to one of the carriages. I suspect it's a ruse to get away, something I intend to prevent." Savoie motioned two soldiers to come over, and then quietly issued his instructions. They in turn removed their shouldered rifles and readied them. "But only shoot if they ignore my warning," their superior added. "In that case, make sure to only wound them. I want them alive so we can question them."

At last, the trio arrived at the aforementioned carriage.

"Only one at a time," commented Poirier. "You're the strongest, Monsieur. Climb in and take the wounded man by the shoulders."

Franz had expected something of the kind. He nodded his agreement, but in no wise felt outsmarted. *I'm going to go along with it*, he thought, *but it's you two who are heading into a trap*. Franz grasped the wounded man and carefully backed into the carriage. The other two lifted and pushed. But before the wounded man was half-way into the carriage, they let go of him, forcing Franz to shoulder more of the weight.

"It's now or never. Let's go!" whispered Poirier.

He turned around, and followed by Caron, sauntered along the side of the carriage, hoping to reach its end and duck behind it and then disappear down the unattended slope. But the watchful officer had anticipated their move.

"Hold it, you two," he called up to them. "Stop!"

They pretended as if they hadn't heard him and kept walking.

"Stop! Or I'll shoot," the captain hollered.

Poirier looked back and whispered to Caron. "Damn! They somehow suspect us. But before they actually get the first shot off, we'll be safe behind the wagon. Let's go!"

Both men ran to the end of the last carriage.

"Fire!" Savoie commanded.

Franz, still preoccupied with the injured man, had of course noticed their hasty departure. He leaned out the door, just in time to see them round the end of the carriage. *Just as I thought*, he mused. *They want to head down the other side. Just wait you two.* He walked to the back of the wagon, opened the rear door and jumped out. Armed with the revolver in his right hand, he rushed to the end of the last wagon when he heard the captain's order to fire. Two shots rang out, but instead of hitting the culprits, they struck the wooden side of the wagon.

"Welcome!" Franz yelled to the two perpetrators who came bounding around the end of the carriage. "What's your hurry? Stay for a while."

Both men recognized their immediate danger. Poirier drew back his fist, intending to strike the revolver out of Franz's hand, but before he could do so, he was knocked to the ground by Franz's powerful blow, momentarily losing consciousness. Caron wasn't about to give up and upped the ante by pulling his knife, charging determinedly at Franz. Yet the brave Ulanen sergeant met him with a well-placed kick to his solar plexus, so that he stumbled backwards, dropping the knife. Franz quickly pocketed his revolver and stood over both men, holding them down. He looked up to see several soldiers come running around the end of the wagon.

"Ah! There they are," called out the captain, catching up to them.

"Yes, and quite compliant," laughed Franz. "Perhaps it would be best if you had them tied up."

The officer balked, not liking the tone of his voice. "I thought it was my place to determine what needs to happen next?"

"I won't stand in your way, Captain," Franz replied evenly, standing up and collecting his hat. "But please, sir, exercise more caution from now on."

"About what?" Savoie asked indignantly.

"I heard your order to shoot at those two vagabonds, but the bullets missed them entirely and struck this wagon instead. What if I had been hit?"

"Pah! It would have been your own fault. How could I have known that you were back there? Who told you in the first place to go after them?"

"I didn't need anyone's permission, Captain! Had I not pursued them, then these two rogues would have escaped. By the time your men would have shown up, they would have scampered down the slope, and likely have found refuge in the brush."

"I rather doubt that, Monsieur."

Franz was not to be deterred. "And furthermore, there were injured people in that same carriage. What if they had been hit? You should have taken that into account before you issued the order to fire."

"Really? And who are you to point out such matters?"

"That's beside the point. The main thing is to ensure that these two men are in custody." Franz nodded curtly and headed back down the embankment.

The captain felt he had been reprimanded and fought to suppress his anger. He ordered the suspects to be tied up and moved to an empty wagon. Once they were confined inside, he ordered the placement of a sentry.

The two vagabonds weren't about to give up and resorted to boldness in the hope of extricating themselves.

"Captain," started Poirier, "what have we done to deserve this treatment? We haven't done anything wrong."

Franz returned just then with the conductor and the American in tow.

"Maybe you should direct your questions to these gentlemen," Savoie replied. Both men stared at the American, as if they had seen a ghost.

"You plundered this man," Chaisson said pointing at Deephill.

"We don't know anything about it," Poirier replied, trying to suppress his growing unease.

"Oho!" exclaimed Franz. "The audacity of the man. It was he who had removed the billfold and stuck it in his own jacket." He jumped onto the wagon and searched Poirier's coat pocket. "Here it is, Monsieur

Deephill. Why don't you check to see if anything's missing? Those two scoundrels spoke of large banknotes."

Deephill opened the billfold and examined the contents. "Nothing is missing," he said, smiling. "Besides, the thieves made a huge mistake. These aren't actual banknotes, rather they represent instructions to my bank. I have to sign them before they can be tendered for cash. As it stands now, they're not worth one sou."

"That in no way diminishes their guilt," Chaisson declared. "They planned this whole thing, derailing the train and thereby plundering this man's pockets. They're responsible for the deaths and injuries of countless people. They're guilty of the crime and deserve no mercy."

"Prove it!" shouted Caron. "We have an alibi. We were close to a railway worker when the tragedy occurred."

"We know all about it. Your accomplice actually placed the rocks, while you arranged for your alibi. You're not going anywhere. Where is your friend?"

"We don't have one."

"Fine. Lie all you want. We'll find a way to make you confess. Captain, please arrange it so they won't be tempted to leave a second time."

"Don't worry. I'll see to it," Savoie confirmed.

The captain stationed an armed guard at the open window. The soldier stood on the running board and kept a watchful eye on the prisoners. He was given explicit instructions to shoot, should either one attempt to get away. Satisfied, the entourage headed back down the embankment to lend assistance where it was needed most.

Though tied-up and confined, the two criminals conversed quietly.

"Hey Poirier, we're done for," said Caron.

"I wish the devil would strangle that fellow who got in our way. Who could he be?"

"I've never seen him before."

"Me neither. We almost got away. Damn him!"

"They seem to know everything about us."

"I know; even about Lefleur," conceded Poirier. "How could they have found out?"

"There's only one explanation: someone must have overheard us."

"But who?"

"I suppose we'll find that out at our trial."

"Heaven and hell! Once we end up there, it'll be over for us."

"Don't I know it."

"Wait just a minute!"

"What? You have an idea?"

"Yes, but keep it down. I don't want that guard to know that we're talking."

"Don't worry. Those down there are making plenty of noise for us not to be heard. So, what's your plan?"

"Well, so far no one seems to know who we are."

"That's true."

"If we managed to get away, time would be on our side, and grass would grow over this affair. We would have to disappear for a while, maybe a few years."

"Of course. But how can we get out of here?"

"If you've noticed, they're only keeping watch on one side, but not on the other—"

"What use is that?" interrupted Caron hopelessly.

"If we could only open it?"

"But the soldier won't turn away long enough."

"So, we'll have to come up with a way to distract him."

"Yes, I see that's the only way; but we're still tied up. How can we open a window or slide that large door?"

"I know. Even if we managed to get out, it would be impossible to run, tied up like this."

"Tarnation! If we only had a knife."

"That's what I was thinking. I've lost mine. Let's give it some thought. It's our only chance."

"I just thought of something," Caron said.

"Really? What?"

"Do you suppose that the old man would leave us to our fate?"

"Well, I would think that our rescue would be just as important for him as for us."

"Of course! But that old captain is unpredictable."

"Surely he must realize that we will implicate him if he abandons us."

"I don't know. It depends on the circumstances."

"Quiet back there!" admonished the sentry, who finally realized they were talking.

"We weren't talking," Poirier replied insolently.

"Shut up! I saw you and I'm warning you. If you speak again, I'm going to put a gag in your mouths."

They shot him angry glances, but in the end had to comply.

CHAPTER FIFTEEN

A TIMELY ESCAPE

Back at Castle Ortry, Baroness Adeline de Sainte-Marie was in a foul mood. Anticipating that her stepdaughter Marion would be chastised by the captain, she took to the news badly and though she tried to suppress her disappointment, ended up with a headache that threatened to turn into a migraine. A servant had been dispatched to Thionville to find Doctor Bertrand and persuade him to pay the distressed lady a visit.

As Philippe Bertrand was also engaged as the Baron's personal physician, he postponed his afternoon appointments and rode out to the castle without delay. He was still occupied with attending to the ailing baroness, when a horseman rode into the courtyard, inquiring after the doctor. The doctor excused himself from the baroness's chamber and headed to the foyer. The rider dispensed with the usual formality and appealed directly to the doctor.

"Doctor Bertrand," he said without preamble, "you need to come right away. All doctors are urgently needed. A train has derailed."

All those present, with the exception of the baroness, were sitting in the dining room, witnesses to his proclamation. They paled at the news. The old captain lifted his head and looked expectantly at the messenger.

"You say a train has derailed," queried the doctor. "Where exactly?"

"Just before Thionville. Someone had deliberately placed rocks on the railway tracks."

"Dear God!" Philippe exclaimed. "What an awful deed. Does it look bad?"

The messenger nodded. "Many have been injured. There are also some deaths."

"Then I must leave immediately. Captain, please excuse me. I have to leave *sans façon*."

The captain's eyes had a sinister glow. *How did they already know it was deliberate?* he thought. *Did my men handle it poorly? There's a lot at stake. I'll have to go and see for myself.*

"Yes, by all means," he said out loud. "There's no need for you to apologize. Is your horse in the stable?"

"Yes," confirmed the doctor, turning and heading for the door.

"If you can wait for one minute, I will accompany you. In such circumstances, you can never have enough helpers. It might be best if we dispense in going back to town and head directly to the accident site."

He opened a nearby window and issued instructions to saddle his horse.

Marion de Sainte-Marie was visibly shaken. "Dear God!" she managed to say. "But that's the train that Madelon was planning to take."

"Madelon? Who is that?" Albin asked quickly.

"Nanon's sister."

"Oh, you mean the German governess. Well, don't concern yourself too much with her."

"What kind of a statement is that?" asked Marion, rising from her seat. "Only a devil could say such a thing."

"Be quiet girl," he admonished her. But she wasn't about to be deterred and pushed her chair back.

"I can't just sit idly by when Madelon could be in danger. I have to go as well."

"No! You are staying," Albin instructed.

"You know very well what we discussed yesterday. Doctor Müller," Marion said, turning to face the educator, "will you accompany me?"

"I am at your service, gracious lady," he said bowing.

The captain faced him. "And if I forbid you to come along?" Albin retorted, the veiled threat barely skin-deep.

"Would you really consider sending a lady without protection to such a place, Captain?" Richard offered.

Debating with himself, the old man played with the ends of his moustache. "Alright! I will allow it. But next time I'm going to insist that she comply with my wishes." Then turning toward Bertrand, he added. "Let's go, Doctor."

Two minutes later, the two men galloped toward the perceived accident site. They took a path through the open fields, thereby avoiding having to follow the street through town. They reached the general area and jumped from their mounts. They left their horses at the bottom of the gulley, scaled the embankment and headed down the other side toward the staging area. The old captain was acknowledged by the site commander, Savoie, who of course knew him, while Bertrand was welcomed by two colleagues who were happy to have another physician helping out.

Bertrand came prepared, his satchel in hand, and immediately went to work. He spotted a beautiful woman that was occupied in rendering aid to a man whose leg had been horribly crushed. He approached her and offered his help.

"The poor man," she said looking helpless. "He must have passed out from the pain."

"Perhaps it's best that way," Philippe commented standing up. "Let's move on to another victim. We can't do anything for this man right now. I fear the leg will have to be amputated."

As the lady rose, Philippe was able to fully see her face. "Could it really be?" he said taken aback. "It's too much of a coincidence. You have to be—" He stopped speaking and looked around to see if he could be overheard. "Why you're Fräulein von Löwenklau."

"Yes," she said smiling. "And you must be Doctor Bertrand who in 1866 was miraculously—"

"—rescued by your brother," he said, finishing the sentence for her. "It was then that I had the pleasure to make your acquaintance. But for heaven's sake, aren't you placing yourself in danger by showing up here?"

"I had to risk it," she clarified. "And if I may be so bold, I was hoping for your assistance."

"I will gladly do what I can for you, Fräulein."

"It was my intention to look you up in Thionville. But I too was involved in this unfortunate accident, the consequences of which—"

"What?" he interrupted her. "You were on that train as well?"

"Unfortunately, Doctor. But I don't want to place my needs above those here who require help far more than I do. I was going to ask for your hospitality, by allowing me to stay in your house for a few days."

"Of course, gracious Fräulein."

"I should point out that I'm travelling as an Englishwoman and going by the name, Harriet de Lissa."

"Does your brother know that you're coming here?"

"No, he doesn't."

"What about his servant, that man over there?" he said pointing to Franz.

"I've already spoken to him. But for now, shouldn't we move on?"

After these clarifying words, they resumed their work.

⁂

Meanwhile, Savoie had extended his hand to Richemonte in greeting and after the usual pleasantries, steered the conversation to matters at hand.

"So, you've already heard about the tragedy?" Savoie asked.

"Unfortunately, yes. But what I see is beyond description," the captain said, pretending to be appalled by the gruesome scene.

"I'm afraid so. These bodies, and the mutilation…" replied the officer motioning with his hand, "it's indescribable."

Richemonte nodded. "Tell me, who was at fault? The employees?"

"No, not at all. Someone had placed rocks and debris on the tracks."

"*Diable*! Probably youths who derive pleasure from such things. Not only that but it was a passenger train that happened to come along."

The captain shook his head. "No, Monsieur, it's worse than you think. I believe it was done on purpose."

"On purpose?" asked the old man, pretending to be shocked.

"Yes. The rocks were intended to derail the train so that a robbery could take place."

"Is something like that possible?"

"Yes, it was a devilish plan. Still, we managed to capture those responsible."

The old captain narrowed his eyes momentarily. "How fortunate. But do you have the right ones?"

"Yes. We found a stolen billfold on them."

"Do you know them?"

"No. They can't be from around here."

"Really? Is it possible to see them? Perhaps I could find something out."

"I would be most pleased to show you the prisoners."

"Where are they being kept?"

"In the rearward coupé of the second-last carriage. I'll accompany you, but first I have to look after another matter."

Savoie turned around and left. The old man cast a cursory glance at the coupé in question. He spotted a guard keeping watch from the running board. From his vantage point, Richemonte noticed that there wasn't a sentry on the far side of the carriage. A fiendish smile played across his lips. Instantly, he conceived his plan and was determined to carry it out. He reached into his coat pocket and removed a small folding knife. He opened it and held it in the palm of his right hand, ensuring it was completely concealed by his coat sleeve. He cast a quick glance at the captain, relieved to find him in conversation with a sergeant. The old man sauntered toward the wagon, as if the commander's return was taking too long. But instead of going up to the sentry, he walked around the corner of the last wagon, pretending to evaluate the security measures the captain had undertaken. No one was there. Another look around satisfied him that he wasn't being watched. He quickly walked up to the closed door of the coupé that housed the prisoners, and quietly released the latch, so that it could easily be opened from the inside. He then retraced his steps, assuming the disposition of a man who was inspecting the integrity of the carriage.

No one had paid him the least bit of attention; not even the sentry was aware of his actions, but the two vagabonds became alert, having heard something.

"Caron, did you hear that noise?" whispered Poirier without moving his lips.

"Yes, someone was at that other door."

"Zounds. Really?"

"Yes. I can see a small crack. I think it's unlocked."

"Who could have done that?"

"I'm not sure; no doubt it was for our benefit."

"Possibly. Let's wait and see."

Just then the old man approached the coupé from the other side. The guard noticed him and saluted smartly.

"Do you recognize me?" queried Richemonte.

"Of course, Captain."

"Good. Let me have a look at those two vagabonds in there."

The guard jumped off the running board, allowing Richemonte to climb up. He hung onto the ledge of the open window, and ensured he occupied the entire opening.

"So, these are the two men who caused the disaster," he said out loud. "We should pry their mouths open with pliers."

Without the sentry's knowledge, the old man had tossed his small knife inside, so that it landed at the feet of the closest prisoner. He then jumped down from the platform allowing the guard to resume his former station. The guard now felt duty-bound to direct some of his attention toward Richemonte. With the guard being distracted, the two prisoners had the perfect opportunity to converse with each other.

"It's the old man himself," whispered Poirier.

"Unbelievable. What daring."

"I know. What did he toss on the floor?"

"A knife."

"Really? How clever of him and how fortunate that they never tied our hands behind our backs."

"Isn't it? When he's not looking, cut my rope and then I'll cut your bonds."

"Sure. We need to be ready to bolt. If only that damned soldier wasn't so conscientious. I wish he would disappear for a couple of minutes."

"Don't worry about that. The old man is clever enough. He'll work it out."

Savoie approached the wagon. "Well, Captain Richemonte," he began. "Did you have a chance to look at those two?"

"Yes, but only for a moment."

"Did you recognize either one?"

"No, I'm afraid not."

"Perhaps they know you? I'll find out right away." He stepped forward and climbed up, taking the sentry's place. "You two in there," he called out. "Do you know the gentleman, the one who was just at the window?"

There was no answer.

"If you fail to answer me, I'll find a way to get you to talk. I have some rope, handy for suspending you both upside down from the roof. I'm asking you again if you know him?"

"No, I've never seen him before," was the short response.

"So, you're not from around here?"

"No."

"Where are you from?"

But before either man could reply, they all heard a loud, rolling sound.

"Captain, it's the relief train," Albin alerted him.

The officer turned around automatically, and watched the previous locomotive return, pushing several carriages. "Pah! I'll stay where I am," he added with resolve. He had managed to solicit a few responses from the vagabonds and wasn't about to let the opportunity pass him by. "So, where do you both come from?" he asked, facing Poirier.

"From the Verdun region," replied the latter.

"What about the other man, your accomplice?"

"There's no one else."

"Don't lie to me!" Savoie admonished him.

"How can we have an accomplice if we haven't done anything wrong?"

"I'm convinced it's just a matter of time before we catch him as well. You could spare me a lot of aggravation if you fess up."

"I've already told you that we haven't done anything wrong."

Just then, the locomotive pushed the newly appropriated carriages up to those in place. Even though the machinist was being careful, they still bumped the ones standing still and pushed them a short distance down the track. The captain hadn't anticipated the movement and was not able to hang on, jumped off and ended up jogging after them.

"Now!" whispered Poirier to Caron. Several quick slicing movements by the knife and both men were free of their bonds. "Is anyone on the far side?" asked Poirier.

Caron, who was closer to the door, slid over and peered out through the crack. "No one. Let's go!" he replied, easing the door fully open. He jumped out with Poirier close behind. The wagon had nearly come to a stop, with the wheels protesting in response to the braking. The quick-thinking Poirier slammed the door shut, hoping the noise would be covered by the screeching brakes. The two men scrambled down the embankment and disappeared into the safety of the bushes.

Meanwhile, Richemonte had caught up to Savoie.

"The two prisoners claim to be from Verdun," related the officer. "Do you find that believable?"

"It's possible," the old man replied. "But please, continue your interrogation, Monsieur."

"You're right. One has to strike while the iron is still hot. I'll prepare them for the magistrate." He climbed back onto the running-board, with no more than half a minute having elapsed since he had jumped off. "Listen up, you vagabonds, I'm telling you—tarnation!" Savoie stopped in mid-sentence, visibly agitated.

"Well, what is it?" asked the old captain. "What do you see?"

"Nothing," the officer replied, staring ahead. "They're gone."

"Impossible."

At last Savoie turned around to face Richemonte, his face ashen-grey. He looked at the old man helplessly. "I don't understand it."

"How could they have gone? I don't understand you."

"I'm telling you; they're gone."

"Let me see for myself," the old man said, pushing him aside while climbing up. "Unbelievable. I don't see them either. Maybe they've crawled under the seats."

"Under the seats?" asked Savoie, whose cheeks looked a little less pale at the sound of the hopeful news.

"Yes. What other explanation could there be?" replied Albin, trying to drag out the scene, thereby giving the perpetrators more of a head start.

"But why?" asked the officer.

"Simple. They're trying to fool us into believing they've escaped. While we look for signs of them on one side, they could sneak out on the other."

"I'd like to see them try that. I'll flush them out."

"Yes, let's satisfy ourselves," Richemonte chimed in.

Savoie opened the door and looked in, peering under the benches. As he pulled back, his face paled again. "Damn! They really are gone," he said in frustration.

"*Sacre bleu*! But they couldn't have just disappeared, could they?"

"I... I can't explain it," Savoie added dumbfounded.

"Could the window have been left ajar?" the old man offered.

"No. I had checked it myself."

"What about the other door?"

"I'll go and see," the officer said, walking over to examine it. "No, it's still firmly closed, like before."

"Then only the devil can make sense out of it. Can you see any sign of them out the window?"

Savoie lowered the window for a better look. "No, I can't see either one."

"Then it's a mystery to me. I can't explain it."

"Me neither," Savoie said as he emerged from the now empty coupé. He was sweating and looked embarrassed. "The prisoners' confinement had been entrusted to me."

"But you had them watched and even participated in the same," Albin said, pretending to be sympathetic. In reality, he was stalling for time, thereby distracting Savoie from commencing a search.

"And still, it occurred under my watch. They just disappeared," Savoie said, shaking his head in disbelief. "It must have happened when I jumped from the moving carriage."

"They couldn't have escaped on the far side," offered the old man. "It's all closed."

"Well, they certainly couldn't have come out this side. We were here the entire time."

"What about the floor, or the walls?"

"They're solid and haven't been tampered with."

"Well, I'm not going to get all worked-up over it."

Richemonte was about to turn away, when he noticed the arrival of another official. The train had brought more people with it, personnel to deal with the injured, but also investigators charged with conducting a proper investigation. The gentlemen had purposed on attending directly to the accident site, but after being advised that the perpetrators had been apprehended, they decided to postpone their 'field' examination. Although the old man had observed them earlier, he pretended not to notice them. But now, seeing them approach, he removed his hat in greeting.

"Ah, Monsieur Procurator, it's you," Richemonte said, bowing.

"Yes, it's me, Captain. A most tragic affair, one that requires my presence. I stand at your disposal, sir," he said, turning and addressing Savoie. "I've just learned that the culprits have been apprehended."

"Evidently, Procurator," the officer replied pulling a handkerchief from his pocket and wiping the sweat from his brow.

"I see you've been entrusted with their custody."

"Yes…unfortunately…I mean of course," he stammered.

"What do you mean by unfortunately?"

"I no longer have them."

"So, you've arranged to have them transferred?"

"No."

"I don't understand. You mean you no longer have them in your custody?"

"Right. You see, they... they're... gone," he stammered embarrassed.

"Gone? Then you had them removed, under escort?"

Savoie pulled himself together, but before he could respond another spoke in his stead.

"No, they've escaped," Albin interrupted.

"What? Escaped?" asked the procurator. "Gentlemen, I certainly hope that there's been a mistake. Surely, this isn't your idea of a joke, at the expense of suffering people."

"It's no joke. They've managed to escape."

"Dear God! Captain Richemonte, is this really true?"

"Yes. There's no doubt," nodded the old man decidedly. "Let me tell you what happened."

The procurator's eyebrows furrowed. "I'm obligated to seek a fuller explanation about this," he said sternly.

"You see," Albin continued, ignoring the embarrassed officer, "I was advised about the horrible train wreck, and quickly rode over here, as I was expecting a business associate to arrive on this very same train. Concern and fear drove me here. When I arrived, I learned that those responsible had been caught. Captain Savoie was kind enough to let me see them. They were sitting in that coupé," he said pointing it out, "behind closed doors, tied up and under the watchful eye of a guard. The captain was just starting to interrogate them but had to jump off for a moment when the arriving locomotive bumped the carriage. Less than one minute later he climbed back onto the running board, but they had disappeared."

"Where to?" asked the procurator.

"I have no idea."

"Surely you have an idea how they managed to get away?"

"That's what is so frustrating. The door was closed on the far side. Over here, we kept watch, and still they managed to escape."

"Escape could only be possible from the other side."

"But both the window and the door were secure."

"Perhaps the door lock was inadequate."

"I'm sure I would have noticed it if that were the case," Savoie replied in his defense.

"Well, it will come to light soon enough. The culprits have escaped. That much is certain. Captain," he said sternly, addressing the young officer, "if you would be so kind as to arrange for a search, commencing on the far side of the embankment. The rest of us will head over to the wreck site."

The tone of his words left little doubt that Savoie, who was responsible after all, had committed a blunder. The procurator turned away, and along with his team of investigators headed for the wreck leaving the two officers to ponder matters. But before Richemonte could lay further blame on the young captain, Savoie headed toward his men to issue the necessary orders for commencing a search.

Richemonte slowly followed the investigators, intent on fulfilling his quest to find the American.

CHAPTER SIXTEEN

THE ENGLISH LADY

As Captain Richemonte made his way over to the wreck site, he recognized Nanon now occupied with bandaging an injured man's arm.

"So, did your sister survive the ordeal?" he queried.

"Yes. She's alive. Thank God."

"Pah! What does God have to do with it? I'm more concerned with a gentleman, an American, who was also on the train."

"Do you mean Monsieur Deephill?" she asked, ignoring his jibe.

"Yes, that's the one. Is he still around?"

"I believe so."

"Where is he?"

Nanon looked around and pointed. "Over there, beside the English lady. He's bandaging that injured passenger."

"Ah, the gentleman with the dark hair?"

"Yes."

Amelia had removed her mantle. As she moved about in her dress, her figure was more accentuated by the movement, revealing her beauty. The old man considered himself an admirer of womanly beauty and noticed her right away.

"An Englishwoman?" he asked, scrutinizing her appearance.

"Yes, Captain."

"Was she also on the train?"

"She occupied the same coupé as my sister."

"Really? And both were spared from serious injury? It would seem that fate was gallant in favouring the lovely this day." He approached the group and removed his hat. "I was told I could find Mr. Deephill here," he said politely. "Was my information accurate?"

The American businessman stood up and likewise removed his hat.

"Of course, Monsieur. I am that gentleman," he replied.

"Did you come from New Orleans?"

"Yes."

"Are you looking for Captain Richemonte?"

"Indeed."

"Well, then you've reached your goal. I am Albin Richemonte. I knew of course that you planned on arriving on the noon-day train. When I learned of the calamity, I immediately rushed over hoping I wouldn't find you among the dead. To my relief, I heard that you had survived. You can thank your lucky stars."

He extended his hand, giving credence to his words.

The American shook his hand and said, "Captain, your concern for me elevates me in your sight. May I entreat you to pay me a visit today or tomorrow?"

"Only a visit? No, Monsieur, I would be honoured if you would be my guest. I trust you will accept my offer to stay at Castle Ortry."

"I would be delighted to accept."

"Very good. I've come to meet and accompany you to my estate. When do you wish to depart?"

"I must ask for a slight postponement," he said allowing his eyes to settle on Amelia. She had of course looked up on hearing the name Richemonte, and cast a quick glance at the old man, but then again occupied herself with bandaging the injured woman. The captain noticed Deephill's approving look.

"Ah, beauty always has its admirers," he commented.

Amelia blushed yet pretended not to pay attention to their discussion. The American's brows furrowed slightly. "Monsieur," he began taking offense, "is it your intent to speak of beauty, here in this place, surrounded by the injured and the dead? Misfortune often has a stronger pull than bliss. I couldn't possibly leave until I'm satisfied that I've done my part."

Instead of agreeing with him, the old man shrugged his shoulders. "Don't worry. There are plenty of volunteers," he replied coolly.

"That's still no reason for me to abstain. The more hands there are, the faster the job will get done."

"You might have something there. If I may be so bold, would you do me the honour of introducing me to this lady?"

"Certainly. We first met on the train, coincidentally occupying the same coupé. Captain, may I present to you Miss de Lissa from London."

"Ah, an Englishwoman," Albin said, removing his hat and bowing before her.

Meanwhile, Amelia had risen and turned to face Richemonte. Here she stood, face to face with the most cunning and destructive enemy her family had ever encountered. But there wasn't the slightest trace of ill-will against him visible on her face. She looked at him openly and unpretentiously, as if she wanted to imprint his features into her memory; then she bowed to him. She was struck with a formidable idea, one borne out of inspiration and sought to put it to use right away.

"It really is a pleasure," she said smiling, "to finally meet the gentleman whom I've heard so much about."

"Really? You've heard about me, Miss?"

"Yes."

"Perhaps you've confused me for someone else. Richemonte, after all, is a common name."

"I was referring to Captain Albin Richemonte, who resides at Ortry."

"Well, then you've found the right man. May I inquire in what capacity or by whom you have heard about me?"

Amelia smiled coyly. "Perhaps later, should we see each other again. You see Captain, I belong to a Women's Suffrage Association, the *Sisters of Mercy*."

The old man's eyes lit up. "Ah!" he exclaimed a little louder than he intended. "So, are you travelling on behalf of the order?"

"Indeed, Monsieur."

"That is interesting, most interesting," Albin said, pulling on the ends of his moustache. "May I inquire as to the destination of your trip?"

"Thionville."

"*Sapper*—I mean, really. Please forgive my outburst. So, you're heading to Thionville. Are you expected anywhere in particular?"

"No. I'm free to arrange my own affairs. However, I'll be staying at Doctor Bertrand's house."

"Are you acquainted with him?"

"No. He was recommended to me."

"Did you know that he's here, engaged in his professional capacity? I believe he's up there in that carriage," he said, pointing it out.

"I know, Captain," she acknowledged with a smile. "I have already spoken to him, thank you."

The old man could barely keep himself from staring at her lovely features. He didn't know what had come over him.

"Forgive me, Miss de Lissa, for bombarding you with all these questions," Albin said contravening his usually harsh and cutting speech. "But there's something about your face, your speech, your mannerisms that leads me to believe that we have seen each other before. If I may be so bold, would you indulge an old man and give him the opportunity of getting to know you better? Have you ever been to France?"

"No, never," she said, surprised at his warm entreaty.

"Then I must be mistaken. Perhaps I will be fortunate to meet you soon. Are you planning on staying for a while in Thionville?"

"That's still uncertain. But for now, I beg your leave so I can return to my task." Amelia bowed and returned to bandaging a passenger.

The captain, still captivated by her, pulled the American aside.

"Did you overhear what the lady said?" asked Albin.

"Naturally, Captain."

"And your purpose in coming here was out of political considerations?"

"Of course."

"It strikes me that the Englishwoman came here for similar reasons."

"It would seem so. Yet we never discussed the purpose of her trip. After I had introduced myself, the conversation immediately steered toward the derailment. Think of it—it was planned."

The old man listened up. "A planned derailment?" he asked surprised. "That implies you had knowledge of a plot?"

"Exactly."

"But sir, how is that possible?"

"I managed to come to that conclusion only moments before we reached the fatal place, so that it was impossible to prevent the outcome."

The old man needed all his self-control to keep his rising anxiety in check.

"May I ask," he continued, "how it was that you drew your conclusion?"

The American hesitated with his answer. He stared pensively in front of him, his face unmoving and sombre. He debated with himself how much he should reveal.

"Monsieur," he finally said, "they weren't interested in the train—they were after me."

The captain's face paled at the revelation, as he tried to conceal his shock. "After you?" he asked. "Not possible!"

"Oh, quite possible, once you understand the facts."

"But it's unthinkable."

"Actually, it's quite straight-forward. The perpetrators knew I would be travelling on this very train and that I would be in possession of considerable sums of money."

"Really? Please, go on."

"Those in the know had decided to arrange things so that the train was bound to derail, and then recover the money from my person… from my dead body."

Richemonte couldn't believe what he was hearing. He coughed, then played with the ends of his moustache before looking away.

"But that sounds absurd," Albin managed at last.

"Perhaps, but it's the truth."

"Do you have any proof that would confirm your suppositions?"

"Certainly. While I lay in the badly damaged coupé, two men went through my pockets and removed my billfold."

"Hang it all! What audacity to do such a thing."

"Yes, that's what I thought."

Richemonte looked away, pretending to evaluate the rescue effort going on around them. If truth be known, he was deeply affected, shocked at what he was hearing all the while trying to maintain his composure. After a lengthy interval, he glanced back at the American businessman.

"But it still doesn't prove it was done on purpose," the old man said.

"What do you mean?"

"I suspect they were just two ordinary thieves, opportunists looking for a way to improve their lot in life at another's expense. They probably came across you by accident."

"Hmm," was all Gaston managed, reluctant to reveal what he knew. He didn't like the captain's countenance at all.

But the old man continued, trying to gain the other man's confidence. "So, you see that your earlier assessment may not be correct."

"Perhaps. But I still can't understand how they learned about my itinerary and the large amount I was carrying in my billfold."

"Only two men were privy to that information: Count Rallion and myself; no one else."

"I can't imagine either one of you revealing the true nature of my trip."

"Of course not. But Monsieur Deephill, what happened to your billfold? Was it lost?"

"It was, but only for a short time. The officer in charge retrieved it from the thieves."

"You don't say. Could it be the same ones who have just escaped?"

The American's face paled at the news. Up until now he had been engaged with Miss de Lissa in rendering aid to the wounded rather than being concerned with other issues.

"Escaped? You mean absconded?" Gaston asked in disbelief.

"Yes. Both of them."

"You're talking about the two that were confined up there in the coupé?"

"I'm afraid so. The officer has been negligent and had not adequately supervised their custody, allowing them to escape. I believe they're mustering soldiers for a pursuit."

"What utter carelessness! It's reprehensible of him—" Deephill stopped speaking and stared ahead, deep in thought. "Still, I hope they'll be able to catch them soon," he continued after a moment.

"Quite likely, Monsieur. Now then, you'll be my guest of course. Unfortunately, my presence is required back at the estate, and I must leave. How are you planning to leave this place?"

"I expect to obtain transport in one of those wagons."

"Alright. If you will permit me," Albin offered, "I will send my coach to collect you at the railway station in Thionville."

"I would be most grateful for your hospitality."

"Then adieu for now."

They shook hands. The captain left Deephill and went to look for his horse, finding it grazing on the lower part of the embankment.

※

When word spread that the prisoners had escaped, a number of soldiers were assigned to the search. Franz joined them, and Like Deephill, was incensed that the officer had been so careless. However, since much time had elapsed, he realized he wouldn't be able to contribute much to recapturing the fugitives. He decided to return to the accident site.

Just as he was about to emerge from the brushwork, he spied the old captain heading for his horse. At about the same time, Franz spotted two riders at gallop, coming across the meadow. He recognized the two as Baroness Marion and Doctor Müller. The captain also noticed their approach and decided to wait for them. They reined in their horses in front of him. Richard jumped from his horse, intending to help the baroness dismount.

"Leave that! Can't you see I'm here," Albin barked at him. He helped his granddaughter from her horse and escorted her up the embankment. Marion accepted his offered arm and showed no sign of having a row with him earlier.

"Is it up there?" she asked him as they climbed up.

"No, it's down the other side. Remember, it was you who insisted on coming out here. I hope you'll be strong enough to bear it."

"I'm sure I will."

"Then come."

When they arrived at the top, he stopped momentarily to give her an overview of the carnage below. Marion shuddered at what she saw.

"I suppose you're going to faint now," he mocked.

"Not if I can help it," she replied, composing herself. "It must take a cold and unfeeling heart not to be affected by what you see."

"Ah, I understand you; I'm supposed to have such a heart?"

"So it would seem."

"Pah! I'm not suffering by it," Albin sneered. "Have you seen enough?"

"What do you mean by that? I intend to help of course."

"What?!" he replied angrily. "You, Baroness de Sainte-Marie, are willing to get your hands dirty?"

"Yes, me! A baroness has just as much responsibility to help those in need as any other woman."

"Hmm. That sounds more like the rhetoric of social democrats. If that's what you have in mind, I have no objection. However, I have one stipulation."

"So long as it doesn't interfere with my work."

"*Sacrement*! You've all of a sudden become quite emancipated. I'll see to it that from now on your wings will be clipped."

"Then I better make use of my wings before they're touched by any scissors."

"We'll see about that. I expect you to heed my instructions. Do I make myself clear?"

"Yes, even though they won't have much impact and are entirely unnecessary. A simple plea or wish would suffice."

"*Sapperlot*! So, I'm no longer able to issue instructions?" he scoffed. "What's next?"

"Isn't it obvious? Respect is the first rule of friendship and even more so with intimate relationships. Surely you must know that by now."

Richemonte abruptly let go of her arm and spun around. He was about to retort with a scathing remark, but Marion cut him off with an imperious gesture, with the words dying on his lips.

"Be quiet!" she admonished him. "There are people nearby who don't have to witness your tyrannical outbursts. Now then, what are you asking of me?"

The captain barely managed to suppress his rage. "Have a look down there," he replied. "Do you see that gentleman and the lady beside him presently putting a sling around that man's broken arm?"

"Yes."

"That man is Monsieur Deephill, an American. He will be residing with us on the estate, and I hope you'll allocate him more courtesy than you have me."

"That all depends on him. Rudeness can never hope to elicit respect and politeness."

"Fine. Just leave your philosophising for someone else. That lady beside him is English, Miss de Lissa."

"Does she come from an influential family?"

"Certainly. She intends to reside at Doctor Bertrand's house. I would *prefer* that you make her acquaintance—"

"Ah, am I supposed to play the part of a diplomat?" she cut in.

He nodded. "Get acquainted with her and try to sound her out. Do you understand me?"

"Very well. But I don't have your kind of talent for spying on people."

"Just see to it," he said ignoring the jibe. "I'm going now. I hope to hear upon your return that you've spoken to the lady. Adieu."

By the time he reached the bottom, Richard was nowhere to be seen. Richemonte mounted his horse and left Doctor Bertrand's mare to graze, while he rode back to Castle Ortry.

☙✠❧

Earlier, when Richemonte and Marion climbed the slope, it had been Richard's intention to follow them. He hobbled[161] both horses and allowed them to graze near the bushes. He was about to leave when something caught his attention.

"Psst!" he heard a subdued voice, coming from the brush.

Richard forged through the sparse foliage and spotted Franz lurking nearby. "Ah, it's you. So, you weren't able to prevent the catastrophe?"

"No. Who could have anticipated that those scoundrels planned to derail the train?"

"You're right. Did you arrive with the first-aid train?"

"No. I came with the original train."

"What? The one that plunged down the embankment?"

"Yes. Like we discussed, I caught the early train to Trier and met up with Madelon, forewarning her about our presence here."

"Good. I'm glad you managed to meet up after all," Richard noted.

"Yes. I also thought I might be able to locate the American, Deephill."

"That shouldn't have been too difficult, assuming he was travelling on the same train."

"Actually, I met up with him earlier, inside a *Gasthaus* in Trier."

"Were you able to warn him of the imminent danger?" probed Richard.

"I didn't get the chance. Worse yet, I got into an argument with him. We ended up going our separate ways. I only learned of it later, when we ended up sitting in the same coupé."

Richard smiled at the way things had unravelled. "Then you did travel together?"

"Yes. The two of us, along with two ladies."

"Was Madelon in the same coach?"

"Yes, she was one of the ladies."

"And the other one?"

"An English lady, Miss de Lissa from London."

"Go on."

"The American introduced himself to the lady by handing her his business card. That's when I spotted his name. Naturally I sought to warn him of the planned robbery."

"Did he believe you?"

"No, not at first," Franz reflected. "But then I told him about the millions he was supposedly carrying and about his two confidants, Richemonte and Rallion; that finally swayed him."

"And then?"

"Once we explored the gist of what I had discovered the previous night, he stumbled on the notion that perhaps they might be planning something drastic, like derailing the train in order to claim their prize."

"Dear God!" Richard exclaimed. "It all makes sense to me now."

"I know."

"What happened then? Quickly, out with it."

"We were close to this place," Franz said gesturing at the accident site. "I reasoned that if they really were determined to carry it out, it would probably happen close to Thionville."

"Of course. Go on."

"There was no time to lose. We opened both doors, and stepped out onto the running board, one on each side. Just as we were about to alert the engineer, the machinist hit the brakes and sounded the alarm signal. From where I stood, I could see a pile of rocks and boulders on the tracks ahead."

"My God! What happened then?" asked Richard, caught up in the story.

"We couldn't just leave the ladies to a horrible fate. I pulled Madelon out of her seat, with Deephill taking hold of the English lady. We both jumped from our respective running board, bearing our precious cargo, and not a moment too soon. We barely hit the ground when the train with all those on board plunged down the embankment."

"Thank God that you both managed to jump. I've just arrived, but it must be a horrible sight over there," Richard said pointing toward the accident site.

"It's too terrible to put into words," Franz replied sombrely.

"Were many injured?"

"Yes, quite a few. Unfortunately, a number of people lost their lives. Miraculously, a few escaped with virtually no injuries."

"So then, with all this planning and execution, did those two *franctireurs* come looking for the American?"

"Of course. But here's the best part," Franz said, grinning. "I convinced the reluctant Deephill to play the part of a dead man. The vagabonds easily found him and helped themselves to his billfold. They would have gotten away, if I hadn't stopped them. The officer on site ensured they were tied up and confined in one of the coupés."

"Thank God that they were apprehended."

"*Sapristi!*" Franz cursed. "Richard, you won't believe what happened next."

"I'm afraid to ask," Richard said, looking at him quizzically.

"They were in custody for a short time, *only* to escape. I've just returned from a fruitless search."

Richard was taken aback. "But how did they manage to get away? Surely there were people everywhere, making any escape attempt futile."

Franz nodded. "There were plenty of people milling about including those from the nearby villages who came out of curiosity. But consider the following. The officer in charge placed those fine fellows in a coupé and tied them up nice and proper. He stationed a guard on the active side but failed to post a sentry on the far side."

"How careless of him," noted Richard.

"Yes. Something that only a glory-seeking Frenchman could come up with."

"You're right. Back home, a sheepherder would have had more sense," Richard agreed.

"I can't believe we're dealing with such stupidity," Franz said, still agitated.

Richard tried to steer him away from this contentious issue. "So, you managed to rescue the lovely Madelon?"

Franz nodded. "The American even carried off the pretty Englishwoman."

"Good for him. But it doesn't concern me as much."

"Not as much?" asked Franz, looking puzzled.

"It's not that I don't care; I just don't know the lady."

"I seriously doubt that."

"What do you mean?" asked Richard, taking an interest.

"Well, to begin with, the English lady is travelling incognito."

"You mean under a false name?" Franz nodded. "But she's still English, right?"

"Actually, no, even though she speaks the King's English. Can you imagine that she… er—?"

"That she what?" Richard interrupted.

"That she comes from Berlin."

"From Berlin? And yet she pretends to be English? There's more to this story."

"Well, I'm in a position to fill you in on the details," said Franz, grinning.

"I see. What does she look like? Is she attractive?"

Franz nodded. "More than just attractive; beautiful in fact."

"So, do you know her name?"

"I managed to overhear her first name."

"Let's hear it."

"It's Amelia."

"Hmm. Just like my sister's name."

"Apparently, she stems from nobility. Her family name reminds me of an exotic animal. Now what was it again?" He thought about it. "Tiger, or panther... something like that."

"What? I've never heard of a name like that."

"I must have gotten it mixed-up. Let me think. What's another name for an animal's paw?"

"You mean like a beast's foot, a lion's claw?"

"Yes, yes, but not in French—in German."

Richard thought about it, looking puzzled. "Like… löwen-klau?"

"Yes!" Franz nodded enthusiastically. "That's what it sounded like— Löwenklau."

"Franz, what the devil are you getting at?" Richard said, becoming annoyed. "If I didn't know better, I'd say you were describing my own sister."

"Heavens!" quipped Franz. "So that's why she looked so familiar."

Richard looked at him, not knowing what to think. "Be serious for one moment. Tell me honestly, who is this lady?"

"I stand by what I said. She's Amelia, your sister."

"What! *My* Amelia?" Richard blurted out, looking dumbfounded.

"Yes, Fräulein Amelia von Löwenklau," he said, gloating over Richard's consternation.

"Dear God! What is she doing here in Thionville?"

"I haven't a clue," Franz said, smiling.

"I can't think of anything else, other than she's accompanying her friend to the funeral. But surely my grandfather wouldn't..."

"Your grandfather wouldn't have given his consent for that reason alone."

"That's probably true. There has to be another reason."

"I suspect we'll find out soon enough."

"Without question," Richard said thoughtfully. "But if we should meet, I fear that she will unintentionally reveal herself."

Franz shook his head. "It's possible that she'll fear it'll be Doctor Müller who will unintentionally reveal himself."

"But thanks to you, the good doctor has been forewarned. Still, unforeseen things could happen if we were to meet unexpectedly. I have to speak to her alone, and I want to find out what motivated her to take this trip."

He was about to leave, but Franz held him back. "Just one more thing before you leave."

"You can fill me in later," Richard replied dismissively.

"Well, for what I have to say, we may have the time later, but no opportunity to discuss it privately."

"Alright, then out with it."

"Well, I had a terrible toothache last night," Franz quipped.

"A toothache, with your healthy teeth?"

"I know. I was forced to see Doctor Bertrand last night. Fortunately, he was still awake. I explained to him that I was in pain. His remedy startled me. He wanted to pull the offending tooth."

"Ridiculous. You have the finest molars I've ever seen."

"Exactly what I thought. I asked him if there was an alternate remedy, like medication that could help the affected area. That's when he supplied me with a little flask. Here, take a look," he said, handing Richard a vial.

Richard examined it. "But it's still full, Franz," he said.

"Of course."

"You didn't take any of the drops?"

"I wouldn't dream of it. They're far too potent."

"I'm not following your logic," Richard said, looking puzzled.

"Well, five drops will take the pain away. But if you should accidentally take forty or so, then—"

"Really? Wait a minute. The one who's only supposed to take five isn't going to miscount by that much."

"That's true. But the one who ends up taking forty will become ill."

"Become ill? What are you getting at?"

"Well, he becomes so sick," Franz added with a devilish grin, "so that he ends up confined to his bed, likely for two or three days."

It was as if a light went on in Richard's head. He recalled the substance of their previous conversation. A satisfied smile crossed his face. "Scoundrel," he said, laughing.

"Who me?" Franz mocked.

"So, Doctor Bertrand gave you the vial?" Franz nodded. "Does he know what you need it for?"

"I told him it's meant to keep someone incapacitated and confined to his bed."

"I meant," Richard clarified, "if he suspects who the intended recipient might be?"

"Sure, he knows we've singled out the captain."

"Alright. We owe our Austrian friend a great debt. Perhaps the time will come when we will be able to repay him for his thoughtfulness. Now then, let's wrap this up. I suspect this derailment has somewhat altered your plans. Are you and Nanon leaving with the next available train?"

"Yes. We hope to leave with the four o'clock train."

"That begs the question if my sister will accompany you both. I *really* must speak with her. Let me leave first, since we can't be seen together."

Richard stepped out of the brush and climbed up the embankment. He came across a throng of onlookers and was about to be turned away by a sentry. However, once he identified himself as the baron's educator he was allowed to proceed. What he saw was reminiscent of a battle scene. As a seasoned soldier he was accustomed to seeing calamity and kept walking, his eyes searching for Marion. He spotted her, kneeling beside a blonde woman. Both ladies were occupied with rendering aid to a young child. As Richard approached them, the blonde one turned around to look at the newcomer. It was indeed Amelia, his sister. Yet she didn't jump up or acknowledge him in the least. He saw that both women were in tears.

"Doctor Müller," Marion said, crying softly while pointing to the child. "I'm glad you've come."

"The poor boy," Richard said sympathetically.

"So young and innocent," she added, "and now he's dead. His chest was crushed."

"Where could his parents be?" Amelia wondered.

"They likely perished as well," Richard replied.

"Dear God! Why would you say such a thing?"

"If either of his parents had survived, they would be frantically searching until they had found him."

"Yes, you're probably right," Marion acknowledged. "So long as either one was still alive, they wouldn't have left their child."

Richard cast a quick glance at Marion. He sensed her compassion came from an inward conviction, since she herself hadn't experienced such a loss. He wondered how she managed to feel such tenderness, not having been raised in a loving environment.

"If no one comes forward to claim the child's body, then I will see to it that he's properly buried," she announced.

"Indeed," Amelia added. "It would be a shame to place him in a grave, unmarked and untended. Please, allow me, dear baroness, to assume the role of his mother along with you."

"Of course, my dear Miss Harriet," Marion agreed. "I would have rather looked after him in life than in death. How quickly suffering and compassion bind two hearts together. We've barely known each other for one hour, but…"

She stopped speaking but Amelia understood her. She reached for her hands and continued in her stead. "But already we've become quite fond of each other. Is that what you meant to say?"

"Yes, indeed. It seems that the most beautiful flowers can be found in a cemetery, and here, at this place of mourning, one's innermost thoughts tend to evolve so quickly."

"Please, allow for time to heal the broken-hearted. Or do you feel uncomfortable in making friends under such circumstances?"

"No, not at all."

The two women hugged and kissed each other. In life, there are beings who are destined for each other. As soon as they meet, they sense a kindred spirit and embrace a lifelong friendship, while others, familiar with each other for many years, never develop a longing for a deeper relationship. Out of respect, Richard had chosen to stand a few paces behind them. He quietly contemplated the pair kneeling before him, both beautiful in their own way.

Suddenly, Marion became aware of him standing behind her and blushed.

"Forgive me, Doctor Müller," she said rising to her feet, "for neglecting my duty. Doctor Andreas Müller, my brother's educator, may I present Miss Harriet de Lissa from London."

Brother and sister bowed to each other, as if this were the first time they had been introduced. Initially, Amelia wasn't sure how to proceed, but Richard, the quick-thinking officer, was ahead of her.

"I overheard the ladies wish to assume responsibility for the boy's body. Unfortunately, this will likely require awkward, perhaps cumbersome proceedings, which may prove unpleasant for any lady. If you will permit me, I can look after those arrangements."

"Gladly, Doctor Müller," Marion replied. "I don't understand much about such matters and would be grateful if you will undertake it. Look, there goes the man who saved Nanon's sister. I have to speak to him and offer my thanks."

Marion left the two standing there and headed to intercept Franz who was purposefully walking past them. That left Richard alone with his sister.

"Amelia!" he exclaimed in a subdued voice. "I was shocked to learn of your presence. Still, it's wonderful to see you, but I'm afraid I dare not hug you."

"I know, Richard. Who told you I was here?"

"Franz."

"Are you cross with me for coming?"

"How could I be? I still don't know the nature of your visit. Has grandpa given you permission to travel?"

"Of course."

"Then why would I be displeased with your coming?" he said with a smile.

Amelia breathed a little easier. "Richard, I've come here for two reasons."

"And they are?"

"The first one concerns Franz, the second Marion."

"Hmm, what about Franz?"

"He's in possession of one of the lion's teeth."

"I already know."

"You don't say. You've known all along, and you haven't told us?"

"No, you've misunderstood me," Richard added, pacifying her with his hand. "I just found out myself. Besides, not having any proof, could I risk bringing you false hope? Do you know the connection between Franz and the lion's tooth?"

"Yes, somewhat."

"Who told you?"

"Nanon mentioned it to her sister in her last letter, and then Madelon told me. Of course, we had to share the news with grandpa. You should have seen the look on his face when he read her letter. He was beside himself and paced back and forth in the study, threatening to wear out the carpet. As you can imagine, it brought up the whole thing again, the anguish and sorrow over the loss.

"Naturally, Madelon was unaware of all that had transpired so long ago, so we did our best to fill her in. I'm still shaking when I recall reading your news of how Bajazzo, that scheming circus clown, had deliberately staged Eloise's fall within their highwire routine during the performance in Thionville. Imagine, sending your own daughter to her death. And why did he do it? It was his selfish way of concealing the true story behind the boys' disappearance all those years ago."

While Amelia was recounting the tragic events, Richard's thoughts returned to the time when he was just a young boy. He recalled the uproar in the Goldberg family home when it became clear the boys' sudden vanishing was no accident, but rather that the twins' disappearance had been staged. Then came the frantic yet organized search conducted by his uncle Kunz, who offered a large sum for any credible information leading to their whereabouts. Yet despite all their efforts and all the prayers, there were no leads, no sightings. There was nothing to go on, not even a shred of evidence to point toward the identity of the kidnappers. The twins had simply vanished without a trace.

"It all seemed so senseless," Amelia concluded. "What was most peculiar was that there was never a demand for ransom. Ever!"

"Well, I might as well tell you," Richard said, his thoughts returning to the present. "My intention was to first find that rogue, Bajazzo, and persuade him to part with the truth. Then I would at least be in a position to make further inquiries and risk bringing the matter out into the open."

"Have your efforts amounted to anything tangible?"

"Not yet. But I haven't given up hope. Now then, what about your second reason for coming here? You said it concerned Marion."

"Yes, dear brother."

Richard briefly looked uncomfortable. "In what way?"

"You'll have to forgive me. During a recent conversation with grandpa, I'm afraid I was a little too explicit."

"Explicit about what?"

"Well, how you encountered Marion on the road to Blasewitz."

"Oh no. How did he take the news?"

"He said he wouldn't tolerate a French girl as his daughter-in-law."

Richard nearly broke-out laughing. "As long as I've been alive, I've had to put up with French women. First, my mother, not to mention my aunt and grandmother."

"That's more or less what I've told him."

"So, what did he say?"

"He said that in France women are worth more than men, while in Germany, men count more than women."

"Yes, that sounds like something Blücher would have said, and now he's embellishing it. But don't worry, he'll come around once he's gotten to know Marion."

"That's why I've come," she replied coyly.

"*Sapperlot*! So that's it. You've come as a spy," Richard said waving his finger in jest. "But have you considered what difficulties your presence might present for me?"

"Of course. You don't have to worry about me; I've prepared myself beforehand. Besides, I don't intend on staying here for long."

"Are you planning to disembark in Thionville?"

"Yes. Where else?"

"I thought your main reason for this trip was to accompany Madelon."

Amelia shook her head. "No, grandpa wasn't in favour of it."

"But where will you stay?"

"At Doctor Bertrand's house."

"Really? Why there? I'm already deep in his debt. How can I repay his hospitality?"

"It's quite simple. We met here at the accident site. Once he recognized me, he invited me to stay in his house and I accepted." She paused, appraising her brother. "Richard, if we hadn't met at this terrible place, I would have laughed about your appearance long ago."

"Why? What's wrong with it?"

"That hump; it's grotesque."

"Oh, I'm quite used to it."

"And that gipsy-like face."

"It gives me that rugged look."

"What about the wig?"

"Why can't you ladies leave my hair alone and fuss with your own?"

"Ah, I think I've struck a nerve," Amelia said, giggling.

"I'm not used to my family making fun of my appearance," he replied, feigning being hurt. "There are plenty of people here who talk about my looks behind my back. I will try to look you up at the good doctor's house."

"Oh, it won't be necessary," she said decidedly.

"It won't?"

"No. We can see each other at Ortry."

"No, not there," Richard objected. "It's much too dangerous. What if the old man spots you and connects you to our family?"

"There's no danger of that happening. I've already spoken to him," she admitted openly.

"What!? You've risked too much, Amelia."

She smiled. "He thinks that I belong to a women's suffrage movement from London."

"Really? Perhaps he holds you as a representative, who came here to seek clarity about women's rights and the state of war preparations?"

"Yes, something like that."

"How did he act around you?"

"I must have left a favourable impression. He said he hoped to see me again. And now, that I've made Marion's acquaintance, it stands to reason I will be invited to the castle for sure."

Richard was visibly relieved. "Just make sure that you take the necessary precautions."

"Of course. You can depend on me."

"Amelia, don't be too sure of yourself," Richard cautioned. "There are dangers about that place—in and around the castle—that you're not familiar with, ones that I'll have to explain to you." He stopped speaking and smiled at her, clearly happy to see her.

Just then, Marion came back. "I've just learned the machinist is stoking the locomotive's boiler, meaning the relief train will be leaving soon."

The coupés were now filled with people. The train was ready to depart, bound for Thionville, carrying the less severely injured to town where they'll receive further care. Meanwhile, the volunteers laboured one last time, hoping there were no more bodies to be found. Several railway workers were busy clearing the last of the debris and had reconstituted the damaged rails so normal rail traffic could resume.

Amelia climbed aboard with Nanon and Madelon. Marion de Sainte-Marie bid Miss de Lissa a farewell, promising to visit her at Doctor Bertrand's house in the near future. She then accompanied Richard back to where their horses were grazing. He helped her onto her horse, mounted his own, with both riding back to Castle Ortry.

⁂

As soon as Marion had dismounted and left her horse with the groomsman, Richemonte came out of the house into the courtyard.

"Did you meet with the American businessman?" Albin asked her.

"Yes, I did."

"I've sent my carriage to collect him at the railway station. He should be arriving soon. What about the Englishwoman?"

"I like her. She's a cultured lady, one of standing."

"Really? I'm glad we share the same opinion. Excellent."

"She's staying at Doctor Bertrand's house. I plan to visit her soon, perhaps tomorrow."

"Very good. I'm glad to hear of it."

"And if you'll allow me, I would like to invite her here for a future visit."

"Of course," he said, nodding. "I would be pleased to see her again. I still don't understand why she's staying at the doctor's house. We have plenty of room here."

CHAPTER SEVENTEEN

THE PORTLY PAINTER

Back at Trier station, Hieronymus Aurelius Schneffke surveyed the mess around him, the result of taking yet another unforeseen tumble. He was still lying prostrate on the platform, when he was rudely interrupted in his musings.

"You, there. Why don't you get up?" a voice barked.

He turned over and fixed his gaze on the impertinent waiter, who in his mind was responsible for him tripping over his own suitcase.

"Get up, why don't you, you bumbling fool?" the waiter repeated rudely.

Much faster than anyone would have thought possible, the portly painter jumped to his feet and challenged the ruffian.

"What did you call me, a fool?" Hieronymus demanded.

"Yes, who else," the unwise waiter retorted.

"I'll show you what any fool can do." Schneffke slapped the waiter's face so soundly that he careened backwards and fell down. "Well, now you're in the perfect position to collect the fragments."

Hieronymus brushed himself off and walked to the restaurant to pay for the broken plates. He then headed into the city to procure new eyeglasses and drown his frustration in a glass of Bordeaux over missing the train. By the time he sauntered back to the station it was nearly three o'clock. It was then that he realized he had left his sketchpad in the coupé of the previous train. He headed to the telegraph bureau and made his inquiry through the following cable:

Noon-day train, coupé 125, left sketchpad behind. Will collect with next train at 4:30. Hieronymus Schneffke, painter.

Just as an attendant announced the imminent arrival of his train, word came telegraphically that the earlier train had derailed near Thionville, leaving many passengers dead or badly injured. This placed the normally good-natured Hieronymus in a state of consternation. He paced up and down the platform, gesticulating like a madman.

"The governess… the governess," he lamented. "How did she fare? Is she dead, half-dead, injured, unconscious, alive, even unscathed? That damn train is taking forever. If she has died in the meantime, I'll blow up a bunch of these tracks myself."

At last, the train pulled into the station. Schneffke ran toward one of the open doors, nearly turning a summersault in his hurry to come aboard. He was overjoyed to have the coupé all to himself, yet his anxiety left him no peace. Like a caged animal, he ended up pacing back and forth within the confines of the small compartment.

"Damn dawdling train!" he cursed out loud to no one. "I could run ten times faster."

The train passed Karthaus, Wellen, Winchergen, Nennig, Sierck, and finally Königsmarchen as well. Not being able to contain himself any longer, Hieronymus opened the window for a better look. The train was slowing down as it approached the accident site. He spotted workers near the tracks, removing the last of the rubble. There at the bottom, he saw the remnants of the wagons and the half-buried locomotive. Pressing all around the perimeter were row upon row of bystanders, clamoring for a better view of the rescue effort.

"You there," Hieronymus called out to a nearby railway employee.

"What do you want?" replied the man, glancing up at the passing carriage.

"Have you seen an injured governess?"

"Of course. There were five of them."

"All governesses?"

"Yes. Three old ones and two young."

"What bad luck!" he mumbled more to himself than the worker, pulling his head back inside. *Five governesses; who would have thought that? Then she must be one of them. And I can't make inquiries in Thionville since I have to keep going to Metz. I'll just have to conclude my affairs in Etain as soon as possible and then head back. But I want to see her before they bury her.*

Disappointed, he plunked himself down in his seat and hung his head, trying to console himself. A poem came to mind:

*'If two hearts have to part,
ones who were meant for life
then follows a deep sorrow,
unyielding and far from tripe.'*

The sound of a distant bell brought him out of his musings. A locomotive came into view, the wheels screeched, and the train rolled to a stop in Thionville station.

"Thionville! One minute stop," the conductor instructed. "All passengers climb aboard."

Schneffke wasn't paying any attention. He wanted to check on his sketchpad and alighted.

"Monsieur, there are only a few min—" the conductor called after him.

Hieronymus wasn't concerned and headed for the main office. On the way, he spotted a man wearing a cap, a vest, and sporting white sleeves.

"Are you a porter?" he asked.

"Yes, sir."

"Do you have my map folder?"

"What map folder, Monsieur?"

"I left it on the previous train."

"Ah! You're the one who missed his train and telegraphed ahead, right?"

"Yes."

"Please, check over there in the office bureau."

Schneffke walked in and greeted. "Have you seen my map folder?"

The employee scrutinized him carefully before he delved under the counter for a piece of paper. Having found the right one, he scanned the contents. "Are you Hieronymus Schneffke?" he asked, reading from it.

"Yes, I'm the painter from Berlin; I cabled from Trier."

"Very good. We've managed to save your folder. Here it is," he said reaching into a box and retrieving something resembling a paper and cardboard sandwich which had been rolled together and tied with string.

Hieronymus stared incredulously at the oddity.

"Wha—what is that thing?" he managed, finally finding his voice.

"Your map folder, sir."

"My… my folder?"

"Indeed."

"But that's like no folder I've ever seen."

"Perhaps, but this is yours. It's a little worse for wear since it didn't escape the trip down the embankment. Surely, you're relived that we've been able to recover it."

"Well, if that isn't a fine looking present. Listen to me, Mons—"

"Hold it, my good man," the employee cut him off. "There's no need to thank us. Are you staying or are you travelling on?"

"I'm going further."

"When?"

"Well, with *that* train," he said, gesturing over his shoulder.

"Oh no. The machinist has already given the signal. Please hurry if you want to catch it."

In his habitual hurry, Schneffke bounded out the door leaving his hat behind. All the doors had been closed, and the wheels were already in motion."

"Wait!" he bellowed. "I'm coming as well."

"Sir, get back!" cautioned the station chief. "It's too late."

"Monsieur Schneffke," he heard a female voice call out to him.

Hieronymus looked for the originator of the summons, and spotted Madelon waving a handkerchief from an open window. He ran alongside the moving train to get a closer look.

"Is she among the injured, among the crushed?" he hollered.

"Who?" Madelon asked.

"The governess."

"No, she wasn't crushed. She's alive. She's staying in Thionville with—"

That was all he caught. The rest of her words were swallowed by the noise of the train's rolling wheels, which was now going considerably faster than he. Hieronymus stopped running and steadied himself on a lamp standard, catching his breath.

"Thank God she's alive," he said with relief. "I haven't lost her yet. Perhaps this is God's doing in that I've missed the train again."

He spotted his handkerchief on the platform and went to fetch it. All that exertion had raised his internal temperature. He felt hot and wanted to wipe the sweat from his forehead. He reached for his hat, normally firmly in place, but it was strangely absent.

"*Sapperlot!* Where is my Calabrese hat?" he mumbled to himself. He looked around the platform but couldn't locate it. *Hmm! Where could it be?* he thought. Just then an idea struck him. *I must have left it in the telegraph office.*

The painter headed back to the bureau.

"What do you want now?" asked the clerk a little abruptly.

"Forgive me, but I seem to have left my hat behind."

"It's over there. So, you missed your train."

"Unfortunately."

"You should be happy. If you had left as scheduled, you would have left your hat behind and been forced to send another cable."

"That's true. When is the next train?"

The clerk checked his schedule. "It departs at nine thirteen, about five hours from now. You'll have plenty of time to look around town."

"I intend to. Would it be permissible for you to accept a small gratuity for having to put up with my questions for a second time?"

The clerk's stern face brightened considerably at the prospect. "I don't normally accept tips," he lied, "but so as not to appear ungracious, I will make an exception."

"Well said. Would you then allow me to present you with the remnants of my treasured map folder, the one you managed to rescue?

If you take the time to repair the pages and leave the folder with an accomplished painter, he could transform the pages into something you could treasure for a lifetime. Good day, sir."

Schneffke tucked the unsightly sketchpad under the clerk's arm in one swift motion, turned around, and disappeared out the door. The haughty clerk stood stiffly in place, not believing the painter's arrogance in withholding the expected monetary tip and saddling him with the decrepit folder. He stared for just a moment at the closing door through which the benevolent painter had left and then grabbed the dilapidated folder, hurling it into the furthest corner.

"Damned irritating fellow," he cursed. "He won't get away with that a second time. If he dares to show his face in my office, I'll see to it that he feels the blunt end of my cane, something *he* won't treasure for a lifetime."

∾✠ℐ

Schneffke decided to use the five hours to conduct inquiries about the governess. He went up and down the streets, visited all the bars and restaurants and even ventured out to the accident site, all without the desired result. If he accomplished anything at all, it was that time sped by. It was nearly nine o'clock. He only had a few minutes to spare before he had to head back to the railway station. By coincidence, he ended up on the street where Franz Schneeberg lived.

Two women came around the corner. He stopped in his tracks by what he saw.

Unbelievable, he thought. *One of them has to be my governess.* He rushed toward her, removing his hat. "God be praised, Fräulein," he started. "You're still alive. I heard you had perished in the accident, and I felt—" Schneffke stopped speaking. The lady cast a fleeting glance in his direction, but then shrugged her shoulders and walked into a nearby house.

Hieronymus removed his spectacles and rubbed his eyes. *Wasn't that the governess?* he thought. Replacing his glasses, he noticed the house had two doors. The outer door had a glass front, adorned with a prominent sign, *Apothecary*. The second door presumably facilitated an entrance to a private residence. He made a beeline for the glass door. As he entered, he noticed a lad standing behind the counter, watching him with amusement.

"Did you happen to see two ladies?" Hieronymus asked him, unable to suppress his irritation.

"Of course," replied the young man, eyeing the newcomer.

"Do you know who they are?"

"Hmm," mumbled the young man, rubbing his back on a doorpost.

"Well, it seems that you know them?"

"Indeed. But aren't you here to buy something, Monsieur?"

"No. I don't need anything."

"Well, good night then."

The clerk was about to close-up for the evening, when Schneffke seized the opportunity. He was willing to buy a trifle, rather than walk away empty-handed.

"Hold on," he said. "I just remembered that I do require something."

"How can I be of service," replied the clerk, returning to the counter.

"I need some Russian ointment, along with a little information."

While the clerk busied himself with packing the ointment, the painter asked away. "Who lives here?"

"Doctor Bertrand."

"Anyone else?"

"Well, the plant-collector Schneeberg and I."

"What about those ladies?"

"Here you are," the young man said, handing him the package. "Spread it liberally over the dressing and place it on the affected area. Don't remove it. When the wound has healed the dressing will fall off on its own."

"Thank you. So, who was the blonde lady?"

"Do you require anything else?"

"No, not tonight."

"Then please excuse me. Good night."

"Hold it! I'd like to purchase a small quantity of the yellow powder."

"Very good."

"Now then, who was the blonde mademoiselle?"

"She's visiting my mistress, the doctor's wife."

"What's her name?"

"Madame Bertrand."

Schneffke's jaw dropped. "No, not *hers*, the visitor's name."

The clerk thought about it for a moment. "Miss de Lissa," he revealed.

"But that's impossible."

The clerk shrugged his shoulders. "That's what I was told. Here is your product. It's best to apply it directly to the infected area; it's good for keeping inflammation down."

"I know. Who is she then?"

"Do you require anything else?"

"*Sapperlot*! Do you want me to purchase the entire inventory?"

"No, sir. But I'm only supposed to converse with customers."

"Fine! Just give me a little of that salve on the counter. So, tell me, where is the lady from?"

"England."

"It can't be. Who was the other lady with her?"

"Dr. Bertrand's wife."

"Did the blonde one escape injury on today's noon-day train?"

"Yes, Monsieur. Just make sure to apply the salve properly and allow for the air to circulate."

"Fine. How long was she planning to stay?"

"I don't know. Will there be anything else?"

"No, that should do it."

"That will be two francs and eighty centimes."

"Heavens! Those are expensive expenditures. Actually, I don't need this stuff," Hieronymus said, laying out the money.

"Then why did you buy the items?" asked the inquisitive clerk.

"So, I could prolong our conversation."

"Well, in that case," said the enterprising clerk, "I am prepared to buy them back for fifty centimes."

Schneffke gaped at the man's shrewdness. "Man, you're something else," he finally managed. "I take my hat off to you. If I knew that you were in need of the ointment for yourself, I would accept your offer. But perhaps I can make use of this stuff. Good night."

Hieronymus left the apothecary and not a moment too soon. He arrived at the train station with only minutes to spare. He had barely sat down in the second- class coupé, when the whistle blew, and the train started to move. He was pleased with himself for not having to share the coupé. He stretched out on the seat and fell asleep, not waking until the train arrived in Metz. After disembarking, he headed for a nearby hotel where he stayed overnight.

Early the next morning, he inquired about transportation to Etain. The mail carriage had long since left. The friendly porter suggested that a man who wasn't in a hurry could cover the distance by walking and taking in the sights along the way. Schneffke allowed the man to talk him into going on foot. Before he embarked on his outing, he purchased a smaller map folder with paper, along with a portable field stool. He enjoyed the scenery but found the journey too long. Arriving hungry and tired in Etain, the painter sought out the first available guesthouse and after checking in went directly to bed. Strangely, he never told anyone about his sojourning experience. Perhaps it had been so pleasurable that he didn't trust himself to render it justice.

CHAPTER EIGHTEEN

NANON FORGES AHEAD

Franz Schneeberg was required to submit a detailed protocol of his involvement to the commission at the accident site. He managed to evade the more pressing questions about how he had come to learn of the impending plot and was eventually allowed to proceed with Amelia and the Charbonnier sisters into town. At the train station, Amelia said her goodbyes and headed for Doctor Bertrand's house. The good doctor had thought of preparing his wife for the upcoming guest by sending a messenger ahead of her arrival.

Nanon, Madelon, and Franz waited until the train from Trier pulled in. They climbed into the next available coupé, settling in the second-class carriage. It was Madelon who first spotted the large, blue satin handkerchief.

"I've seen this napkin before," she laughed. "Now we're in for some fun."

"Who does it belong to?" asked Nanon.

"Monsieur Hieronymus Schneffke, the man whom I've told you about. He must have come on this train from Trier and momentarily stepped off. I hope he doesn't miss his train."

Just then the machinist gave his signal. The doors were shut, and the wheels started their laborious circular movement. Madelon spied the portly painter come running down the platform, a sight in itself; but it was too late for him. She was forced to relinquish the satin handkerchief and tossed it out the window.

"No, she wasn't crushed," Madelon voiced, responding to Hieronymus's query regarding the governess's fate. "She is alive. She's staying in Thionville with Doctor Bertrand's family."

"I've got to have a closer look," said Franz, peering over her shoulder. "I know that fellow."

"Really? Isn't he hilarious?"

"Indeed. But I can tell you that he's not as clumsy as he pretends to be. He likes to leave that impression, but in reality, he is actually quite clever."

"Where did you get to know him?" the perceptive Nanon asked.

The question proved a little awkward for Franz, who wasn't free to divulge his real identity to her just yet. "I ran into him years ago, on a trip," he replied extricating himself quickly. "He was a student at the time, learning his trade."

Under other circumstances, a lively conversation may have ensued among the three young people. But the tragic events of the day had tired the two sisters, and Franz was quite happy just to enjoy their company without divulging too much. Each one sat, leaning back in their seat, occasionally making a passing comment. Yet, over and over, Nanon's eyes drifted over to the disguised Ulanen sergeant. She had only seen him dressed in his plant-collector garb, and today he was attired in a fine suit. He had the appearance of a refined gentleman. It became difficult for her to refrain from looking at him. Madelon of course noticed her sister's attentiveness and coupled with the uncanny instinct women have about such things correctly assumed their relationship was far from casual.

The train pulled into Metz station at about six o'clock. Franz arranged for a carriage that would take them to Etain. Since both ladies had brought some luggage, Franz was forced to sit up front with the coachman. The horses were fresh and kept-up a good pace so that they reached their destination before midnight. They alighted from the coach in front of one of the best hotels in the area. Franz arranged for the rental of two rooms, one for himself and the other for the sisters. Once they were settled in, they took part in a simple meal together. Later,

Franz excused himself and retired to his own room, leaving the sisters alone to catch up on their recent escapades.

"At last, we're alone together, just the two of us," Madelon began. "Now we can talk without interruption."

"We don't have to keep any secrets from Monsieur Schneeberg."

"Do you really think so? You have that much confidence in him?"

"Yes, I trust him implicitly."

"Who is he actually?" prompted Madelon.

"An orphan, just like us. I've written you a few things about him, but I can elaborate further." Nanon related about Franz, and how she often met him in the woods during her excursions. But she wasn't as forthcoming as she had been with Baroness de Sainte-Marie.

"Isn't that peculiar," Madelon commented. "Just a few days ago, I met a man who is the spitting image of Franz."

"Really? Me too. What a coincidence."

"Who was your double?"

"An artist by the name of Haller. He came from Stuttgart and spent a day at Ortry, painting a portrait."

Madelon nodded thoughtfully. "What did you think of him?" she asked.

"I found him appealing and interesting."

"Quite likely it's the same man."

"Really, the same one? Are you saying that Haller is now staying in Berlin?"

"Yes. If I knew you to be discreet, then I could be more forthcoming."

"Madelon? Are you trying to insult me?" Nanon replied, her cheeks reddening. "Whatever things my sister divulges to me, I can certainly keep to myself. We've faced all sorts of calamity in our lives together. Even though we've had to live apart, our hearts have always acted with one accord. Should we now harbour mistrust toward one other?"

"No, my dear Nanon. I hadn't intended to hurt you," Madelon said, looking steadily at her sister. "You see, Herr Haller, purporting to be a novice painter, is in reality a French officer."

"You don't say!" Nanon exclaimed.

"Yes, not only an officer, but a spy. France is itching to start a war with Germany. The French emperor has authorized vanguards to fan out across Germany, disguised and equipped to scout out Germany's readiness."

"I wouldn't have thought that of him. He looked like such a kind man."

"I took to him as well, and now I feel sorry for him. You see, Nanon, he's boarding in our house."

"How interesting."

"Isn't it? I received him in a friendly and trustworthy manner. We even had a few conversations together. Then, just before I headed for the train station, he came to see me and made vague references about our upbringing, intimating he knew something about our past."

"Oh, that would be wonderful, if only it were true."

"He promised to explain further, but only after I returned from my trip."

"Do you place much stock in it?"

"I'm not sure what to make of it. I have to be patient and wait. I'm holding out some hope for tomorrow though."

"Not me," replied Nanon.

"Really? I can't shake the thought that our former caregiver knew something about our lineage. I can't imagine him dying and not having told his son beforehand. That's what I'm hoping for."

"So, you think Charles will divulge something?"

"Yes, don't you?"

"No, not at all. I know that Charles Berteu better than you."

"He always struck me as a stubborn, yet helpful boy. He hadn't caused us any harm when we lived there."

"Up until we parted, no. Remember, you obtained your position before I did, while I stayed behind at Castle Malineau. Do you recall how fond he was of me?"

"Sure, I still remember."

"Well, after you left, he became more overt in his feelings for me. He kept after me, hounding me, to the extent that he made a marriage proposal."

"A marriage proposal?" Madelon asked stunned. "Charles, our stepbrother?"

"Yes, Madelon. Naturally, I turned him away. After all, I was still very young. He took it badly but wouldn't give up. After I had obtained my position at Castle Ortry, I received correspondence from him there. He wrote about his affection for me and of our future together. I only replied once, hoping to get him to stop. But when I realized it only spurred him on, I stopped writing altogether."

"I had no idea, dear Nanon."

"Oh, but there's more. He even travelled to Ortry a few times, waiting for me while I went out for walks. It wasn't easy for me to get away."

"That's despicable."

"During my employ, I was fortunate enough to accompany Marion on a few trips, giving me some breathing room. Shortly after my return however, I received another letter from Charles, informing me he planned on paying me another visit. I was afraid to set foot in the forest, if it weren't for my protector."

"Who is that?" Madelon asked with interest.

"Franz Schneeberg, Doctor Bertrand's plant collector."

"Ah, him."

"You know, Madelon, he was always close-by when I went out for walks, even though we never planned on meeting. No sooner had I entered the forest than he showed up. I never would have contemplated going to the funeral without his watchfulness."

"Are you afraid that Charles will renew his advances?"

"I'm convinced of it."

"Will Monsieur Schneeberg watch over you?"

"I hope so."

"How will he manage that?"

"I don't know."

"Were you thinking of billeting him in the castle?"

"No. I can't see us doing that."

"You're right. How else can he stay close?"

"I'll have to leave it up to him. It's best that I'm up front with him and the sooner the better."

"What? You're not thinking of seeing him tonight, are you?"

"Yes, why not?"

"Nanon, it's past midnight. A young lady visiting a man in a *gasthaus?*"

"Madelon, it strikes me that there must be awful people living in Berlin for you to take that view."

"Why?"

"You don't place much trust in him. Monsieur Schneeberg is so good, so honorable and modest. He never says a word that makes me feel uncomfortable."

Madelon smiled a little sheepishly. Naturally, she couldn't divulge that it was this same man who came from Berlin and stemmed from military circles.

"Then do what seems right to you. Clearly you know him better than I do."

"Alright. I won't be too long. Who knows if I'll have an opportunity of speaking privately to him tomorrow."

"Then you better get going. I'm going to bed. I haven't slept since we left Berlin."

Nanon left their room and quietly walked a few doors down the hall.

❧✠☙

Meanwhile, Franz sat at the open window staring out into the starry night. Even though he didn't get much sleep the previous night, he didn't feel fatigued. He had extinguished his light so he could better observe the rising stars, yet he would have gladly traded them all for the one that had risen within him. He was interrupted in his musings by a soft knock. Surprised, he spun around and in a half-loud voice beckoned, "Come in, it's not locked."

The door opened slowly, but only a fraction. "Are you still awake?" a timid voice asked. "Oh, but your light is out..."

Instantly, Franz recognized the visitor's voice. As if having received a shock, he catapulted from his chair. "No, I haven't gone to bed, Mademoiselle Nanon. I'll just re-light my lamp. Please, come in."

He lit a match, and as the wick began to burn, he saw her standing in the doorway, unsure if she should stay or leave.

"Are you afraid, Mademoiselle?" he asked.

"No, not at all. But the hour is late, and I wasn't sure if I should intrude upon you. It was dark and I didn't know if I had found the right room."

"Please, have a seat on the sofa," he said smiling. "I'll pull up a chair."

Nanon was reassured by his offer and took a seat on the sofa. Franz closed the window and seated himself on a nearby chair. Nanon appraised him with a warm smile.

"You didn't have a light on, Monsieur," she said with amusement. "Weren't you bored sitting there by yourself?"

"Not at all."

"What were you doing in the darkness?"

A slight redness spread over his face. "Oh, nothing spectacular, and completely harmless. I was gazing at the stars."

"Really, the stars? Monsieur Schneeberg, tell me, do you consider yourself a poet?"

"No, I'm afraid not. I don't have the skill for rhyme."

"Perhaps you're an astronomer?" she suggested.

"Even less so. Astronomers have to be good mathematicians, while I tend to lose track of numbers. How then would I fare with complicated calculations?"

"Did you know that one can be a poet without being skilled in rhyme or syntax? A good wife, who adorns her home with the harmony of satisfaction and peace, is perhaps a better poet than one who amasses an entire stack of books on prose."

"You may be right, Mademoiselle. Such a woman is worth more than all the treasure on earth."

"Likewise, one can aspire to become an aficionado without bothering with complex equations. Anyone can gaze at the stars."

"That's true. In fact, I needn't look toward the heavens for a star. It's much closer, Mademoiselle Nanon."

She blushed. His eyes rested on her with a deep longing, almost with a pleading expression. But her trust in him was firm and unshakeable, so that she didn't perceive his longing as something repulsive.

"Now then, you're an astronomer," she continued. "I like the sound of that. But even if you weren't one, and still gazed at the stars, that only leaves one possibility."

"And that would be?"

"Can't you guess?"

"No."

"Well, lovers are captivated by the stars."

"Really? I suppose that's true. Yet I lean toward one who's captured my heart."

"A soft and tender heart is a gift from God and can be complemented by a strong and energetic will. Those two, namely a genial disposition and strong character, I can attribute to a man that would make a girl happy and content. Just today, you've demonstrated yet again your prowess and resolve by rescuing Madelon from the brink of death. How can we possibly repay you, my good, Monsieur Schneeberg?"

He looked embarrassed for the briefest moment.

"Mademoiselle Nanon," he replied, "I wish I could demonstrate my devotion to you in such and even more ways. But I feel content when I see your smile. It tells me that you're satisfied with me."

"What? More service?" she smiled. "And yet that's why I've come to you at this late hour, to ask you for one more favour."

"Anything, anything at all."

"I'm afraid that I'm imposing on you," Nanon said, hesitating.

"Please, tell me. I want to be useful."

"Very well," she breathed relieved, "I'm going to be candid with you. There's a man whom I can't stand and one who's determined to force me into becoming his wife."

Franz's good-natured expression waned, turning into one of concern.

"Mademoiselle Nanon, I won't tolerate you being taken advantage of."

"Unfortunately, my sister and I will be traveling to his house tomorrow."

"I don't understand. May I at least know who it is?"

"He's the son of my deceased stepfather."

"So, in effect, he's your stepbrother."

Nanon nodded and then told him about the unwanted letters, the proposals, and lastly the few times that Berteu tried to get close to her.

"Did any of this occur while you were at Ortry?" asked Franz.

"Some of it, yes."

"It's fortunate for him that I wasn't nearby."

She smiled. "This was before you came to work for Dr. Bertrand."

"I see."

"But Charles threatened to pay me another visit."

"He had better dispense with it. However, from what you've just told me, you and your sister are forced to travel to his place because of his father's funeral."

"I'm afraid so, Monsieur. He's determined and unpredictable."

"One shouldn't just judge the outward appearance. I know of a nobleman, a Ulanen officer, without whom I wouldn't walk into a closet.[18.1] Is your stepbrother tall and strong as well?"

"No, not too tall, but he's stocky and strong. That combination is supposed to be formidable. Now, consider that I have to spend the better part of the day in his house."

"When is the funeral service?"

"At three in the afternoon."

"What if you and your sister appeared just before the commencement of the service?"

"His own stepdaughters? Oh no, that wouldn't be fitting. People would quickly find out that we were being hesitant, even though we were on hand."

"Surely there will be other people around?"

"Quite a few, or so I would expect."

"Then there's nothing for you to worry about."

"Don't be too sure of that. He'll look for an opportunity to speak to me privately."

"And that makes you uncomfortable?"

"During the day, no."

"Are you planning to stay into the evening?"

"Yes, though not overnight. There's to be a reception after the service, and it wouldn't look proper if we left prior to that."

"Hmm," said Franz rubbing his chin. "I'm beginning to understand your concern, Mademoiselle Nanon. How far is it from here to Castle Malineau?"

"About one and a half hours."

"Is his house far removed from the others?"

"An old mill, surrounded by a forest, is ten minutes away, and on the other side about the same distance lies the village, which belongs to the castle."

"What is it called?"

"Malineau. In order to reach the castle, we have to travel through the town."

"Is there a guesthouse or hotel nearby?"

"No, just a small tavern."

"How were you and your sister planning on reaching the castle tomorrow?"

"On foot. Someone else could follow with our little luggage."

"My wish for you is that you change your plans."

"I don't see what else we could do without imposing on anyone."

"There's always an alternative. If you engage a carriage for the day, you can use it to transport both of you to the castle. Once you've gotten off, the coachman can head to the tavern and wait for you there. When you've finished at the reception, you can send word to him at the inn. The driver will then collect you both and bring you back to Etain."

"Along with you, right?"

"No."

"No?" she asked surprised. "It's because I need your protection that I've come to you at this late hour."

Franz smiled reassuringly. "Have no fear, Mademoiselle. I intend on arriving before you at the castle. And even though you might not see me, rest assured that I *will* be there and keep an eye on you both."

"Really? Will you promise me that?"

"Of course. Here is my hand," he said extending it.

"Thank you. I feel much better now. But I'm still concerned for you."

"Don't worry about me. I'm convinced that tomorrow will end as peacefully as it will begin."

"God willing. And since you've been so kind and accommodating to us, I want to share something with you; it's a hope of sorts."

"I pray it comes to pass."

"Madelon has reason to believe that our stepfather, our caregiver, knew something about our past. He may have passed it on to his son before he died."

"So, you think that your stepbrother, Charles Berteu, will reveal something tomorrow?"

"Perhaps, but I have my doubts and told Madelon as much. If I'm right, at least she won't be surprised by his reluctance. What do you think, Monsieur?"

"I don't wish to give you false hope either. I suspect that you won't find out anything."

Nanon nodded thoughtfully. "But what use can it be for him to conceal it?"

"Actually, quite a lot."

"I'm not following you," she said puzzled.

"That's because you don't know what he's been told by his father. Yet one thing is certain: he's fashioning a weapon against you, a terrible weapon."

"Dear God! You're frightening me, Monsieur."

"Please, just hear me out," pleaded Franz. "I'm not referring to a weapon which he can wield with his hands, but one that will overcome your resistance toward his efforts to marry you."

"He couldn't possibly win."

"You don't know that. What if he bribed you with riches?"

"He's not rich."

"Or with honour and position?"

"Whatever honour he might possess is worthless to me."

"Mademoiselle, I wasn't speaking about his riches or his honor, rather to that which he's kept back and may belong to you and your sister. Your father may have been a nobleman."

"Do you really think so?"

"It's entirely possible. When I look at you, Mademoiselle, it's as if you came from a distinguished family. Everything about you is so fine, so pure and wholesome. You remind me of a star, whose light casts an extra blessing on whomever its light illuminates."

Nanon placed her hands in her lap and looked at him expectantly. "Monsieur," she said, "you've allowed your kind heart to speak of things it perhaps should have kept hidden."

"Alright. But what if your father had been wealthy?"

"That's entirely possible, since my mother had many valuable items, ones she was forced to sell over time."

"There, you see. And now this new proprietor, Charles Berteu, demands that you give in to his proposal. If you consent, you become rich, but if you spurn his offer, he keeps the information to himself, and you remain poor."

"I would rather remain poor than to give in to that arrogant man."

"What about Mademoiselle Madelon? Shouldn't you take her side into account?"

Nanon stared ahead into the night for a few seconds, contemplating her options. At last, she came to an inward resolve. "Madelon would rather remain poor than to see her only sister unhappy."

"God bless you for your honesty and resolve. One more thing: where does Berteu live? In the castle?"

"No, in the house next door, the one set aside for the administrator and his family."

"Are you familiar with its layout?"

"Very well, since we were raised in it."

"Is it significant in size?"

Nanon thought about it for a minute, her mind going back to her childhood. "There's the ground floor and a second story."

"Do the windows have shutters?"

"Only the ones on the ground floor."

"Is there a balcony?"

"No. But there is a veranda around the entire house, supporting the lattice work for the wine branches."

"Ah, I see now. Does the veranda extend up to the second floor?"

"Yes."

"So, the house sits unencumbered by other buildings. Is there a garden?"

"No. But why all these questions?"

Franz smiled. "I haven't formulated a plan yet, but it's wise to be prepared beforehand. At what time were you planning to leave tomorrow?"

"Oh, mid-morning."

"Then I will arrange a coach for you both."

"I knew that you would do even more than we would have dared to ask. We continue to fall deeper into your debt."

Franz shook his head and waved his hand dismissively.

"I know of a young lady, who is so rich that each friendly glance contains countless diamonds. Shouldn't such a glance be worth more than I could ever hope to possess?"

Franz heard soft, golden laughter. "May I know who this young lady might be?" she teased.

"Why you yourself, Mademoiselle Nanon."

"Then from now on I will endeavour to pay you by radiating dazzling diamonds from my eyes."

She stood up from the sofa while he rose from his chair. She held her small fine-boned hands out to him which he tenderly gripped.

"You're no ordinary man, but strong, dependable, and steadfast. In fact, you're a man without falsehood and arrogance. I'm only telling you this because I know you. Despite your modesty, you seek a higher ideal. You desire to speak from your inner being without imposing on me. I'm just a poor, lowly girl. I don't know what another would do in my stead, but I desire you to be happy and inwardly blessed."

Before Franz had time to respond, Nanon pulled his head toward hers and pressed her lips to his, so that he felt her passionate kiss.

"Goodnight, my dear Franz," she said, freeing herself from his embrace and headed out the door.

Franz barely heard the door close behind her. He simply stood there, rigid like a statue, not able to move a single muscle. After a long pause, he turned from the door.

What a chaste woman, he thought. *Pure as an angel in heaven. That was a kiss worthy of a duke or prince, and she kissed me. Me, an orphan, a lonely sergeant with the Ulanen, one who has few prospects and will likely end up being a policeman or worse, a tax collector.*

CHAPTER NINETEEN

CHARLES BERTEU

Toward the end of the last century, Castle Malineau had nearly been destroyed by fire. The owner at that time was wealthy enough to rebuild and did so in the splendour of the Renaissance period. Being a proud aristocrat, the count didn't want the caretaker to dwell under the same roof and so he had decided to build a secondary dwelling, one set apart from the main structure.

A peculiar aroma emanated from the interior of this smaller dwelling, reminiscent of wood shavings and resin, not uncommon by-products in the manufacture of coffins. Charles Berteu, about twenty-six years old, sat in a gabled upper room. He wasn't particularly tall yet possessed a stocky build leaving little doubt he could handle himself. A large head, thick neck and small wary eyes left the impression he was physically strong but lacked in the mental faculties. A book lay open before him, the pages displaying rows upon rows of numbers. He was resting his head in his hands, as if the mere act of looking at the figures gave him a headache. Charles, the son of the recently deceased caretaker who was to be buried later that day, had a dour look on his face and was in a poor frame of mind.

The door opened, and his mother, a short, wiry woman, walked in. Louise was strong-boned, and the recessed lower chin suggested she no longer had any teeth. Her skin had a leathery-like appearance, and a sallow complexion further detracted from her appeal.

"Well, Charles," Louise began. "How is the supply of wine?"

"Oh, Mother!" he erupted. "Not that damned wine again. You know full well that we don't have a single bottle to spare."

"What about the bottles in the estate's wine cellar?" she suggested.

"Well, that's what I've been studying for the past hour, to see how many bottles we can appropriate for ourselves. It's not easy to falsify the records."

"Then look after the entries later. There's no time now."

"But what if the count should unexpectedly show up and find the books are not in order?"

"He won't come that quickly."

"Really? Don't you remember that the count had written he intended to come within four weeks? But since then, we've had to cable him regarding father's death. It's quite likely he'll come sooner, with the express purpose of reviewing the accounting books."

"Still, it shouldn't pose a problem for us. He has no idea that my husband kept two separate books, one for himself and one for the gracious count."

"But that's what's giving me a headache. He always kept the books to himself, rarely giving me a glimpse into how he managed things. Now that he's gone, it's not easy for me to make sense of it. So far as I can tell, he wasn't able to save much."

"I know, we're not rich," Louise sighed.

"Don't I know it. But before the count shows up, I have to replace nine hundred francs. The only problem is where to get them."

"I would have thought that the old captain…?"

"Well, yes, the latest order for the gunpowder will give us some cash, but it's like digging a bigger hole in order to fill a smaller one."

"It's not exactly the way I thought this would work out. We should have been well-taken care of after your father's death."

"That was always his plan. But then those birth certificates just disappeared. Where on earth could they be?"

His mother's face didn't look hopeful. "We've searched everywhere and found nothing," she lamented.

"Are you sure they were here in the first place?"

"Yes. The girls' mother had kept them safe at an undisclosed place."

"Did our father know?"

"Of course."

"Did he know their true identity?"

"He knew everything."

"It's even more aggravating that he died so suddenly, without revealing one word," Charles complained.

"We could have obtained a large amount for those documents."

"What? Don't be daft, Mother," he admonished her. "Were you really thinking of selling those papers back to the girls? I want to have it all."

"And now you have nothing."

"Don't be ridiculous. Sooner or later, I will come across those documents. The main thing centers around my stepsisters. Once I've married Nanon, I'll be assured of the rest."

"I've yet to hear that she's accepted your proposal."

"Be quiet! She'll have to bow to my will."

"Don't be so sure of yourself, Charles."

He looked irritated for a moment. "Look! I'll prove it to you. If Father hadn't died, I would be underway right now with another shipment of gunpowder. The old man would've been helpful, since it would be to his advantage for Nanon to leave. He complained to me before how Marion has been using her friend Nanon as a crutch, resisting his efforts to facilitate an engagement. Now that we're faced with the burial, I'll just have to rework my plans. If not through persuasion, then through coercion. It'll be decided tonight. She'll be mine, whether freely or by force."

"Just be careful, Charles."

"Pah! Wasn't I chosen to be one of the leaders of the *franctireurs*?"

"What if Nanon doesn't show up?"

"Don't worry, she'll come. She didn't know our father's true nature and consequently held him in high regard."

"And when she becomes your wife—then what?"

"Then I'll tear this whole house apart; I'll find those papers eventually."

"What about Madelon? Remember, half belongs to her."

"Let me deal with her," he said in a dismissive tone. "She won't get one franc. I've already formed a plan. I don't mind telling you that I would marry Nanon even if she had no money. She's a mouth-watering delicacy, a beauty like no other. I can hardly wait to get her for myself."

Just then they heard noises downstairs, stemming from horses being reined in.

"Who could that be?" asked his mother.

"Go down and find out."

"What if it's Nanon? Aren't you going to greet her?"

"No. It doesn't suit my plan. She's the stepdaughter, while I'm the rightful son. It's up to her to greet me, not the other way around."

Louise left, closing the door behind her. What followed were sounds of happy women's voices emanating from the kitchen. After a few minutes, the voices died down and Berteu heard approaching steps.

His mother opened the study door and proclaimed, "Charles, what a surprise. Look, both girls are here."

Berteu turned around and came face-to-face with two beautiful young women, Nanon and Madelon, standing in the doorway. His brow furrowed in disapproval. This wasn't turning out according to his plan. Nanon was welcome, but Madelon could get in his way. He composed himself and stood up.

"You've come at a sad time," Charles began. "This place has turned into a house of mourning. Still, I bid you welcome. I was hoping Nanon would be able to come, but I hadn't expected to see you as well, Madelon. How did you manage to come all the way from Germany?"

Both women looked composed and serious, but not because of the upcoming funeral. He sensed they felt uncomfortable in his presence.

"Nanon cabled me," replied Madelon. "As for my part, I requested a brief holiday and then headed directly to the train station."

"Well, you both could have dispensed with it; Nanon with the cable and you Madelon, with that long trip."

Nanon ignored her stepbrother's jibe and instead replied heartily. "It wasn't just on your account, Charles. We haven't seen each other for quite some time and wanted to use the opportunity for a little reunion."

"Well, if you aren't full of surprises," he mocked. "But for now, go downstairs. Mother will put you to good use. I have work to do."

Louise headed downstairs. They turned around intending to follow her, but he called after them. "Wait a minute. Did you walk, or arrive by way of coach?"

"We procured a coach," Nanon answered.

"Who does it belong to?"

"A coachman from Etain."

"Is he heading back right away?"

"No. He's going to wait for us at the tavern. Then in the evening he'll collect us and take us back."

"*Sapperlot!* You're leaving tonight already?"

"Yes."

"I won't hear of it. I want you to stay for a longer visit."

"I'm afraid we can't do that. We both managed to arrange for a furlough, but a short one at that. We must leave tonight."

Berteu scratched his head. "So, you're really having the coachman wait for you at the local inn?"

"Yes."

"And who's going to pay him? Surely not I?"

"No, we will. We hired him," confirmed Madelon.

"Alright. You may go."

They left without questioning his abrupt manner. Meanwhile, Charles kept writing and going over the accounts. After a good hour, Louise came up to advise him about some matter concerning the funeral. They settled it quickly, but before she left Charles asked her to send Nanon upstairs—by herself.

"Are you going to broach the topic of a proposal?" Louise asked.

"Yes."

"She's going to turn you down."

"Let's wait and see."

"Charles, listen to me. She seems to have turned into quite a different girl. She's no longer the quiet, meek girl we used to know, but surer of herself and independent."

"I've also become more independent. We'll see who's going to win."

Louise left, with Nanon coming upstairs shortly after her. She of course suspected what he had in mind but didn't show the least bit of concern or uneasiness. Charles had taken a seat on the sofa and motioned her to join him.

"Ah, there you are, Nanon. Please, take a seat," he said, pretending to be hospitable. "We have a little time for a visit before the funeral."

"Thank you," she replied evenly. "But I like to conclude simple errands while standing."

His eyebrows went up. "If you're under the impression that this concerns some little errand, then you're mistaken. Actually, it's quite an important matter I wish to discuss with you. Won't you have a seat?"

"Alright," Nanon replied taking a seat on a nearby chair, not on the offered sofa.

Surprised, Charles adjusted his seat so he could face her. "Well, I must confess," he started, "that you've turned into a nice-looking and respectable girl. Wouldn't you agree?"

Ordinarily, Nanon may have simply ignored such a leading comment, but in this case, she felt that a response was warranted.

"Yes, isn't it obvious," she said matter of fact.

"*Sacre bleu!*" he replied, not expecting such a comeback. "Aren't you the all-knowing one? So, you're aware of your own importance?"

"Just as you are of yours."

"That's fine with me. I see that we're like-minded. Do you think we should pull our resources and come together?"

"No, thank you," she replied without hesitation.

"No? Why not?"

"Charles, are you implying by your less than aesthetic comment, which most prudent people would refer to as a betrothal or engagement, that I should seriously consider your proposal?"

"Yes, of course."

"It surprises me to learn that you've chosen the least flattering expression, rather than trying to impress me with a more, noble one. It's not so much that each one of us is aware of his or her own worth and culminating in a happy union, but that one is convinced of the other's importance. Actually, I haven't even contemplated a betrothal. I certainly have no interest in a simple togetherness. That much should be obvious to you."

"Aren't you the refined and eloquent one," he retorted. "You speak like you're reading from a book. So, you're talking about recognizing each other's value. How high would you rate mine?"

"I have yet to notice your worth, therefore I can't render a proper opinion."

"Alright. You'll soon come to appreciate mine. After all, the highest qualities are the ones often hidden from view. You can find all sorts of rubble lying about, but the precious stones, the real gems, those you have to dig for. I'll give you an opportunity to dig for treasure and you'll be amazed by what you will find."

"I'm not in the mood to start digging up rough-hewn stones. I'd rather devote my time in attaining unblemished gems."

"So, do you suppose that I'm rough and uncut?"

"I don't even know if you're worth polishing?"

"Heaven and hell!" he exclaimed angrily. "You're a feline that knows how to make use of her claws."

"Perhaps. Still, a girl has to protect herself from unwanted advances."

"Suit yourself. We can dispense with all this unproductive talk. It doesn't amount to anything. Let's look at my proposal objectively, much like a business arrangement. Now then, I have an inclination to marry you."

She looked at him steadily. "Yes, I can see that. But I don't share in your desire for marriage."

"I admire your openness. I trust we can quickly reach a consensus. Do you already have a suitor? Are you betrothed?"

"Even though I don't feel obligated to answer you, I want to come to an understanding. No, I don't have one."

Charles looked at her steadily. "Why don't you like me?"

"You don't appeal to my taste in a husband."

"Really? So, you want to marry according to your preferences?"

"I don't consider you as the man who would make me happy."

"Pah! And yet you're mistaken. Don't you know what you owe my father?"

Nanon sighed. "I've heard it so often, and Madelon as well, that it's like we're beholden to you for life."

"You should be grateful," he persisted.

"I don't see why I should forever grovel at your family's feet because of your hospitality. My mother sold her jewels in order to pay your father. Furthermore, I suspect she had left money with him, which has been kept from us."

"*Sapperlot*! If that isn't too bold."

"I have no reason to pretend. Least of all, I don't have to explain myself to you."

"Let's leave all this bickering. Now then, you won't marry me, whether out of love or gratefulness. How do you feel about prudence? A clever and wise joining can prove to be advantageous."

"No, thank you," she said, rolling her eyes.

"I could talk to you about... your family name," he said, baiting her.

"Do you really know it?" Nanon added quickly.

"Well..."

"That's no answer. Be specific."

"Alright. But only after you've become my wife. Only then will I reveal your name, your legitimacy and your right toward the inheritance you're entitled to."

Nanon was shocked. "What? You want to benefit by my good fortune by becoming my husband?"

"Of course," he said, grinning. "I won't deny it."

"First prove to me that you're in possession of our baptismal records?"

"Don't you believe me?"

"No. I've only known you as a cheat and an opportunist."

"I would never cheat you, Nanon."

"Spare me your platitudes. Instead, show me my birth certificate."

"Later, perhaps," Charles evaded.

"Then our business here has come to an end," Nanon said, rising from her seat.

Startled, Charles jumped out of his seat. A desperate, covetous feeling welled up within him. He grabbed her arm, holding her back. "I'm going to have you, one way or another. Do I make myself clear, Nanon?"

Rather than capitulating, Nanon shook free and faced Charles with a resolve he hadn't expected. "If *you* so much as touch me again," Nanon threatened, "I'm going to instantly leave this place, funeral or not. And that goes for my sister as well."

"Well," he said looking a little sheepish, "at least you owe me a kiss, a brotherly kiss."

Charles opened his arms to embrace her, but instead of a sweet kiss, he received a sound slap to his face, so that he staggered backwards. Not deterred, he was about to grab hold of her again. Nanon picked up a plate from the nearby table and smashed it on her insolent stepbrother's head, with the pieces scattering all over the floor. By the time he recovered, she had left, joining her sister downstairs.

Charles raised his clenched fist and threatened the departed girl. "You'll pay for that. I'll see to it that you'll become my wife, whether out of love, or convenience, or simply out of retribution."

From that point on, the day played out much like any other bereavement day. Friends and family came to offer their condolences and to take part in the procession to the graveyard. After the coffin had been lowered into the grave and the priest had concluded the ceremony with his customary prayer, many filed back to the house for a little gathering.

As stepchildren of the deceased, it fell upon Nanon and Madelon to serve the guests. Charles excused himself and headed for the stables. There he found the idle stable hand who in many ways was cut from the same stock as Berteu and with whom he had carried out the odd prank.

"Have you seen the foreigner, the coachman who earlier brought my stepsisters?" Charles asked.

"No, I haven't."

"Not even his carriage and horses?"

"Not them either."

"Then head over to the tavern where he's taking a rest. I want you to have a good look at his horses, the carriage, the way he's attired—in effect, everything."

"What for?" he asked casually. But then he caught a glint in Berteu's eyes. "Wait a minute. Are you planning another one of your pranks?"

"Yes. One that will net you twenty francs."

"You don't say! Then I'm your man."

"Good. I want to find out if you could pose as that coachman tonight and swap my wagon for his."

"Ah, so it's to be a switch. That should be funny. You can count on me. But Monsieur, I'll need a few francs to tide me over if I'm going to sit in the tavern for a while."

"Alright, here you go," Charles agreed, handing him the money. The stable hand happily pocketed the few coins and sauntered toward the inn.

∽✠∾

Meanwhile, Franz travelled on foot from Etain and had already walked around the castle grounds, becoming familiar with the layout. After imbibing a little refreshment at the tavern, he was planning on having a look at the flower mill. Having preceded the stable hand to the inn, he noticed right away the man was giving more than just passing attention to the coachman from Etain. Franz saw him head out to the adjoining stable, and after his return, examine the foreign-based carriage. But when the stable hand approached the coachman and offered to buy him a drink, Franz suspected he wasn't just being friendly but did so for a reason.

During their lively conversation, Franz overheard the newcomer was also a coachman and was employed by Berteu. His suspicions grew and he concluded that he and Berteu were planning something that involved the sisters' coachman and his carriage. He expected that the stable hand would soon leave and head back to the castle, but that wasn't the case. Berteu's servant engaged others at the inn in a card game. As the game drew on, Franz became restless and decided to go outside, taking the opportunity to explore the surrounding area. He was convinced that if anything was to take place concerning his pretty charges, it would happen later, probably at night.

After a short walk, he found the mill nestled in the middle of a small forest. A wide path connected the mill with the castle. It was all quiet at the mill, with no obvious signs of activity. Franz guessed it was out of respect for the deceased caretaker with no work having been planned for the day. With dusk approaching, Franz decided to head back to the tavern. There, he spotted the stable hand, still sitting at the same table. But after a short time, the man got up, paid his bill and after saying his goodbyes, headed back to the castle. Franz followed at a distance, ensuring he wasn't spotted. The man headed directly to his room, which was attached to the stable.

It was now quite dark outside. Franz felt he could risk a little time to reconnoitre. He climbed the cross-members of the lattice work until he reached the metal covered platform on the upper level. From there he could look into any of the windows. He slowly worked his way around the platform, taking his time to observe the mourners and the two sisters who were serving them. As he surveyed the different rooms, he recognized which one likely belonged to Berteu.

Charles was sitting with his guests. As long as he was occupied with them, Nanon and Madelon had nothing to fear. Franz made himself comfortable, while keeping a watchful eye on the proceedings. After a while, Berteu stood up and stretched. He left the main room and presumably headed upstairs to his own. As Franz crawled around the parapet toward the one he suspected belonged to Berteu, he heard a man's voice call out from an open window.

"Matthieu, are you there?"

"Yes sir," a voice answered from below.

"Then come up, quickly."

Franz remained where he was. Prostrate on the flat platform and out of view, he was close enough to hear a door open as the stable hand entered.

"So, did you keep your eyes open?" Charles asked.

"And how; the better the pay, the sharper the eyes."

"Was the carriage anything special?"

"No. It looked like one of the less expensive kinds; much like ours."

"What about the horses?"

"He's got two brown ones. They're nearly identical to ours."

"And the coachman?"

"About my stature. He's tall and muscular."

"Do you think we could exchange our team of horses, along with the carriage, for his?"

"Certainly, so long as we stay out of the light."

"That shouldn't pose a problem. Can you guess what I have in mind?"

"Well," said Matthieu grinning, "I would think it concerns the two ladies who came with that coach from Etain."

"Quite right, you old fox. I want to play a trick on my stepsisters, but one that no one can find out about. Now, let's discuss the details."

The servant listened attentively, whistling his approval.

"I have to tell you," Charles continued, "that I want to find out something from them, something they're not prepared to tell me openly. Therefore, I have to twist their arms. The best way to do that is by scaring them a little, without actually causing them any harm. With girls like that, the mere presence of fear can often work wonders. That's where I'll need your help."

"Of course, so long as it doesn't get me into trouble," qualified the stable hand.

"No, don't worry. You don't even have to know what this is all about."

"I like that, since some of your pranks haven't turned out the way you've planned."

"That sounded like a reproach."

"Umm, I was just thinking about our last escapade."

"Never mind. Just remember that this little prank deals with their confinement."

"*Sacre bleu!* Is it dangerous?"

"No, not at all. I intend to speak to them and then free them right away."

"I can handle that. After all, a joke between a brother and his sisters is allowed now and then."

"Good, then we're in agreement. I can tell you that both girls are planning on leaving tonight. I pleaded for them to stay longer, but they didn't want to hear of it. Later, they're going to call for their coach so they can head back to Etain. My plan is to make sure they don't arrive there, but at another place, from where they'll have no choice but to come back here. This way I still get my way and keep them home a little longer."

"I still don't see how I can help you. They're going to call for their coachman and naturally he'll take them where they wish."

Berteu looked at him in surprise. "Idiot! Don't you realize why I've sent you to the tavern?"

"Well, I suppose to compare our carriage and horses to theirs."

"And why do you suppose I wanted you to do that?"

"I don't know?" replied Matthieu, still offended by the remark.

"Can't you guess? I want you to take their coachman's place."

"*Sapperlot!* That could prove to be difficult."

"Not at all. Look! As soon as I notice my sisters are ready to depart, I'll let you know. Then you get our carriage ready and wait nearby. Are you following me so far?" Matthieu nodded. "Good. My sisters will likely send a messenger into town, but he won't go that far. Instead, he will head directly to you."

"Ah! Now I'm beginning to catch on," Matthieu continued. "I'll leave from here, disguised as their coachman."

"Exactly. That's why everything has to look the same."

"I can fetch my coat since their man has one like it."

"Right. Just make sure to turn up the collar so they won't see your face."

"But where am I taking them?" his servant asked, looking puzzled.

Berteu pretended as if he hadn't gotten that far with his plan.

"Hmm, where to?" he asked, thinking. "Good question. Naturally, not into town. I don't want you stumbling across the real coachman. We have to pick an out of the way place, one that will force them to turn back."

"Yes, that makes sense," Matthieu nodded. "So, it can't be just any house."

"Can you come up with a suitable place?" Charles prompted him.

"What about the flower mill?"

That was exactly where Berteu was hoping to lead Matthieu. "Ah, the flower mill," he said thoughtfully. "It could work."

"It's the best place. No one will be out there on this dark night."

"Alright then. Once I've given my farewell to my sisters and they've climbed aboard, I'll quickly make my way to the mill. I'll bring my friend Ribeau with me, just in case. Make sure you take the long way around."

"Good. I'll pretend that I've made a wrong turn and lost my way. I'll knock on the outer door, and you can let me pull the team inside."

"Right. We'll open the main gate, and after you've driven in, we'll close right away, so they won't be tempted to leave. Naturally, I won't have a light on. Ribeau and I will lead them to my little office, where I'll have a lantern ready. That's when they'll recognize us. You can imagine the shock on my sisters' faces."

"What should I do then?"

"You can wait for a few minutes until I've notified you if we'll be heading back in your coach or on our own. In the last instance, you'll head back first, and we'll meet up later. Then we can celebrate with a good bottle of wine."

"Just one more thing. It concerns the place where I'm supposed to wait for the messenger."

"Just stop a little way along the road to the mill. No one will see you there."

"Alright. I'd love to see the shocked look on their faces when they realize this isn't an out of the way farmhouse but their brother's mill."

"Yes, it should be priceless. Just do a good job. Under no circumstances allow my sisters to disembark before you reach the mill. It's possible they could become suspicious underway."

"Don't worry. A lady isn't inclined to leave her coach while it's in motion."

Matthieu left the room, with Charles following shortly. Franz heard every word and guessed the Frenchman's true purpose. *Was Matthieu really that dense,* he thought, *not being able to see through his employer's plan, or was he just pretending? Berteu will likely use the opportunity to corner Nanon with another marriage proposal. Having been turned down before, he's using the ruse of a prank to force her into complying. And since Nanon won't be alone, he's decided to enlist an old like-minded friend to tag along. Heaven help the two sisters if they actually fall into the clutches of those unscrupulous men.*

Franz had heard enough and knew he had to act. He climbed down the latticework and left the grounds without being seen. Once he was clear, he stopped to collect his thoughts.

If I meet with Nanon and Madelon right now and tell them what Berteu purposes to do, they will insist on leaving immediately. We would head to the village, climb into the waiting carriage and head for Etain. I would have saved the day and leave Berteu behind, empty-handed and fuming. But should he get away that easily? No, he needs a more stringent lesson, and I'd like to play the part of facilitator. If only there was a way that I could spoil their little prank, without endangering the two ladies? Wait a minute, maybe there is. A formidable plan began to form in his head. *Besides, I sense that there may be a few things I could learn about this flower mill. And then there's Matthieu the coachman. I can't leave him out of this, unscathed and all.*

Franz was cunning but not careless. He debated with himself, citing all the reasons for and against his plan and finally came to a decision. *I've got two revolvers and my capable fists,* he thought. *More than enough to deal with the likes of these fine fellows, Berteu and Ribeau, even Matthieu. Never mind my personal satisfaction in seeing those three get their just reward.*

Carrying a lantern, he headed for the village and sought out the hired coachman. He explained he was the messenger sent by the young women and that he should expect them in about one hour. It was a precaution, in the event something unexpected occurred. Satisfied the coachman would comply, Franz headed down the road to the mill, looking for the place he suspected Matthieu would use to lay over. He ducked behind a tree and waited for what he hoped would be Berteu's coach. He hadn't been there for long when he heard the sound of an approaching carriage. Concealed behind the tree, he observed as the carriage pulled over not far from him, at a place suitable to turn around. As expected, the coachman climbed down and secured the reins. The man then stretched his legs and eventually headed back to the coach, perhaps opting to climb aboard and relax prior to the messenger's arrival.

This was the opportune moment Franz had been waiting for. He left the cover of the trees and silently darted after the man, laying his strong hands around the man's throat. The attack was so quick and unexpected that Matthieu failed to put up any resistance. As Franz continued to squeeze, the Frenchman let out a gurgling sound and sank to the ground. He removed the hat and overcoat from the unconscious man and laid them aside. He then dragged Matthieu a short distance into the forest, where he tied him to the trunk of an oak tree, using the man's own handkerchief as a gag. This way he couldn't give himself away and hopefully wouldn't be found for a while.

Franz returned to the coach and removed his own hat and coat, stashing them in the space under the buckboard. He donned the other man's coat and hat, untied the reins and climbed up, ready for the messenger's arrival. Berteu's errand boy didn't keep him waiting for long.

"Psst!" the boy said, looking for the coachman.

"Up here," whispered Franz. "Is it time?"

"Yes, but don't rush; it's further from the village than from here."

Franz nodded, then waited for a few minutes as the messenger headed back. He got the horses moving but took his time getting there. He stopped short of the doorway so the light wouldn't illuminate his face. Just as Berteu had admonished Matthieu, Franz followed the advice by turning up his collar and bending the rim of his hat. Coupled with the poor light, his face was unrecognizable. Shortly after his arrival, Madelon and Nanon came out, accompanied by Berteu, his mother and a few guests. The ladies bid their farewells and climbed inside. As they did so, Berteu stowed their luggage and sauntered over to the horses.

"Take your time and give us about half an hour," he whispered to the coachman.

Franz nodded in acknowledgement and drove off, naturally in the direction of the village. The two sisters hadn't noticed anything amiss, ignorant of the looming danger. A short distance from the village, the coach came to an unexpected stop. To their surprise, the coachman secured the reins and climbed down from his seat.

Nanon opened her window. "Is something wrong? Why did you stop?" she asked, the uncertainty in her voice evident.

"I need to talk to you," an unfamiliar voice replied.

A slight fearful shiver went through both women.

"Please, Monsieur!" instructed Madelon, "climb back up. We have plenty of time to talk in the village."

"No, we don't, Mademoiselle Madelon," replied Franz, this time in his normal voice.

"Dear God!" Nanon called. "That's not our coachman's voice."

"Really? And who might that be?"

"Monsieur Schneeberg, is it really you?"

"No one else. Don't be afraid. I'm here to protect you."

"Praise God! We were becoming afraid. But Monsieur, where is our coachman?"

"Down in the village, waiting in his own coach."

"Really? Then this isn't his?"

"No. This wagon and team belong to your dear stepbrother, Charles."

"Heavens! What does he have in mind? Madelon, we need to leave."

"Oh please, wait for just one minute," pleaded Franz.

"But there's something that's not quite right."

"Of course not. His plan was to abduct the two of you."

"Abduct us?" they called out in unison.

"Yes. But I promised to watch over both of you."

"My thanks, Monsieur," Nanon replied with relief. "But how was this to take place?"

"Simple. You were to be driven to the flower mill and met by none other than Berteu and his accomplice Ribeau."

"Ribeau!" Madelon exclaimed with distaste. "I can't stand that man."

Then in detail, Franz explained Berteu's plan as both women listened and shuddered.

"What a wicked plan," Nanon protested. "I wouldn't have survived his barbaric advances."

"Me neither," added Madelon. "Monsieur Schneeberg, we owe you our lives and our freedom. Shouldn't we quickly head to the village?"

"Are you afraid of those two schemers?" he asked.

"No, now that you're here to protect us."

"I'm glad to hear it. This forms the basis of my little plan."

"Please, go on, Monsieur Schneeberg," Nanon prompted.

"I would like to take a little detour to the old mill."

"Dear God! And meet those two connivers?"

"Yes," confirmed Franz, his voice sounding determined and reassuring at the same time.

"But why? I don't understand you."

"To punish them in front of you, what else. Besides, I would like to have a closer look at the inside of that mill."

"But Monsieur, wouldn't you be placing us in danger?"

"Not in the least. Don't you trust me?"

"Of course, we trust you. You're strong, courageous and resourceful."

"And prudent," he added. "I've no intention of placing you in circumstances that are beyond my control."

"I don't doubt you," Nanon said. "But I'm uncomfortable with that out of the way mill and those ungainly men."

"Shouldn't they be punished?"

"Actually, yes. What do you think, Madelon?"

"Yes," her sister nodded, "they deserve to be punished."

"So, are you willing to accompany me there?"

"Yes, so long as Monsieur Schneeberg promises to protect us."

"What will happen there? What shall we do?" asked Nanon.

"I will play the role of their coachman," Franz advised. "I'll drive to the mill and pretend that I've lost my way. They will open up and allow me to drive in, locking up behind us."

"But we'll be trapped, won't we?"

"Don't worry. Then they will escort you both to the office area."

"All alone, without you?" asked Nanon.

"Only for a short time. But you'll still be under my protection. Have you ever held a revolver in your hand?"

"Yes," both ladies replied.

"I have one for each of you. Conceal them for now, but don't be afraid to use the revolvers if they fail to heed your instructions. I will deal with the consequences."

"But to shoot a person?" Madelon asked, wavering.

"Don't worry. It likely won't come to that. Once those two see the weapons in your hands, they'll quickly lose their bravado. These kinds of men are usually nothing more than cowards. Where is this little office located? You've been there before, right?"

"On the far side of the entrance. Won't you be close to us?"

"Please, don't fret. I'll bide my time and make my way inside circumspectly, ready to act at a moment's notice. Will you abide by my plan?"

Madelon hesitated. "Will you give your word to protect us, Monsieur?" Nanon interjected.

"My solemn word. They won't touch you."

"Alright. I'll gladly accompany you and tell those scoundrels what I think of their under-handed tactics. Now that each one of us is armed with a revolver, the risk doesn't seem as great. Let's go then, Monsieur Schneeberg."

Franz climbed back up and turned the carriage around, heading back in the direction of the castle. When he reached the smaller side road, he turned into it, heading for the mill. Having been there earlier in the day, he was somewhat familiar with the layout and steered directly for the main building. Just shy of the main gate, he stopped the horses, smacking the whip in the air several times.

"Holla! Is anyone there?" he called, disguising his voice. Franz repeated the call several times. He perceived noises coming from inside and someone opened a door within the large gate.

"Who's out there?" a man's voice asked.

"We're lost. Where is this place?"

"Lost? And with a carriage yet," the man said. "Where were you headed?"

"Toward Etain."

"And where did you come from?"

"From Castle Malineau."

"Then you've really taken a wrong turn. Climb down for a bit, I'll clean up and show you the right way."

"Thank you. I'm sure the ladies won't mind."

"Ah, you have passengers? That's too bad. But pull in and it shouldn't take long. Unfortunately, there's no light in here. If the ladies will wait for me, I'll go fetch a lantern."

This conversation between Ribeau and Schneeberg, was conducted more in subdued voices, each man doing his best to disguise his voice. Ribeau opened the gate fully, allowing the carriage to pull inside. He then quickly closed it. The two women climbed out, no doubt debating inwardly if they had made the right decision after all. Each one felt a manly arm guiding them through a nearby door.

Initially, Franz pretended to remain where he was, high up on his seat, but when he could no longer hear their steps, he climbed down from his perch and secured the reins. He pulled the pocket lamp from his coat and lit it. As he did so, he noticed that the gate was locked by means of a single wooden bolt, which he could easily remove. He ventured ahead, walking through the same door the ladies had used a minute earlier. He was now standing in the main section of the mill. He crossed the open space, heading for the far corner, where he spotted another door. As he came closer, he heard loud, manly voices, alternating with the soft delicate tones of female voices. He suspected that he was at the entrance to the office. He quickly extinguished his lamp and crept forward listening to the unfolding conversation with interest.

❧✠☙

Earlier, after having concluded his conversation with Matthieu, Berteu joined his guests. Among these was a younger man, Berteu's friend, Jacques Ribeau, not a bad looking sort, one who exuded a certain amount of sex appeal. His face had that rugged look, suggesting a lifestyle that usually brought with it more criticism than praise. He stood somewhat removed from the others, so he could watch Madelon who had drawn his interest. He seated himself at her table, hoping to make her acquaintance.

Madelon caught Ribeau's frequent looks and did her best to carry on without showing him any attention. She arranged it so that he was always served by Nanon, though on one occasion she couldn't avoid him, as he had lifted his empty wine glass, inviting her to replenish it.

"Mademoiselle," Jacques addressed her as she refilled his glass, "did you know that you're quite appealing?"

"Is that supposed to be a compliment?" she replied coolly.

"No, it's the truth. Are you staying on?"

"No, my sister and I are heading back tonight."

"That's too bad."

"Actually, I'm happy to be leaving." Although she could have left his side, she felt an inner stirring to rebuke him for his forward comment.

"You're happy to be leaving?" Jacques continued. "Don't you like it here?"

"No, I don't."

"Isn't the castle and the surrounding area to your liking?"

"Yes, it is. But some people here tend to be ill-mannered."

"Really? Can you be more specific?"

"Of course. There's a young man who can't seem to control his wandering eyes. He doesn't realize that his stares could be viewed as impolite, even insulting. Is that clear enough for you?"

"Ah!" he said grinning at being found out. "You're a clever little snake. But your pointed words won't produce their desired effect; on the contrary, they have an intoxicating appeal on me."

"Well, in that case, watch out for their sting."

Madelon left his side, just as Berteu walked in, heading for Ribeau.

"Jacques, what's the matter with you?" asked Charles. "You look a little frustrated."

"Is it that obvious? I had a little encounter that got me worked up."

Charles paid him closer attention. "With whom?"

"With your sister, Madelon."

"Ah! Was it a gallant conversation?"

"On my part, yes. She, however, was anything but cordial."

"Don't take it to heart. She now lives abroad, in Germany."

"Evidently in the land of boors," Jacques lamented. "I suppose I shouldn't expect her to be civil. Still, she is something to look at," he said, his eyes following her figure, allowing Berteu to catch his lustful look.

"So, she appeals to you?" Charles asked.

"Like no other. You know me. Even though she's your stepsister, she shouldn't concern you, and so I thought I could—"

"Oh, don't get embarrassed," Charles cut him off. "We're old friends, while the two sisters are virtually strangers to me. Besides, I can tell you that Nanon appeals to me as much as her sister does to you."

Ribeau looked at him sideways. "Really? Do you suppose that we could arrange a little adventure, involving both of them? Like the ones we've carried out before. Hmm."

"Well, are you in or out?" Charles asked.

"Well, there are complications. I have to consider my reputation and be discreet about it."

"Come now, old friend. You know I can keep my mouth shut. Besides, they plan on leaving tonight."

"Yes, that's what Madelon told me." Jacques looked at his friend with a knowing look. "I know you too well. You're in love with Nanon, aren't you? She's leaving tonight, and yet you speak of adventure. I'm beginning to sense that something is in the works."

"What?" asked Charles, not able to keep himself from laughing.

"I think you've already thought of something, maybe even put it into play."

"You're not far off."

Ribeau leaned in conspiratorially. "Hold it, friend; and be up front with me. Does your little outing only concern Nanon?"

"No, both of them."

"*Sacre bleu!*" Jacques exclaimed. "I'm your man. What's the plan?"

"A love ménage for four. Out by the old flower mill."

"What, in that old place? I thought they were leaving?"

Berteu smiled. "I see that I'll have to explain it to you." He took him aside, where he quietly outlined his plan. Ribeau listened attentively without interrupting him once.

"Listen Charles," he said after his friend had finished, "we've carried out a few pranks here and there, but this time you've outdone yourself."

"Are you interested then?"

"Need you ask after all that we've been through? Of course, I'm in. I only ask that you leave that slippery little Madelon for me."

"Go right ahead, so long as you can capture her interest."

"Don't worry. She was patronising to me earlier, a sure sign that she's interested."

That settled the matter. Berteu made his rounds as host, and later when his sisters announced they were ready to leave, Ribeau was convinced he would add another feather to his cap. After the carriage had departed with both ladies, Berteu headed for the kitchen to speak to his mother.

"I'm going out for a while," he announced matter of fact.

Surprised, Louise asked. "And if one of our guests should ask for you?"

"Just tell them I'm not feeling well that I'm upstairs lying down."

"What if they insist on speaking to you?"

"Then be firm and tell them I'm not available."

"At least tell me where you're going."

Charles's initial thought was to put her off, but then changed his mind.

"Sure, why not. I'm going to collect my bride."

His mother looked at him, not knowing if he was serious or making a joke. "I'm not following you," she said at last.

"There's nothing else to explain. I stand by what I've just said. I'm going to find a wife."

"Where?"

"At the old flower mill."

"Way out there?" Louise asked, looking puzzled. "Is this going to turn into another one of your adventures? On the day of your father's funeral?"

"No, it's not an adventure; a business arrangement is what I have in mind. I'm meeting Nanon there."

"Nanon?" his mother asked, clearly shocked. "But she just left."

"I know. But she's not heading to town just yet. She's being driven to the old mill by Matthieu, where I'll meet up with the coach. One way or another, she will end up giving her consent."

His mother, by now used to his schemes, supposed this was more of the same. She also realized that she no longer had the influence she once had over him. With her husband gone, Charles was bound to carry on, orchestrating events that would sooner or later prove to be his undoing.

"Please, no carelessness, Charles," she pleaded.

"Don't fret. In just a short time, Nanon will become my bride."

"Has she changed her mind?"

"It doesn't matter. She'll have to give her consent. The reasons are secondary," he said stubbornly as he walked out, dismissing any further objections.

CHAPTER TWENTY

THE OLD MILL

Berteu picked up two bottles of wine, along with four glasses. He gave Ribeau a wink to follow him. Both men left the house and headed down the lane, turning onto the gravel road. Not far away, Charles heard a muffled, moaning sound.

"Listen!" he alerted Ribeau.

"What is it?" Jacques asked, straining to hear.

"I'm not sure. It sounded like moaning from over there."

"Pah! Probably nothing more than the wind bending a tree's boughs."

They continued on their way, not realizing the sound had come from their bound coachman, Matthieu, who was desperately trying to free himself.

Once the two men arrived at the old mill, Charles unlocked the door and they headed directly to the small office. Berteu proceeded to light the lamp, while Ribeau looked around the sparsely outfitted room.

"Not bad," Jacques commented, a cynical smile forming on his lips. "But two rooms would have been better."

"Pah! We're friends and they're sisters. Let's light a couple of cigars while we wait for their arrival."

"What? With all that gun powder around?"

"Relax. There's no danger. The powder kegs are safely tucked away in the cellar and there's no flammable material up here." He opened a drawer in his writing desk and fished out two cigars. Once they were lit, the two scoundrels sat down on the chairs, propping up their feet on the table. "I can hardly wait to see the surprised looks on their faces," quipped Charles.

"We have to make use of their fright," Jacques acknowledged. "Fear has a way of paralyzing resistance. I bet I can kiss Madelon ten times before she manages to utter one word."

"Perhaps it'll turn out differently than you think."

"How else could it turn out? They'll complain, then plead for leniency, and finally give in. Listen!"

"That has to be our coachman using his whip to announce his arrival."

"Yes. Let's go and see."

They headed for the front gate, where Ribeau conducted the short discussion. Once the sisters had disembarked, the men escorted them through the cavernous mill toward the office. Charles opened the door, with the ladies preceding the men. The culprits were expecting shouts of fear, anything but what was about to transpire. Without saying one word, Madelon and Nanon crossed to the far side and sat down on the small sofa. This way, they had the wall behind them and the writing desk between them and the men. Perplexed, Berteu looked at Ribeau, who himself couldn't hide his surprise. Both men looked on, now shocked by the women's calm demeanour.

"*Sapperlot!* It's you two," Charles said, finding his voice. "Who could have imagined both of you paying me a visit. How did you get so mixed-up in your directions?"

"It's obviously the coachman's fault," replied Nanon.

"Then you must have engaged a simpleton for the job."

"Either that or you had him replaced with a cunning man."

"Do you really think so?" he said, unable to suppress his amusement.

"Yes, I do. Either very stupid, or very deceptive."

"Well, what's the use in denying it? If the man was really stupid, then he wouldn't have followed my instructions so well. You see, we wanted to have the pleasure of your company for a little while longer. I could start by telling you all about how we managed to pull it off. But first, we'll take a seat beside you. I hope you won't object."

"Not at all," Nanon replied. "Assuming you have no objection to these."

She pulled a revolver from under her cloak, with Madelon doing the same. Charles stopped in his tracks. "Hang it all! They're armed," he called out, stating the obvious to Ribeau.

"You weren't expecting that, were you now? I'm warning you, if you try to touch either one of us, we'll be forced to shoot you down. I mean it."

"Nanon, don't be ridiculous. And where did you get those weapons? You didn't have them earlier."

"When dealing with people the likes of you, one always has to be prepared for the worst."

"That's true," replied Jacques, nodding and slowly moving forward. "But you have to know how to use them." Ribeau was much more agile than Berteu. Quite unexpectedly he lunged forward, and in one swift motion grabbed both revolvers, negating the sisters' advantage. A twofold cry erupted from both women, followed by laughter from the men.

"Well, well, now we're the masters here and you're going to abide by what we have in mind."

"Not quite," a manly voice announced from behind him. Ribeau tried to turn around but was felled by a powerful blow so that he collapsed like an empty sack. Berteu starred in disbelief, thinking he was dealing with his own coachman.

"Damn it man!" he cursed. "What's gotten into you, Matthieu? I'm going to—"

He didn't get any further because another powerful blow dispatched him as well, so that he ended up on the floor beside his companion. Only then did Franz remove his hat and coat.

"Now then," Franz said, smiling, "these two Messieurs won't be in a position to hold a decent conversation for some time. Hmm, I'd like to sample this fine wine. And you ladies?" he asked holding the bottle up for them to see. Both women were still dazed and shook their heads. He shrugged and opened one, pouring himself a glass. He nodded his approval once he had sampled it. Then he collected the revolvers which Ribeau had confiscated and then dropped.

"Oh, how wonderful that you showed up," Nanon said, pulling herself together. "Ribeau took them from us. But now what? Wouldn't it be better if we just left?"

"Mademoiselle Nanon, a little patience, please," he pleaded.

Franz opened a desk drawer and looked inside. He found some packing thread, which he used to tie up the unconscious Frenchmen. Then he moved them behind the sofa, so they wouldn't be able to see what he was doing. He took his time going through the contents of the drawer. As he did so, his face reflected his mounting satisfaction. Madelon, aware that he was a Prussian soldier, guessed why he examined the ledgers and corresponding papers with such thoroughness. Her sister however, had no idea, and was surprised at his curiosity.

"Do you find the manufacture of powder so fascinating?" Nanon ventured to ask.

"No, I'm not that interested in the operation of this mill, rather the paperwork behind it. Is this signature familiar to you?" Franz asked, laying out a few letters for her.

"Yes, this is Richemonte's signature," Nanon confirmed.

"What about this one?"

"It belongs to Count Rallion."

"It's the letters that interest me. I'm going to copy a few. I won't stretch your patience too far, Mademoiselle."

He looked through the other drawers and found a quill, ink, and loose sheets of paper. Nanon was surprised to see the skill Franz employed with the quill. It was a peculiar situation: two bound men lay in the corner, still unconscious while the two sisters sat quietly a few paces removed from Franz, who was happily copying journal entries, as if nothing were amiss.

"Now then," he announced after a while. "I'm finished; it's time we left." He stuffed the copied papers in his coat and returned the originals to their proper place in the desk. He was about to extinguish the lantern when he heard a distant noise.

Nanon heard it too. "Someone is knocking," she said.

"No, that's not knocking," Franz corrected her. "Someone is hammering against the gate. Did you hear that? They're hollering, demanding that we open the doors. Could the coachman have managed to free himself and find help?"

"But that shouldn't pose a problem for us," offered Nanon. "Should we comply and open the gate?"

Madelon was more astute than her sister, realizing Franz could be in grave danger. "No, don't let them in," she warned.

"But why not?"

"I'll explain later."

Franz nodded in agreement. "At the moment, you're not in any danger," he said, "but the same can't be said about me. After all, I've tied up the coachman and incapacitated Malineau's two upstanding citizens."

"It's getting worse out there," Madelon noted. "What can we do? They're pounding harder."

"Let's go, then," Franz prompted. "It's time to find out what they want."

He left the appropriated coat and hat behind and stuck the two revolvers in his waist band. He led the two ladies through the dark hall until they reached the horses. The banging was more pronounced now, as if they intended on forcing their way inside the mill.

"It's too bad that you've brought your belongings with you," he whispered.

"We can leave them behind," suggested Nanon.

"No, I have a better idea," Franz said, having thought of something. "It's fortunate that there's enough room to turn the carriage around. Please, climb aboard. But first, I want to have a few words with these unruly visitors." He approached the door. "Who's out there?" he called out.

Many voices responded at the same time, drowning each other out.

"What do you want?" Franz continued.

"Where is Monsieur Berteu?" an insistent male voice asked.

"In his office, having a nap."

"And Monsieur Ribeau?" asked the same man.

"Also, in the office."

"What about the stranger who choked me and tied me to a tree?"

"I'm right here."

"I demand that you open this instant," Matthieu demanded.

"I'll be happy to oblige."

Franz quickly retreated and turned the wagon around. As he did so, he noticed that the large doors opened outwardly. That would explain why the crowd had been unsuccessful in forcing them open. As they struggled and cursed, they couldn't hear that Franz had quietly slid the bolt back. In no time at all, he was back on the buckboard, holding the whip in his right hand, with the reins and revolver in his left. One smack of the whip urged the horses forward so that they nudged the doors open, knocking a few bystanders over.

"Get back!" Franz shouted. He followed up with several revolver shots in quick succession. Although the frightened horses reared up, he had a good grip on the reins. A few more smacks of the whip and the coach shot forward and out through the gate. The startled horses galloped down the forest road, leaving the crowd's angry shouts far behind.

Franz laughed out loud, relieved it had worked out so smoothly. None of the townspeople had any hope of catching up to the fleeing coach. He reached the main road, and without slowing down, guided the team into a tight turn, heading toward the village. Less than five minutes had elapsed before he reached Malineau. To his satisfaction, he spotted the hired coachman out in front and waiting for them. Franz slowed the horses, pulled up along side, and addressed him.

"Monsieur, did you look after your tavern bill?" Franz inquired.

"Of course."

"Good." Then facing the sisters, he continued. "Ladies, it's time to switch to our own coach."

With the coachman's help, they transferred the luggage and helped the ladies climb into the waiting carriage. The whole transfer took less than five minutes. Franz reclaimed his own hat and coat, making himself comfortable, as the coach pulled out into the road for the trip back to Etain. He explained to Nanon and Madelon that it probably wouldn't be safe to spend the night in Etain. Once they arrived, he located their previous coachman and instructed him to harness the horses so they could depart for Metz the same night.

❧✠☙

Franz was waiting outside in front of the guest house, accompanied by the two sisters. Just as the luggage was being stowed, a window opened up above and a head poked out.

"You, down there, wait up," a voice called down.

Amused, Franz looked up to see if the caller had meant them.

"Yes, you, please wait," the same man pleaded, pulling his head back.

"I suppose he wants a word with us," voiced Nanon.

"So, it would seem. Alright. Let's wait a couple of minutes," agreed Madelon.

The foyer and landing were lit up. A short, plump man descended the steps, wearing a large Calabrese hat and girded only with a red tablecloth. In his hurry, the man's feet became entangled in the cloth so that he lost his balance and tumbled down the last two or three steps. Now sprawled on the floor, his red tablecloth came undone, revealing he was only wearing underwear and a night shirt. This of course generated some interest from onlookers.

He composed himself quickly and jumped up faster than many would have expected, covering himself with the tablecloth and donning the large hat.

"Hold it. Just wait a moment," he called, covering the short distance to the door.

"Were you addressing us, Monsieur?" Franz asked annoyed.

"Of course, who else?"

"Who are you?"

"I sir, am Hieronymus Aurelius Schneffke, landscape painter from..."

"Ah, so that's who you are," said Franz laughing.

"What? You've heard of me?"

"Yes, as per the Renommeé and the Distance."[201]

"Ah, wonderful, wonderful. Are you perchance accompanying the ladies?"

"Yes, I am."

"Would you permit me to speak to your charges for a moment?"

"Of course, so long as it suits them."

"Please, Mademoiselle Madelon, may I pose a question?" Hieronymus asked, stepping onto the running board.

Perplexed, Madelon nodded, not sure what the painter had in mind.

"Is she really an Englishwoman?" he queried.

"Who?"

"The governess."

"Oh her! Yes, she's English," Madelon laughed, forcing herself to part with a little white lie.

"Oh dear. That's dumb like pudding. And she really goes by the name, Miss de Lissa?"

"I'm afraid so."

"Then I no longer want anything to do with all these governesses."

Hieronymus spun around and was about to jump off. He paused, then changed his mind and faced the ladies again. "May I inquire where you've just come from?"

Ordinarily, that would have seemed a little intrusive, but Madelon was strangely drawn to the portly painter. "From Castle Malineau," she offered without hesitation.

"Heavens! Who would have thought that."

"Do you know the place?"

"Somewhat. It's where I'm heading."

"Really? You've come all this way just to see the castle?"

He contemplated if he should be more forthcoming. His mind returned to a conversation not long ago, one where he was given a peculiar assignment by an old acquaintance. Underhill, a cranky old man in his seventies, had been harboring a dark family secret for nearly twenty years. With the unfortunate death of Castle Ortry's caretaker, Albert Berteu, the entire sordid affair may become public, something that Underhill wished to avoid all costs. Therefore, Underhill had instructed Schneffke to undertake the long journey to France and ferret out the truth from Berteu's surviving son, Charles. But then Hieronymus remembered that he had promised Underhill to be discreet.

"Herr Schneffke?" Madelon prompted.

"Umm. The castle was recommended to me. Since I plan to be in the area, I've decided to do some sketching. That reminds me. Does a certain Monsieur Berteu reside there?"

"Which Monsieur Berteu?"

"The caretaker of the castle."

"Albert Berteu has recently died and was only buried yesterday."

"Ah! Were you at his funeral?"

"Yes. That was the purpose of our trip."

Schneffke appraised her with a quick glance. "Are you related to Monsieur Berteu?" he continued.

"He was our caregiver, our stepfather," she replied, with Nanon nodding assent.

"And where are you going now?"

"Back home. But first I'm going to visit with my sister at Castle Ortry, near Thionville."

"Ah, Ortry! Well, Mademoiselle, here is my hand. Please, accept my apology for these probing questions. I have a feeling that we will see each other again, hopefully under happier circumstances. Adieu, and I wish you both a safe trip."

Schneffke returned to his room and looked out his window just in time to see the carriage depart. Then he went about cleaning up the mess in his room. Earlier, he had heard noises and the usual sounds that accompany a waiting carriage. He had looked outside and recognized Madelon and made up his mind to speak to her. In his haste to see her, he hadn't bothered to get dressed, thinking he could use the tablecloth as a temporary covering. He had snatched it from the table, but in doing so, scattered everything onto the floor.

The following morning, he looked for his wallet, and found it lying beside his pince-nez, in a most unconventional setting, next to an overturned night pot. Fortunately, he hadn't availed himself of its use during the night.

281

CHAPTER TWENTY-ONE

THE STEWARD

It was a beautiful morning and Hieronymus Aurelius Schneffke used the opportunity to take a leisurely walk toward Castle Malineau. He headed for the local tavern and enjoyed a hearty lunch after the morning's outing. Since he considered himself to be on a sort of diplomatic mission, he chose to keep the conversation to a minimum, even though the innkeeper tried his best to fish something out of the portly stranger.

With lunch taken care of, he outfitted himself with his field stool and sketch pad and sauntered toward the castle. He dispensed with going inside, choosing to forego his inquiries by tackling his problem in another way. He looked for a pleasant spot, plunked himself down on his stool, opened his folder and commenced sketching. It wasn't long before he was interrupted by the approach of a young man. The newcomer came closer and greeted him, while leaning sideways to catch a glimpse of the picture on the sketchpad.

"Ah, you're an artist, Monsieur?" he inquired.

"Yes," Hieronymus replied, nodding.

"May I ask in what genre? Perhaps a landscape painter?"

"All aspects."

"Are you French?"

Hieronymus wasn't inclined to be too forthcoming. "I'm Polish."

"Really? And what is your name?"

"Schneffka."

"Are you under contract to paint the castle?"

"No. I'm doing it for my own edification."

"Please forgive my curiosity. You see, my father has recently died, and left us a few paintings, whose value I'm not in a position to judge. A true, accomplished painter has never come through these parts before. I would be honoured if you would consent to have a look at them."

"Where are they?"

"In my father's study. My name is Berteu." Hieronymus couldn't believe his luck yet kept a straight face. "Would it be convenient for you to accompany me?" Charles offered.

"Sure, why not."

Hieronymus closed his folder, picked up his supplies, and followed the young man to his house. He pretended as if the upcoming visit meant little, but inwardly looked forward to learning more about the family.

Berteu led him to his study, where only yesterday he had struggled with the accounts, argued with Nanon and lastly plotted to trap his stepsisters with Matthieu's help. In the far corner, Hieronymus spotted three small landscape pictures. He recognized right away that they held little value, having been painted by amateurs, or beginners at best. Collectively, they were only worth a few francs at most, yet he chose to examine them in a light that suggested they were worth much more. After all, it was to his advantage if he could spend a day or two with Berteu and obtain pertinent information about his father.

"Well?" Charles asked.

"They're really not bad. Such a shame though."

"What do you mean by that?"

"I would estimate that each piece on average could easily fetch a price near five hundred francs."

Charles looked at him in disbelief. "Monsieur, you're joking."

"I should clarify," Hieronymus said, smiling, "that is what they were once worth, perhaps more. Unfortunately, they show signs of being neglected."

"Oh, no."

"I'm afraid so. In their current state, they're not worth more than ten or twenty francs, but with some work by an experienced craftsman, they could be refurbished to their original state, enhancing their value."

"But isn't that expensive?"

"Of course. However, there are artists, who for the sake of appreciation of an older piece, move themselves to restoring it for a nominal fee, sometimes even dispense with the usual honorarium."

"Yes, I suppose. If only such a man would venture our way."

Schneffke nodded thoughtfully but pretended as if he hadn't caught the inference and occupied himself with the paintings.

"Have you ever been involved in restoration work, Monsieur?" Charles inquired.

"On occasion, but purely out of interest. And then only with landscapes."

"Well, these *are* landscapes," Charles offered.

"Indeed."

"Tell me, Monsieur, are you inclined to stay in the area?"

"I'm not currently engaged in any work therefore I can come and go as I please."

"Perhaps I could persuade you to stay here so that you might devote a little time in restoring these?"

"That might work, though I doubt if I could stay longer than a day or two."

"May I know the reason?"

"Well, it concerns your house. Would there be enough room to accommodate an artist?"

"Oh, don't worry," replied Charles relieved. "If that's your only concern, I can assure you that my mother can fix up one of the guest rooms to your liking. And if you could keep your honorarium to a reasonable amount—you see, I'm not a rich man."

Hieronymus pretended to consider it. "Hmm. Perhaps you could show me the room?"

Charles didn't hesitate but led his new guest upstairs and showed him the best room. It was quaint, but clean and furnished with dated but quality furniture. The large window faced east, beckoning the occupant to catch the sun's first rays of the morning. The painter looked around, clearly impressed by what he saw.

"So, Monsieur, what do you think?"

"If I may be up front, most artists wouldn't do it this way. They would think they're wasting their time and their talent. But I can see you're a hard-working and honest sort and the pictures aren't bad at all. I'll tell you what. I can stay for a couple of days, three at the most, and restore them without charging you my typical fee, provided that you won't let me starve or die from thirst."

"It's a deal, Monsieur," agreed Charles happily.

They shook hands to seal the bargain. Charles was happy to have talked the portly painter into the restoration work for the price of accommodations and a few meals. He wasn't planning to keep the restored pictures but intended to sell them as soon as possible. The easy-going painter suited his purposes, and he asked him to stay on right away.

Schneffke consented and began to work on the pictures that same afternoon. Still, he wasn't about to rush the job. He remembered Underhill's plight, and the subsequent commission to ferret out the truth about the elder Berteu. His benefactor had supplied him with a generous expense account for the journey, something not to be taken for granted. That aside, the lovely governess had inexplicably transformed herself into an Englishwoman. To overcome his disappointment, Hieronymus had a simple solution: immerse himself in his work.

※

The following morning, Schneffke was seated at an improvised easel, continuing with his previous day's work, as Louise Berteu entered with his breakfast. He had selected one of the paintings and was in the process of making the grass greener, the sky bluer and the sun brighter. Louise watched in silence, pleased to see one of Charles' ventures amount to something worthwhile. With the window open, Hieronymus was admiring the castle's side view.

"Madame," he asked, "who does the castle belong to?"

"The Count de Latreau."

"He must be a rich man."

"Very rich."

"Where does he live?"

"In Paris."

"Such aristocratic gentlemen tend to be admirers of fine art and often collect priceless works. Are there any such paintings in the castle?"

"I've seen a few."

"Would you be so kind as to give me permission to view them?"

"I don't have the authority to make that kind of decision," she replied, her face having taken on a passive expression.

"Who else then?"

"The administrator."

"You imply that there's an overseer aside from the caretaker, even when the count is not in residence?"

"Yes."

"Where does he live?"

"Over on the far side, in the west wing."

"What's his name?"

"Melac."

"*Sacre bleu!*" he blurted out.

"Pardon me?" she asked taken aback.

"I can't stand that name."

"And I can't stand him."

"Do you mean the administrator?"

"Not only him, but his entire family. Yet, I'd rather not talk about it."

"Still, I will have to go over there if I want to see the paintings."

"True. But my advice to you is not to pursue it. They would hardly grant a stranger permission. My son and I live in this house, adjacent to the east wing, while those people reside over there. We don't have any dealings with each other."

Madame Berteu then turned around and left. She had spoken in a nearly inconsiderate tone, but he wasn't put out. *Interesting story*, he thought, *but what business do I have in getting mixed-up with family squabbles?*

After Schneffke had eaten his breakfast, he pocketed his sketchbook, grabbed his stool, and headed for the nearby park, situated on the estate grounds. As is typical of many artists, he was an admirer of nature. He liked to wander about, observing a tree's irregular growth pattern or study the blossoms of a particular plant. As he continued on his exploratory jaunt, he was about to step out from behind a bush, when he spied an old man sitting on a park bench. Despite his age, the man had an appealing profile, complemented by a snow-white beard that reached to his chest. In no time at all, Schneffke sat down on his stool, opened his sketchpad, and began to draw the noble face on his paper.

Later that evening, only after he had worked on Berteu's pictures, did he pull out his earlier unfinished portrait, and began to complete the work. When he was finished, he examined it carefully content with the knowledge it was probably the best sketch he had done so far in his career.

The next morning, he headed for the park again, and quite unintentionally ended up at the same place from where he had sketched the old man. The bench now was empty, so he took a seat and admired the surroundings. It wasn't long before he heard a clear alto voice singing.

'A man shouldn't rely on land and purse
for the circumstances in life can be harsh.
To the one, the God-given talents come easily,
like gifts plucked from a tree,
while the other has to dig for them,
deep in the crusty earth.'

She sang beautifully and in the German tongue, here in the middle of France. Schneffke thought this most peculiar. He simply had to see the singer. He stood up and headed for the place where the sound came from. He spotted another bench and the one who occupied its space, a girl about twenty years old. She was dressed quite simply—in a white skirt with a white jacket. She was neither tall nor slim, but rather short in stature, and had a full figure. She had blond hair, a sweet round face, blue eyes and a lovely mouth that beckoned to be kissed. Her lap was full of flowers she had collected and was now arranging into a bouquet. She started to sing again.

> *'I'm going to the meadow*
> *where the cow chews her cud*
> *and when the lad meets the girl,*
> *he hums along with her.*
> *Up high on the meadow,*
> *with no watchers, there it's peaceful.*
> *Only when the lad meets his girl,*
> *then he exalts in song.'*

Suddenly, she yodelled so clear, that she could have competed with a lark.

"Bravo! Bravissimo!" Hieronymus applauded. He could barely contain his enthusiasm and walked the short distance to meet her. "Forgive me, Mademoiselle, for disturbing you. But when I heard you singing, my heart rejoiced, and I just had to join in your revelry." Hieronymus had, without a second thought, spoken in French.

"And you've come," she replied, "thinking that one can be happier with another than on their own."

"Yes, so it would seem. You, Mademoiselle, have that appeal as if no one could become sad in your presence. "

She fussed with the flowers she had collected, revealing her pearly-white teeth. "You could be right. It's a gift from God. One is happy when he cries, another when he laughs. Which sort do you belong to, Monsieur?"

"To the latter; in other words, to yours, Mademoiselle."

"Really? Then take a seat beside me. I'll make some room for you."

She slid over, so he could take a seat. It was so natural, so unpretentious that he would have liked nothing better than to kiss her.

"Thank you," he said. "I wish I could help you, but I don't have any talent for arranging flowers."

"Oh, that's alright. I'm almost done. This arrangement is for my grandfather, a surprise for his birthday. He loves the wildflowers more than any other."

"Is today your grandfather's birthday?"

"Yes, today," she added.

"Do you live far from here?"

"No, not far."

"Perhaps we'll see each other again before I have to leave."

"Leave? So, you're not from around here?"

"No."

"And yet you speak the local dialect so well."

Hieronymus smiled. "And you, a French girl, singing German songs so well."

"Grandfather has no quarrel with the Germans."

"Is he of German descent?"

"No, as you can tell from our name."

"But Mademoiselle, I've yet to hear it."

"My last name is Melac."

"*Sacre bleu!*" he blurted out. To his surprise, she didn't seem to hold it against him.

Without raising an eyebrow, she looked at him steadily. "It's true isn't it, you're thinking about the man who devastated the Pfalz state."[21.1]

"Yes. It's the same name as the one shared by a breed of bloodhounds."

"We're related to him. He's our forefather, and it's for that reason that grandpapa sides with the Germans. He thinks that he should make up for Melac's past sins by supporting them in principle."

"Then your grandfather is a brave man."

"Yes, I suppose he is. I'm very fond of him. The gracious count favours him as well."

"I see. I understand your grandfather is the castle's overseer."

"Yes."

"Along with your father?"

"I no longer have my parents. That's why I'm living with my grandparents."

Schneffke nodded thoughtfully. "I'm staying at the caretaker's house."

"I heard that Monsieur Berteu has just died."

"Are you on good terms with them?"

"I'm afraid not. They avoid us, even though we haven't done anything to them. I've asked grandfather about the reason, but he can't explain it either."

This confirmed what Schneffke had already suspected. The fact that the Melac family didn't subscribe to putting down the neighbours spoke highly of them and reflected poorly on the Berteus.

"Who taught you German songs?" Hieronymus asked, changing the theme.

"I can thank my grandparents for that. They both speak German. How long are you planning to stay?"

"Only for a few days."

"That's too bad. I'm enjoying our conversation. It's a break from having just my grandparents to talk to."

"Really? Me too," the painter agreed. "If I planned to stay on, I would have liked to meet your grandparents."

"You still can. Grandpapa enjoys talking to those who don't look down on others. Surely you must have seen him around."

"This is only my second day here."

"Well, if you encounter an older, stately-looking man, with a long white beard, then you've found him. He would enjoy meeting you and loves to exchange ideas. Unfortunately, he has little opportunity these days. With the count and his family away, there isn't much for him to do. He sleeps in late, even longer than grandma. He should be getting up soon and I want to surprise him with this bouquet."

The young woman stood up to leave. But Hieronymus sensed she wasn't quite sure how to take her leave.

"I would have gladly picked a few flowers for your grandfather," he said standing up as well. "But I've come too late. However, I could add something to your arrangement, if I knew it would please him."

The girl looked at him expectantly yet was reluctant to voice her question.

"Yesterday, I ended up becoming a thief," he continued. "I spied an older, refined man, and by your description he was your grandfather. I took something from him. I would like you to give it back to him, this day being his birthday, and ask his forgiveness for being presumptuous."

The painter opened his map folder, retrieved the recent sketch and handed it to her. No sooner had she laid her eyes on it, than she stepped back a pace, pleasantly surprised.

"It's him," she beamed. "That's his likeness. What a surprise. You must be a painter, perhaps an artist, Monsieur."

"I've been known to draw a little now and then," he said, smiling.

"It's a masterpiece, a real masterpiece. Would you do me a big favour by paying us a visit, so that he could see it as well?"

"But I've just handed it to you; you can give it to him yourself."

"You mean show it to him?"

"No, it's his to keep, a birthday present from his loving and faithful granddaughter."

Hieronymus noticed that she found it difficult to accept his words at face value. "Really, Monsieur?" she questioned. "Are you serious?"

"Of course, it's yours to keep or give away."

A child-like exuberance enveloped her already radiant face. "Monsieur, I wouldn't have thought such a thing possible. You can't imagine what a delight your gift will produce. It'll be difficult to describe. How can I possibly thank you?"

He smiled. "If I may point out, I hardly know you."

"Oh, please, tell me. Tell me!"

She had adorned her white jacket with one simple decoration—a carnation.

"Would you consider parting with your flower, Mademoiselle?" he asked pointing it out. "I will cherish it as a memento of our meeting."

She turned red but removed the carnation and handed it to him. "But it's so little, so little compared to your generous gift. I wish I could present you with a better gift." Then a thought came to her. "Please, won't you allow grandpapa to thank you himself? Is there a chance you could pay us a visit?"

"So long as I'm welcome, yes."

"You're more than welcome. Please, join us later. My name is Marie. Adieu, Monsieur."

What a girl, he thought to himself, watching her depart. *She's different than the rest: untainted, healthy, genial, and a little more rounded as opposed to slim. I suppose that she could one day attain a figure much like mine. Heavens, what a fine-looking couple we could make. All of a sudden, I don't want anything to do with that governess—any governess. They don't stay the same but are apt to change without notice. They not only change nationalities, but also their names. One ends up running after them, only to keep missing trains. But then such a simple and gentle soul like this one comes along. She is something else. She has life and vitality. This blossoming park flower from Castle Malineau is ripe for the picking and she could become mine one day.* He stopped himself momentarily, but then proclaimed out loud. "Basta! Either that, or I'll remain a bachelor for life."

❧✠☙

Later that same afternoon, Schneffke found himself walking into the castle's right wing, the visit coinciding with the usual visiting time. He spotted the name Melac on one of the doors and knocked. The door was opened by the 'park flower', who beckoned him to enter. It was clear she was pleased to see him. He followed her into the adjoining room. There sat an old, refined gentleman, whose portrait he had sketched. Next to him was a woman of roughly the same age. She had a close resemblance to her granddaughter's build, and it stood to reason that Marie would one day attain the same figure.

"This is the gentleman whom I had met earlier in the park," Marie explained, "and who was kind enough to present me with your portrait, Grandpapa."

Both grandparents rose from their seats, greeting the newcomer warmly, as they would an old friend. This small gesture left a very favorable impression on him. He gave his name, Schneffka, the same name he had given Charles Berteu, and was immediately drawn into an animated discussion. A bottle of wine and leftover cake stood on a nearby table, remnants of the birthday celebration. He was the recipient of some cake as well as a glass of wine, as the three Melacs smiled encouragingly at his easygoing manner.

On a nearby wall hung a pastel portrait of a young man, evidently a man of nobility. Even though it was protected by glass, the picture had lost quite a bit of its original lustre. Pastel paintings are susceptible to air and moisture degradation, their colors adhering like fine dust particles to the surface. They have to be protected from foreign matter and handled carefully while in transit. During their lively conversation, Hieronymus' eyes kept drifting back to the portrait. He speculated that it was no ordinary painting but had been fashioned by a master.

How could this masterpiece, such an expensive painting have ended up in the home of this ordinary couple? he pondered.

Monsieur Melac noticed his preoccupation with the painting. "Does the portrait interest you, Monsieur?" he asked.

"Of course. It appears to be a masterpiece."

"Really? I'm afraid I don't know much about such things."

"Who painted it?"

"I don't know."

"Is there no mark or artist's signature visible?"

"No, not that I can make out."

"Surely you must know who is depicted in the portrait?"

"That too is unknown to me. The picture was a gift. Actually, I'm not even certain if I can consider myself as its rightful owner."

His last answer genuinely surprised Schneffke. "That sounds mysterious."

"Yes, it's a secret."

"Now *that* appeals to me. Nothing interests a painter more than a painting that is shrouded in mystery."

"Unfortunately, I'm not able to penetrate this curtain of mystery. I only received this picture from a sick lady, one who ended up dying before she could explain the circumstances surrounding it."

"So then, you don't know how she herself came into possession of it?"

"No. She was here for only a short time. Her name was Charbonnier; she had two young daughters who—"

"Charbonnier?" Hieronymus interrupted him, thinking about Madelon Köhler, who's surname means Charbonnier.

"Yes, Charbonnier," he continued. "At first, she was living at Berteu's house, but her best days seemed to be behind her. She never discussed her past, even though she spent most of her time with us. I suppose she felt more comfortable here, rather than with the Berteu family. When she became ill, she asked my wife to care for her. We had no idea that her health would decline so quickly and that she would eventually die. Thanks to my wife, she managed to bring this portrait into our house, saying she would explain later. She died the next day."

"Without giving you any clarification about the picture?"

"Regretfully, no. As I recall, she tried to say a few last words to my wife, but they came out incoherent and we couldn't make any sense out of them."

"Do you know anything about the lady's past?"

"No. She arrived one fine day and asked the caretaker if she could rent a room. She must have had some sort of arrangement with him, because after she had died, he arranged for the funeral and began caring for her children. The girls grew up and eventually became governesses."

Hieronymus couldn't believe his good fortune. Here he was, having stumbled onto this extraordinary bit of information. He was careful not to divulge how important this was to him.

"A curious story. I have a weakness for such secretive events. Perhaps the caretaker is in a better position to shed some light on this mysterious lady. No doubt she spent some time with him."

"That's possible, though not likely. Besides, whatever knowledge he possessed, will now remain with him. He's also dead."

"I'm aware of that," Hieronymus acknowledged. "But perhaps he conveyed some details to his son, Charles."

"That's highly unlikely. I suspect that Charles has been kept in the dark."

This is what I've come to find out, Schneffke thought, rejoicing inwardly. "Were you there at the funeral?" he asked to keep the conversation going.

"No. We wouldn't dream of intruding upon them during this time, since we're not on speaking terms. But then you're staying there, haven't you noticed anything about our relationship?"

"Yes. I sensed that there was some tension there."

"It's not our fault. That young Berteu has turned into an ill-mannered and inconsiderate neighbour. At first, he came across as friendly, but we quickly realized his true motivation. He was after our Marie. His advances became so insistent that she appealed to us for help in fending him off. Ever since then, he's given us the cold shoulder and we've been living in enmity with his family. Even though he's given us lots of ammunition to foster our discord with him, we've held back. They even dared to demand that we turn over this picture to them, which of course they're not entitled to keep."

"Surely Berteu has no claim on it."

"Not in the least. The recently deceased Albert Berteu was present when Madame Charbonnier asked my wife to safeguard the portrait. Still, he's always maintained that this was nothing more than a temporary arrangement, and not a gift."

"Perhaps he intended to reclaim it for the benefit of the two sisters?" Hieronymus offered.

"No, it was only a pretext. If truth be known, he only wanted it for himself, knowing its importance."

"Perhaps he suspected Madame had a connection to the picture."

"That's probably it."

"Will you allow me to examine it?"

"With pleasure. Marie, take it down from the wall."

The young woman pulled up a chair, positioning it against the wall, but couldn't quite reach the frame. Hieronymus pulled up a second chair to help her. They stood side by side, and just as Marie managed to free the painting from the nail, her chair started to sway. Supposing she was about to fall, Schneffke leaned over to steady her. But in doing so, he lost his balance and fell. Even so, he had the presence of mind to hang on tight. Likewise, Marie hung on, not wanting the glass to break and so it was that she lost her footing and fell on top of the portly painter.

"Dear God!" her grandfather called, rushing over. "What bad luck; hopefully nothing broke."

"No, the glass is still intact." Hieronymus replied, as he lay sprawled on the floor.

"No, no, that's not what I meant, Monsieur," Melac reiterated. "Are *you* alright?"

"I'll have to check."

Meanwhile, Marie had quickly collected herself. Her pretty face was red from embarrassment. Hieronymus gingerly stood up, slowly moving his arms and legs, one after the other. "It's alright," he said laughing. "I'm not injured and still in one piece."

"Oh, thank God!" Madame Melac said relieved. "It looked like a serious fall."

Schneffke shook his head and discreetly caressed his derriere. "It wasn't all that bad," he replied good-naturedly. "I've always managed to fall softly."

"So, it would seem," laughed Melac. "I believe it was Marie's fault. She should have been more careful."

"No, it was mine," Hieronymus said, defending her. "It's a good thing the painting is still intact. Let's have a look." He picked it up and took it over to the window for better light. "Look at this," he announced after examining it for a few minutes. "Down here in the corner is an 'M' with a stroke through it. It's almost indiscernible. This is the trademark of the famous pastel painter Merlin, from Marseille. He's been dead for several years now. The picture is a masterpiece but has been subjected to humidity and dust and has deteriorated over the years. The colors have faded."

"Can anything be done to refurbish it?" Melac asked.

"Of course. Would you like me to restore it?"

"Really? You're prepared to do that for us?"

"Sure. It should only take me one, perhaps two days at most. Then I can return it and it should look the same as on the day it was painted."

"You mean work on it at Berteu's house? I would rather avoid that."

"*Sapperlot!* Don't you trust me? I will bring it back."

"Oh no, it has nothing to do with you, Monsieur Schneffka," Melac replied reassuringly. "It's Charles Berteu that I don't trust. He might hinder you when you try to return it."

Schneffke nodded. "But what else can we do?"

"Wouldn't it be possible for you to perform the restoration work here, in our house?"

The suggestion made sense and was pleasing to the portly painter. This way he had a legitimate reason for spending time with the pretty Marie. "I'm prepared to do so," he replied, "yet fear I may get in your way."

"Not at all. You're very welcome to stay. However, there is one point we should discuss..."

"Ah, let me guess; it concerns my honorarium, right?"

"Yes," nodded Melac.

"Don't give it another thought. I will gladly do it for my own benefit. On a side note, I can admit to you that I learn while I hone my skills. Do you suppose that I should be paid as well?"

"You're very kind, Monsieur. When can we expect you?"

"Would tomorrow morning suit you?"

"Any time at all, just as you please. But Monsieur, does Berteu know that you're paying us a visit?"

"No, I don't think so."

"Once he learns of it, he may cause you some discomfort, perhaps even try to meddle."

"I'm not concerned. I pride myself in getting caught up in all sorts of discomfort," he said patting his backside. "But for now, allow me to be on my way." He extended his hand toward Marie, who still looked embarrassed. "Are you sorry that we fell together, Mademoiselle?" he asked amicably.

"I was the clumsy one," she replied.

"No, on the contrary, the fall was well-executed. You've no idea how often and how happily I've fallen at ladies' feet. And now I've fallen with you. Can you guess the significance?"

"No."

"There's an old parable, an old wives tale, that suggests if a fellow and a girl, both being single, stumble and fall together, then, hmm— well, a happy wedding is sure to follow."

"Monsieur!" Marie protested in a tone that conveyed more surprise than anger. A subtle redness spread over her cheeks, her eyes masked by her eyelashes.

"Don't worry, Marie," Melac replied, "Monsieur was only making a joke."

He was about to continue when he was interrupted by a knock on the outer door. Hieronymus took this as his cue to leave, but the overseer motioned for him to stay. "Please, Monsieur, you needn't leave," he reassured him. "This likely won't take long."

He walked out into the hall and opened the door, finding a well-dressed young man on the doorstep.

"Pardon the intrusion, Mesdames and Messieurs," he greeted politely. "My name is Martin Tannert, and I come from Rousillon. I represent a notable winery from that region. May I inquire if you would be interested in one of our products?"

"*Sapperlot!*" a subdued voice exclaimed from the corner where Schneffke stood. Hieronymus fixed his gaze on the newcomer, just as Martin looked about the room for the speaker. For an instant, Martin's eyes betrayed recognition, but then, just as quickly, all traces vanished from his face.

"Merci, Monsieur," Melac continued, "but I'm only the administrator here. I myself have limited means, and I'm not in a position to afford such a luxury."

"What about the owner then? Perhaps he can…?"

"I'm afraid His Excellency is not on the estate."

"Is he away on an excursion?"

"No. He lives in Paris. This is his summer residence. Perhaps you've heard of him, the pensioned general, Count de Latreau?"

"Latreau?" the wine agent asked, feigning surprise. "What a coincidence. I've been at his residence on more than one occasion and had the privilege to meet his granddaughter, Countess Ella."

"Really? You know the gracious count?"

"Yes. Haven't you heard what had happened to the countess?"

"Of course! It was in all the papers. Just this morning, I happened to be reading that she has been rescued. We were terribly afraid for her and were relieved to hear that the plot was derailed. I read that a wine merchant was involved in the rescue, a man who—"

Melac stopped speaking, looking a little disconcerted. "Didn't you just say that you were with the count in these last few days?"

"Yes," Martin replied evenly.

"And you're a wine merchant," he uttered, his face looking more animated. "Monsieur, are you one and the same person?"

"Who?" he asked grinning.

"The one who rescued the countess."

"No, that was my master, Monsieur Belmonte; still, I was with him, and I helped a little."

"What? Really? What a coincidence that you've now come all this way to Malineau. Please, Monsieur, don't leave just yet. Would you be so kind to tell us the story?"

"I'd be happy to. Unfortunately, my time is limited, and I need to make further contacts for my firm."

"I can help you there. Have you travelled through this area before?"

"No."

"Then I can assist you, by providing you with the names of all those who usually purchase wine. This way you won't be wasting your time with us. Monsieur Schneffka," Melac said, turning to face Hieronymus, "please, don't leave. Stay and listen to this peculiar tale as well. Gentlemen, have a seat."

Both men complied and seated themselves at the table. As Melac filled their glasses, Martin recounted his adventure. He was a good storyteller and a whole hour had elapsed before he stood up to leave. He thanked the administrator for his helpful information and walked out the door, with Schneffke not far behind.

◈

Once they were out in the open and unobserved, Schneffke couldn't hold back any longer.

"Zounds! I thought I was imagining things," he said.

"And I couldn't believe my own eyes," Martin replied, "to see you here at Malineau."

"You, a wine merchant from Roussillon, by the name of Tannert?"

"Sure, Martin is my first name. And you, Master Schneffka, pretending to be a Pole? What's that all about?"

Schneffke grinned sheepishly. "It's just like the wine merchant who's actually a telegrapher."

"I know. But all sorts of peculiar things are happening around here, my worthy Hieronymus Aurelius Schneffke. I can only guess why you're here."

"Well, go ahead."

"Certainly not because of your sketching."

"No, you're right."

"More likely out of anthropological considerations; people studies, perhaps?"

"Yes, you're getting warmer."

"Could it have anything to do with that appealing little Marie Melac?"

"Possibly."

"Will she take the bait?"

"I hope so."

"Hmm. I'd hate to be the spoil sport, but I don't see it that way."

"Why not?'

"Because I know all about your bad luck."

"Don't be silly. In fact, I've only just become acquainted with a governess, with whom I coincidentally travelled all the way here."

"Naturally you went after her head over heels, right?"

"Of course. I fell for her, literally."

"Go on."

"But then we arrived in Thionville, and the governess changed into the daughter of an English lord."

"Damned bad luck, old boy," he mocked. "Something like that could only happen to the infamous Hieronymus Aurelius Schneffke. But I see that you've already found a way to appease your disappointment."

"Completely. I've had the good fortune to have fallen with her in her house."

"That is a good omen, my old friend."

"One which points to an upcoming wedding."

"Hopefully. But let's be serious for one moment. What are you doing here in the middle of France?"

"It's an actual working holiday, which has coincidentally brought me to the Melac house. What about you? Were you really in Paris?"

"Yes."

"And what about that tale; did it really happen that way, or did you embellish it?"

"Just the way I told you."

"I see," Schneffke replied, not totally believing him. "Who then is this Belmonte fellow?"

"Cavalry Master von Hohenthal."

"*Sapperlot!* Now I can guess the rest."

"So, what can you guess?"

"Well, I'm no fool, and I'm still a soldier."

"A foot soldier with homeland security."

"A non-commissioned officer, you meant to say," Hieronymus corrected him.

"Right. Keep going."

"There's talk of war," Hieronymus added, looking serious.

"I've heard much the same."

"War between Prussia and France?"

"Well, not between Prussia and Honolulu," Martin quipped.

"Which implies that vanguards have been deployed."

"Supposedly."

"I suspect your cavalry master is among them."

"Perhaps."

"What about you?"

"I won't try to deceive you, my friend, especially since I know you're a trustworthy fellow."

"Don't worry about me. Do you think that it will start soon?"

"Very soon."

"*Sapperlot!* Maybe I should think about heading for home?"

"Yes, make your way back. They can use a good man like you."

"But I have to stay for a couple of days."

"On account of Marie?"

"No, because of a painting that I need to refurbish."

"Good. But then you'll head back to Berlin?"

"No, not directly. I have to make one more stop: Thionville. There's supposed to be a castle there, Ortry."

"Ortry?" Martin asked, paying more attention. "What business do you have there?"

"I'm looking into solving a mystery."

"What? You're incorrigible. Listen here, Hieronymus, just make sure you tread carefully."

"How come?"

"I've heard that there could be two of our boys over there. Should you happen to recognize either one, don't give them away."

"Who are they?"

"One is Cavalry Master von Löwenklau."

"*Sapperlot*! A very capable officer."

"The other man is his sergeant, Schneeberg."

"I'm not familiar with him," said the painter, giving Martin a sideways glance. "How do you know all this?"

"We only learned of it yesterday."

"Where is Monsieur von Hohenthal?"

"At Metz. We need to check out the place."

"But why have you come to Malineau?"

"The surrounding area is just as important. Where are you staying?"

"Over there, with the caretaker," he said pointing out the place. "I'm refurbishing his pictures. Do you want to check it out?"

"No thanks."

"What about a glass of wine at the inn?"

"I like the sound of that. But be careful, so no one catches on that we know each other."

"Pah! I'm no yokel. Come on."

CHAPTER TWENTY-TWO

THE PASTEL PAINTING

Equipped with pastel paints, Schneffke headed out to Melac's house the following morning. He was welcomed by a hearty handshake and given a prominent seat at the window. He was itching to get going on the restoration work, but before he could do so, he had to remove the protective glass and separate the picture from the frame. With Marie and her grandparents watching, he turned the frame around and removed the back cover. No sooner had he performed this task, than his eyes fell on a large, yellowed envelope that was tucked in between the back and the canvass.

"An envelope," Hieronymus said surprised, "and it's addressed to the administrator, Monsieur Melac."

"Addressed to me?" questioned the overseer. "Dear God, could this have anything to do with the secret we discussed yesterday?"

"Quite possibly. Here, take it," Hieronymus replied, handing him the package. All four were riveted with anticipation. Melac carefully opened the large envelope, discovering that it contained several documents.

"A child's birth certificate; a girl's, by the name of Nanon de Bas-Montaigne," he read out loud.

"Heavens!" his wife exclaimed. "Surely that must refer to our Nanon."

"And here is one for Madelon de Bas-Montaigne. Yes, it appears to deal with our two girls. Here is a marriage certificate regarding Baron Gaston de Bas-Montaigne and a woman, Amély, nee Rénard."

"This must be what that poor dying woman wanted to reveal to us," offered Madame Melac, clasping her hands together.

"Then there's a receipt for fifteen thousand francs, monies loaned to the caregiver, Albert Berteu. I've always believed the girls were entitled to an inheritance and would come into some money. The money has never been repaid, because the promissory note is still here. I will have to see to this and bring it in order."

"Fifteen thousand francs?" gasped Madame Melac. "That Charles Berteu couldn't repay fifteen hundred."

"We'll see about that. Now, here is a letter that is addressed to me." Melac opened it, and quietly scanned the few lines. He then read it out loud.

"My dear Monsieur Melac,

If you're reading this letter, then I've been spared further suffering, and I have left this world, where I at first found such wonderful love, only to be followed by bitter disappointment. I herewith leave my two daughters in your care. Be their guardian, friend and father, since they have no idea who their real father is. Whether they will ever find out, I entrust to your wisdom alone.

I've enclosed their birth certificates, but perhaps it's best if they never discover that their father stems from nobility. Speak to the caretaker and have him return the money, so that my children can benefit from it. I had arranged it with him, so I could live off the interest, keeping the principal intact for my daughters. What else can I say? You are a gentleman and have always been my friend. I know that you will do what is best for my children, whose father and grandfather have disappeared.

I hereby leave my blessing for Nanon and Madelon. My last thoughts are with them, and I will never cease to pray for them.

Amély de Bas-Montaigne."

When he finished, a solemn quietness descended on the room.

"I was supposed to be their guardian, not Berteu. How sad, that Madame wasn't able to communicate the location of these important documents."

"Yes, and now everything has turned out differently," his wife said, tears forming in her eyes. "Will you reveal to them the contents of this letter?"

"I'll have to think about it."

"Look here," Hieronymus said, pointing to the back of the portrait. "Here is the subject's name: Baron Gaston de Bas-Montaigne. Could that be him?"

"Of course. This depicts the baron, and is the girl's father's portrait," confirmed the overseer. "Their mother had brought it with her. But why did she leave him?"

"Her father-in-law pressured her—no, forced her to leave," Hieronymus added.

"The father-in-law?" Melac asked, surprised. "Even forced her?"

"Yes."

"How could you possibly know that? You're a stranger here. You didn't even know the lady."

"That's true," Schneffke replied. "But you see, I've met the father-in-law."

"Ah! Another mystery."

"Yes. Our gracious God carries his children's destiny in his hand. Allow me to be up front with you. It's for this very reason that I've come all this way to Malineau."

"This reason?" Melac asked. "Were you aware of the circumstances surrounding the children and their upbringing?"

"Not in the least. I was quite ignorant of them."

"You're contradicting yourself, Monsieur."

"No, not at all. Allow me to explain. After what I now know about you, and your family, I'm convinced that I can trust you with what I've learned. A rich old man, a recluse, lives in Berlin. He goes by the name, Untersberg, or Underhill. You speak and understand both French and German. How would you translate his name into French?"

"I would render Unters as Bas… Wait a minute. Could there be a connection between this Underhill and the family of Bas-Montaigne?"

"Definitely. I know this old man, and that Charles Berteu had recently cabled him, advising him of his father's unexpected death."

"So, he kept in touch with Berteu all these years?"

"So, it would seem. Underhill is an old man, indecisive and feeble. He couldn't have undertaken this long journey. It turned out that I was the only one whom he entrusted with the task of travelling to Malineau."

"To attend the funeral?"

"No, far from it. He wanted me to find out if Albert Berteu had, before his death, confided in his son and revealed his secret."

"What secret?" all three blurted out.

"I wasn't told that; he was much too careful, but now I know what it was: the secret of the sisters' heritage."

"I still don't understand—"

"It's quite simple," interrupted Hieronymus. "This old man, Underhill, is their grandfather."

There it was. The three Melacs pondered the reality of that statement. Finally, Melac spoke again. "Unbelievable. But doesn't he care about the girls?"

"No. He doesn't want them to find out anything about their past. You see, he knows that their mother was a commoner, a German girl, not even Catholic. His son had been forbidden to marry her, but when he defied his father, the old man refused to accept his new daughter-in-law. He schemed and pressured her, finally arranging it so that she was forced to pack up and leave with her children."

"Dear God! That sounds like something you would read in a romance novel."

"True, but it's more like a tragedy."

"She left her husband and came here?"

"Evidently."

"How did her husband tolerate her actions?"

"She left secretly, while he was away on business. By the time he returned, she had disappeared."

"Didn't he search for her and his children?"

"Of course, he did. But his own father had lied to him, telling him she had been unfaithful and had left with another man."

"What a wicked thing to say," Marie commented.

"The young baron searched for her," continued Hieronymus, "but then for some inexplicable reason, he left France altogether and even ended up changing his name."

"How do you know all this?"

"Much of it I've been able to piece together; but some of it, I came by it firsthand," Hieronymus said thinking it best to conceal the connection with the kolibri pictures for the time being.

"Are you certain that this Underhill is the sisters' grandfather?"

"Quite certain," Hieronymus affirmed.

"He'll have to swallow his pride and acknowledge their legitimacy."

"I rather doubt he'll consent to it."

"Don't the documents prove that he's Nanon's and Madelon's grandfather?"

"No, they don't."

"But you yourself intimated it."

"The courts demand proof," Hieronymus stated. "Assertions by a claimant, in other words, declarations, aren't sufficient."

"So, how could we prove that he's in fact the Baron de Bas-Montaigne?"

"Perhaps I could handle that."

"Great! Then we've won."

"Not quite. First, show me that this lady, Madame Charbonnier, was actually the Baroness de Bas-Montaigne."

"Why shouldn't she be?"

"And that Nanon and Madelon truly are the children of Baron Gaston."

"I'm not following your logic," said Melac, feeling exasperated.

Schneffke smiled. "I'm afraid that there are probably other points that need clarification. One can't be too sanguine in these matters."

"Then tell us what we should do."

"First, we should determine if Madame Charbonnier is really the Baroness de Bas-Montaigne."

"How can you possibly do that?"

"That part is actually quite easy. I take it you knew Madame Charbonnier?"

"Yes, of course."

"Can you describe her to me?"

"She was very beautiful, slim, had exquisite eyes and magnificent hair."

"Alright. I've seen her portrait. Let's see if they match." Hieronymus took a sheet of paper and pencil out of his folder. But before he commenced sketching, his thoughts drifted back to a recent event. He recalled refurbishing several ordinary paintings of birds, kolibris, for his reclusive friend, Underhill, while in his apartment in Berlin. Accompanied by a fellow artist, Haller, they stumbled upon a concealed painting within its framework depicting a young woman, later identified as Amély de Bas-Montaigne. But the real treasure was the discovery of important documents, detailing the divorce between Amély and her husband, Gaston.

He closed his eyes and thought back to the portrait he had discovered behind the kolibri sketch. Satisfied, he opened his eyes, and the pencil moved with ease across the page, revealing a beautiful face.

"Now then, take a look," he invited as he finished. "Is this her, Amély?"

"Yes, it's her; that's the lady," they all agreed.

"Excellent. This confirms it. Now I can move ahead. You see, the girls have an uncanny resemblance to their mother. Still, we have to proceed cautiously. My thoughts are that we should, at least for the time being, hold back their real identity from them."

"Surely we should do something?"

"Of course. I will be travelling to Castle Ortry."

"To see Nanon?"

"Yes. Madelon is currently with her. Then I can head back to Berlin with Madelon. Who knows what will transpire while we're underway. Once I'm in Berlin, I will head to the recluse's place."

"And force him into an admission?" prompted Melac.

"Perhaps, but I can't say how that will play out. I will certainly write you about the outcome. We have to tread carefully."

"I agree completely. Monsieur Schneffka, how fortunate that we've met. It's quite extraordinary, that you a Pole, have come to see us..." Melac stopped speaking, struck with a thought. "Monsieur, please be honest with us, just like we've been with you. You're not really from Poland."

"Not from Poland? Who do you think I am? An African tribesman?"

"No, you're German."

Schneffke looked pensively in front of him.

"You can tell us the truth," Melac encouraged.

Marie joined in by walking up to him and placing her hand on his shoulder.

"Are you really from Germany?"

"Mademoiselle, don't you despise the Germans?"

"Monsieur, what do you think of me?" she defended herself. "On the contrary, we think fondly of Germany, even though we can't openly support her cause."

"Alright. I admit that I stem from Germany."

All three shook his hand, as a sign that they still welcomed him.

"But why didn't you disclose that fact earlier?"

"Out of caution. People around here speak of a looming war between France and Germany."

"Do you go along with those sentiments?"

"Somewhat."

"Then I should tell you," Melac continued, "that I support the German side and I hope they'll be victorious. I hope Prussia will take back Elsaß and Lothringen, as an atonement for what happened in earlier times. Monsieur, you're just as welcome in my house. So then, what is your real name?"

"It's not that much different. Schneffke, instead of Schneffka. Hieronymus Aurelius Schneffke. That's plain as pudding."

"Just make sure Berteu doesn't find out."

"Don't worry. So, you don't believe that Charles found anything out from his father?"

"Certainly not shortly before his death, since it happened so unexpectedly."

"What about prior to that?"

"That would seem more likely."

"How come?"

"Something happened on the day of the funeral which causes me to reflect."

"Tell me what happened," Schneffke prompted."

"Rumor has it that Berteu lured his stepsisters to the old flower mill at night, apparently in an effort to force Nanon into submission."

"Nanon? Does he want to marry her, is that it?"

"I've heard talk of it. He must know, or at least suspect that she has an inheritance. I expect that he wants to share in it by making her his wife."

"And she doesn't want to?"

"By no means. That's why he was forced to lure her into a trap."

"Heavens! What a despicable man. He should watch so he doesn't wander in front of my Zündnadel, should I be assigned duties near here. Then I would… *sapperlot*!" Suddenly, Hieronymus realized how careless he had been.

"Don't worry, my friend," Melac reassured him. "You're among good people. So, as you've just intimated, you must be a soldier."

"Yes, my regiment is assigned to homeland security."

A small smile crossed the overseer's lips as he surveyed the painter from head to foot. "Are all Prussian soldiers as well-nourished as you, Monsieur?"

"Every single one," Hieronymus beamed. "We're fed exceptional rations. If a whole battalion of such fellows should come into a trot, then they could easily overrun the entire French army. I can hardly wait for it to start. They'll get their due." Turning his attention to the painting, he continued. "But I should work on the portrait and not waste more time."

Schneffke started his restoration work in earnest. The Melacs watched his progress, amazed at his skill. While he worked, he conversed with them until the evening, and finally said his goodbyes feeling as if he had known them for years.

❧✠☙

Schneffke no sooner arrived back at the caretaker's house, than Berteu eyed him with suspicion. "I haven't laid eyes on you all day, Monsieur."

"I know. I've been out," Hieronymus replied.

"May I ask where you've spent the day?"

"Next door, at the castle."

"At the castle? But that's where the overseer lives."

"Evidently."

"Were you with him?"

"Yes, I was."

"Monsieur, what ever for?"

Hieronymus looked at his host in surprise. "I don't like the sound of your tone, Monsieur."

"I have a right to assume whatever tone I choose," Charles replied, his civility barely skin-deep. "Don't you know that you're living under my roof, as my guest?"

"I'm well aware of that."

"Then you should refrain from doing things that go against my will."

"Oho! What sort of things?"

"To begin with, your visit with Melac."

Schneffke looked him in the eye. "Pah! I may be your guest, but I'm not your servant. Actually, come to think of it, I *am* working for you. It should be an honor for you to have an artist staying on your premises. I thought you would have grasped that. And furthermore, it wasn't just a visit; it concerned some restoration work, not unlike yours."

"What? You were working over there?"

"Yes."

"That implies you were painting. Surely not another portrait?"

"Why, yes."

Charles clearly wasn't pleased. He lost all sense of civility and continued his interrogation. "Was it a portrait of the old man?"

"No."

"Then the old man's wife or his chubby daughter?"

Hieronymus shook his head.

"*Sapperlot!* Who then? There are only three of them over there," Charles nearly shouted in exasperation.

Schneffke looked at him without blinking. "When I said I have been working on a portrait, that much is true. But I was referring to an existing portrait, not a new one."

"There's only one painting you could be referring to—a pastel portrait."

"Yes, it was a pastel piece."

"The one that depicts a refined, young man?"

"Yes."

"Do you know the subject?"

"No, I don't."

"I suppose you removed the back?"

"Of course. How else could I have worked on it?"

"Did anything unusual occur?"

"Yes, indeed."

"What? What happened?" Charles asked quickly.

"I was up on a chair, trying to remove the painting—"

"Yes, and then what?" Charles interrupted.

"The nail came out and I toppled from the chair, with the result that I fell on the floor, with the painting coming to rest on top of me. But don't worry, the glass didn't break."

"Yes, and then?"

Schneffke pretended to think back. "Oh yes, Mademoiselle Marie helped me up."

"Monsieur!" Charles exclaimed, irritated.

"What's wrong?"

"Are you trying to make a fool out of me?"

"Not at all. I'm just replying to your questions. Is it my fault that you're so insistent?"

"I wasn't concerned about the glass, nor the frame. So, tell me, you're an accomplished artist, right? Is that portrait worth anything?"

"I should think so."

"How much would you estimate its value?"

"Hmm," Hieronymus considered. "I should think it was worth about six thousand francs when new."

"Six thou—hang it all!" Charles swore. "And now? Does it come close to the same value?"

"When I've finished restoring it, yes… perhaps even more."

"Damn it! What a mistake on my father's part," Charles muttered more to himself than Schneffke.

"A mistake? What do you mean by that?"

"Don't you know how that painting ended up in Melac's hands?"

"I was told it was a gift."

"No, that's not true. The painting was left there for safe keeping. It belongs to my stepsisters. Father should have insisted on having it returned. Have you completed the restoration?"

"No. I need to spend a few more hours on it."

"That means my pictures are being neglected," Charles voiced, unable to hide the sour expression on his face.

"Don't worry," Hieronymus reassured him. "I'll have them done before I leave."

CHAPTER TWENTY-THREE

BERTEU'S PLANS

Since the hour wasn't late, Schneffke had no desire to call it a night. He found himself in a singular state of mind. He felt as if he'd won the state lottery. He had of course met many girls, and each one had left an impression on him. They had all appealed to him, but this Marie—she was something special. He was struck with a curious feeling, as if he'd been lost, and now was found. His spacious room suddenly seemed confining.

Hieronymus retrieved a cigar from his coat, lit it and then left the house. Almost purposefully, he wandered toward the park bench where he had first met Marie. He sat down and reminisced, thinking back on the eventful day. He was so absorbed in his thoughts, that he barely heard the sound of approaching steps. He listened up. The steps were coming closer, and he recognized that it wasn't just one person, but two, perhaps more.

He didn't want to be seen and made a quick decision, one that he wouldn't regret. He snuffed out the cigar, stood up and stepped behind a nearby bush, situated directly behind the park bench.

Two men approached and came to a stop in front of the bench.

"Should we take a seat?" one of them asked, with Schneffke recognizing his host's voice.

"Fine by me," replied the other.

"You're being awfully quiet tonight, Jacques."

"And for good reason."

"Because of the girls?" asked Charles.

"Well, what else."

"Pah! It was just a prank that didn't work out, that's all. No one really knows what happened that night in the old flower mill. No one!"

"How can you say that?" Ribeau objected. "Have you forgotten that we were tied up, gagged, and that's how the villagers found us? All because of those damned girls."

"It doesn't bother me that much," Charles pretended. "But because Nanon managed to get away, I find it hard to overlook. The whole thing has left me out of sorts. And who was that fellow that drove away with them?"

"All I know is that he was tall and not lacking in muscles," Jacques said, rubbing his forehead, as if remembering Franz's powerful blow.

Charles nodded, agreeing with his assessment. "He had blonde hair, I believe. Did you make it all the way to Etain?"

"Yes."

"Well, did you come up with anything?"

"Of course. I had some success."

"Excellent. So, what did you find out?"

"They first arrived the night before the funeral."

"Who arrived?"

"Mademoiselle Nanon Charbonnier from Ortry, and Mademoiselle Madelon Köhler from Berlin. They alighted in front of the best guest house, the Napoleon. They came with a coach they had procured in Metz, and—"

"Who cares about a coach. What about that tall fellow?"

"I heard he came with them. A stable boy remembered seeing a tall, muscular man sitting beside the coachman."

"Ah! So that's how he got here."

"There's more. I managed to have a look into the hotel's registry book."

"Good. So, what's his name?"

Ribeau produced a crumpled piece of paper and read from it. "Franz Schneeberg, from Thionville, *harbossieur.*"

"Schneeberg? That sounds like a German name. I hope he ends up in hell. What does he do for a living?"

"I heard he collects plants for a local doctor."

"*Sapperlot!* That's unusual. Maybe he made it up. Is that all you managed to learn?"

"No, there's more," Jacques said, failing to hide a wicked grin. "I know he's Nanon's lover."

Berteu made a face. "Don't be ridiculous; her and a plant collector?"

Ribeau shrugged his shoulders. "That's what I heard."

"From whom? Out with it."

"Well, one of the hotel's waiters has something going on with one of the chamber maids. They happened to be together late that night, and so as not to be seen by hotel guests, they stood in a dark corner of the corridor. That's when they saw a woman—by their description Nanon—come out of her room and purposefully head down the hall and walk into Schneeberg's room."

"Heaven and hell!" Charles erupted. "I'll strangle that meddling plant collector. Are you sure it couldn't have been her sister who had paid him that late visit?"

"Clearly it was a lover's rendezvous. From what I heard, it had to be Nanon, since Schneeberg doesn't really know Madelon."

"Alright. I'll be in Thionville the day after tomorrow. Then I'll have an opportunity to make my inquiries about this so-called *gentleman*," Charles retorted, nearly spitting out the word. "Anything else?"

"The following morning, the two sisters engaged a coachman to take them to Malineau. But this time, that fellow didn't travel with them. Instead, he went alone, on foot, and he had a good look around the entire region."

"How do you know that?"

"He was seen everywhere. Later, he even dropped in at the tavern and spoke to the hired coachman."

Berteu snapped his fingers. "That explains it all. He *must* have overheard my earlier conversation with Matthieu."

"No doubt. And later that evening, he high tailed it back to Etain with both sisters. Almost immediately, after they had arrived, they changed coaches and headed back to Metz."

"How did people know that?"

"It seems a coach from Metz was already waiting for them. That *Urian* naturally went along." Jacques stopped speaking, as if he'd just remembered something else. "I nearly forgot," he continued. "Something funny occurred just before they left the hotel. There was a short, fat fellow, apparently a painter—"

"No! Really? Did you find out his name?" Charles interrupted.

"Schneffka," Jacques replied, after referring to the same paper. "A landscape painter from Poland, at least that's what it said in the registry."

"Really? But that's the name of the painter staying with me," Charles offered, scratching his head.

"You have a guest? A painter? What's that all about?"

"He's staying with me, refurbishing several of my paintings."

"Then what I'm about to tell you should be of double importance. Just as both sisters were about to climb into the carriage, this fellow came rushing down the stairs. And get this, he was barefoot, wearing only a night shirt, with a red tablecloth wrapped around his waist."

"Unbelievable. What did he want?"

"He spoke to both sisters for a few minutes and then disappeared back into the hotel."

"What did they talk about?"

"I couldn't find out. None of the staff was actually close enough to overhear. But it strikes me as strange that this painter knew the sisters and he's now staying with you."

"That is peculiar. Could he possibly be in cahoots with them? Could he somehow be involved with that Schneeberg fellow?"

"I wouldn't bet against it. Yes, the more I think about it, the more it makes sense."

"Then he can go to hell as well."

"Pah! We can deal with him all by ourselves."

"If he's involved with that Schneeberg, then he's a dangerous fellow, one who may have planned on more than just sketching pictures."

"Like what?" asked Jacques.

"To begin with, where does this plant-collector live?"

"In Thionville."

"Right. In Ortry's vicinity. And Nanon?"

"There as well."

"And Ortry is where we have amassed our cache of weapons and supplies. Haven't you heard about secret emissaries that have been sent out by the Prussians, whose job is to criss-cross our country and gather vital information?"

"Yes, there's been talk about that."

"I've got a hunch that this plant-collector is one of their spies."

"*Sapperlot*! I hadn't considered that."

"It could also mean that the fat painter is working for him."

"Listen, Charles. You might have something there. You'll have to keep a close eye on him."

"For sure. If he is a spy that means he doesn't belong to the ordinary folk, regardless of his outward appearance."

"That means he's some sort of diplomat, perhaps an officer."

"You could be right," Charles replied, thinking it over. "But then he doesn't strike me as someone belonging to the diplomatic corps."

"Even less to the class of an officer. A man who runs around half-naked, covered by a tablecloth, and holds impromptu conversations with ladies in the middle of the night, doesn't fit into my understanding of a cavalier."

"Evidently. In short, the fellow is a mystery and I'm going to solve it. I'll try to speak to him tomorrow."

"Just make sure you handle it well," Jacques cautioned.

"Don't worry. Naturally, I'm going to avoid collapsing like a house of cards. We need to be in the clear about him by tomorrow."

"Why tomorrow?"

"Idiot! Because we won't be here the day after tomorrow."

"Right you are. I had nearly forgotten about the last shipment."

"It would be to our advantage if we could report something useful to the old captain. If I'm not mistaken, we need to deliver the powder kegs to the old stone quarry."

"Yes. That's the most secure place."

"Is it accessible by wagon?"

"Sure. There's an old, abandoned road that we can use. To those who are used to it, it shouldn't pose much of a problem. It's the only quarry in the vicinity."

"What time are we expected there?"

"Punctually at midnight," Charles revealed.

"In the dark? How do we move the kegs to the storage rooms in the dark?"

Berteu rolled his eyes, surprised at Ribeau's lack of foresight. "That's the captain's problem. I suspect there's a connecting passage that leads to the underground vaults."

"Have you ever seen or been down there?"

"No. But from what I've heard, the old man has amassed quite the store house of weapons and ammunition. If those foolish Prussians really want to take us on, they'll be wiped out in no time."

"I suppose they will be the first to strike."

"If they do, it will be their downfall."

"They'll have little choice."

"Our emperor is rumoured to be the most skilful diplomat of our time. He desires war but is clever enough not to accept blame for starting it, and so he'll look for an opportunity and saddle them with declaring it first."

"That could be advantageous. Our side is prepared, while they have no idea what's brewing."

"Exactly. I expect we'll take a leisurely walk toward Berlin, while finding many suitable things along the way for the taking."

"That's the best part," Jacques echoed. "I'm looking forward to the moment when we will finally receive our marching orders. Think of it, I'll be an officer with the *franctireurs*."

"Me too. And a vital part is that we won't be on the front lines. We'll remain behind the regular army, to umm—"

"Well, to what?"

"To keep the lines of communication open. Yes, and ensure there's order."

"Haha, what an opportunity," Jacques said, beaming. "We'll sweep right, then left and appropriate what we can get our hands on. So, Charles, make it a priority to check that painter out and if he strikes you as suspicious, don't let him get away."

"Don't give it another thought. Once I've set my mind to doing something, it gets done. Actually, he's already acted suspicious by conferring with the overseer next door."

"Do you consider Melac a sympathiser of Germany?"

"I should think so. Since he's a descendant of the original Melac, he considers it his duty to make good for the grief that man had caused. But enough about him. We need to get some rest. We'll be starting to load the shipment at daybreak so we can make it to the quarry on time."

Both men rose and left the park. Schneffke waited until their steps had faded into the distance before venturing out from his hiding spot.

"Heavens!" he said to himself. "That was some discussion between those two. Too bad my Hussar friend Tannert couldn't have listened in. What did they call me, a German spy? Ha-ha."

He sat down on the vacated bench to think things over. *Well, I suppose I am a sort of spy, though not political, since I came all this way to ferret things out of Berteu. But a real spy, a vanguard, that I'm not. Unfortunately, I'm not on such familiar terms with Moltke so he can deduce what a clever fellow I really am. So, our friend Berteu wants to find out if I'm an officer or even a diplomat. Fine. Go ahead and give it your best shot.*

Amused, he sat there, recalling how the two men had debated about him. *Perhaps I can turn the spit around*, he mused, *and sound them out, as opposed to them doing it to me. They talked about powder and weapons stored underground at Ortry. Sapperlot! That's more dangerous than pudding, when you consider you're dealing with dynamite. So, these two are organising bands of franctireurs, overseen by the old captain? Just wait you two. I've half a mind to find my friend Martin Tannert, who's—wait a minute. Didn't Martin say that there was a vanguard already in place there, namely Cavalry Master von Löwenklau, accompanied by his sergeant Franz Schneeberg? Could he be the plant-collector they were talking about? Probably.*

I can look to Tannert or Löwenklau if I get myself in a bind. Just wait you two Frenchmen, Hieronymus Aurelius Schneffke will settle your bill—permanently! The day after tomorrow, I should be in Thionville and have time to look for the quarry they talked about. Powder shipments! Underground storage chambers! Secret passages! I've got to find out about these things. That way I'll be assured that their so-called casual stroll to Berlin will encounter a few bumps along the way.

Forging his plans, Schneffke sauntered back to Berteu's house.

⁂

Since the outer door was already locked, Hieronymus had little choice but to knock. Charles himself answered the door, surprised to see the painter awake at this late hour.

"Ah, it's you, Monsieur?" he asked, failing to hide his surprise.

"Of course," the painter replied.

"But it's late. I thought you had retired for the night?"

"Hmm, I didn't think it was too late."

"Really? Well then, we have time for a glass of wine, no?"

Hieronymus was astute enough to realize that the invitation was likely a pretext. The Frenchman's ploy was to draw him into conversation, and with his tongue suitably loosed by the wine, Berteu probably hoped to sound him out.

"Ah, a glass of wine," the painter said good-naturedly. "I like the sound of that. You can wake me up in the middle of the night with an offer like that."

Berteu gave him a forced smile. "Come on then."

"But it has to be good. No painter likes to drink rotgut before he goes to bed."

"Have you ever drunk a bad bottle while staying here, Monsieur?"

"No, I've been most pleased."

"There, you see; please, follow me."

Charles led him to his study and then left to fetch a bottle. He returned shortly, and after uncorking it filled two glasses. "So, let's have a toast, Monsieur. To my country's honor," he announced, all the while looking steadily at Schneffke.

"To France," Hieronymus replied, clinking his glass.

"Health and honor to our great emperor."

"Long live Napoleon. When it concerns the emperor's health, I will gladly drain the last drop."

Berteu refilled their glasses. "So, you're sympathetic toward France?"

"Without question."

"Why is that?" Charles probed.

"Well, I'm more than pleased with the land and its people. That goes for the emperor too."

"Are you serious?"

"Of course."

"Surely you have your reasons for saying that."

"Pah! Tell me, how would a hound appeal to you?"

Berteu looked displeased. "What kind of a comparison is that, Monsieur?"

"I could say the same about a flower."

"Hmm."

"Or a fine-looking girl."

"Then it's a matter of preference, or taste."

"Exactly. Your emperor appeals to me as a matter of good taste."

"Why?"

"*Sapperlot*! Why does one girl draw a man, while another repels him? It's a matter of taste."

"What? I'm not following. You're going around in circles."

"Never mind. Just stay seated. Surely you must know that Poland has always been sympathetic with France. If the great emperor had had his way, Poland would have been free."

"Of course. So, you're Polish?"

"Isn't it obvious?"

"Perhaps more of a German-Pole?"

"What a question. Are there French-Cossacks, or perhaps German halflings? A Pole is a Pole! Understood?"

"You're very passionate about your country."

"Yes, if someone criticizes my country, I can get worked up."

"Yet, you don't strike me as Polish."

"Why not?"

"Well, um... it's on account of your stomach, Monsieur."

"Dear God! What sort of impression have you conjured up about us? Do you suppose that we Poles like to starve ourselves?"

"Well, not really."

"Are we supposed to resemble bean poles or fence boards?"

"No. But I envisioned them to be slim and well-proportioned."

"That doesn't make sense," Hieronymus replied, looking offended. "Am I not well-proportioned?"

"Well, not entirely."

"So, you're saying that I'm poorly proportioned."

"No, it's not that either."

Schneffke looked puzzled. "What exactly do you mean by proportioned then?"

"Your body's dimensions."

"My dimensions? Alright, allow me to elaborate." Hieronymus got up and positioned himself before the Frenchman, legs spread apart. "Do you see me now?"

"Yes."

"Good. I'm glad we agree on that much. Now let's see about my proportions, whether good or bad. Let's start with my girth, since it's the part that catches most people's attention first. Do I have a prominent stomach with spindly legs?"

"No."

"Or perhaps a crooked back with straight loins?"

"No."

"Small eyes and a large nose?"

"Far from it."

"Well then, you can rest assured that you won't find anyone else that's better proportioned than I. I won't go so far as to call myself an Adonis, since I don't fall within the realm of the gods, but in terms of human evolvement and appearance, that much I've achieved. Understood? That's plain as pudding. It should convince you that I'm Polish."

"Yes, Monsieur, but your speech?"

"My speech? What's wrong with it? Naturally we've been conversing in French. If I had the inclination to deliver a litany in Polish, I can certainly do so."

"That's not what I meant. I just wanted to say that you're not employing the customary Polish-French expressions."

"May God prevent me from bastardizing that beautiful French language."

"Poles seem to have different pronunciation."

"Really? Where have you come across this Polish-French mishmash?"

"In Paris."

"That must have been a peculiar type of Pole, Monsieur. Likely an imposter. I doubt you're capable of judging a Pole when he's talking French. I know better."

Schneffke's reprimand didn't miss its mark. If truth be known, Berteu hadn't even met a Pole, much less talked to one. He wasn't getting anywhere and decided to steer away from this sensitive topic.

"You may be right," Charles agreed. "But Monsieur, I've just thought of something. You're a painter, right?"

Schneffke looked at him incredulously. "What a question. Of course, I'm a painter, an artist."

"Just an artist?"

"Of course."

"Nothing else?"

"Isn't that enough? Are you trying to insult me?"

"No, that's not what I meant. I was just wondering if you had another occupation, that's all?"

"Of course, I have."

Berteu felt a sense of triumph, believing he had at last cornered the fat painter. "Alright then. What else do you occupy yourself with?"

"Several things; four actually."

"What? Four jobs? You're joking, Monsieur."

"Not at all. First, I'm a human being, second, I'm a Christian, third I'm a patriot, and fourth, I hope to become a father one day."

The Frenchman felt disappointed. He was hoping that the wine had loosened his tongue enough so that something would slip out. He didn't notice that the portly painter was toying with him."

"*Mille tonnerres!*" he cursed. "None of those things are what I would call an occupation."

"Still, they can occupy a lot of a man's time."

"Fine. Then let's simply call it business dealings."

"That's entirely different."

"So, other than your painting ability, do you support yourself by other means?"

"No."

"And yet, I thought that—"

"What?"

"Well, I've heard of those who paint for pleasure."

"Sure, we all do; but that's not the case with me."

"You paint for a living, yet you won't accept an honorarium from me."

Schneffke smiled coyly. "It's because I enjoy being around French people, and you're French."

"How noble of you to say so, Monsieur. But since you didn't ask for payment, I thought you relied on other means."

"I paint to live, and I live to paint. What other occupation would I want?"

"Hmm! Perhaps that of an advocate?"

"Pah! Laws are too stiff for me. My oil paints are much more pliable."

"A minister?" Charles suggested.

"I'm too sinful a man to consider it."

"A doctor then?"

"What do I know about maladies and bed-side manner?"

"Or... or a diplomat?"

"Don't be ridiculous. If I were a diplomat, I certainly wouldn't be sitting around like this, subjected to being pumped for information like a schoolboy."

Berteu didn't catch the slant and kept right on going. "Maybe an officer?"

"An off—off—officer, hahaha. Are you mad? If I were an officer, I would have challenged you to pistols long ago. Your probing questions are far too intrusive, which many would perceive at the very least as annoying, and in some cases as insulting. Surely you can see that?"

Berteu didn't. "But I'm not offending you, am I?"

"Aren't you? Isn't it considered an insult when you question who or what I am, even though I've plainly told you?"

"You're taking this too personally. Please accept my apology," Charles offered. "You see, I do have a reason to view you with mistrust."

"Whatever for?"

"Is the name Nanon familiar to you?"

"Yes."

"What about the name Madelon?"

"That too."

"And the name Charbonnier?"

"Yes, come to think of it."

"There you see. Then you know the ladies."

"The ladies, which ladies? I'm afraid I don't."

"But you just admitted to me that you knew them."

"I'm familiar with the names, not the ladies themselves. They're three ordinary French names, ones I've often heard before. That's all."

"Monsieur, it almost seems like you're trying to make fun of me."

"Pah! I'm generally a serious fellow. You asked me if I'm familiar with the names, not the people themselves."

"So, the two ladies aren't familiar to you?"

"No."

"And yet you've spoken to them."

"That's possible. One can easily talk to strangers without knowing who they are."

"But your conversation took place in such a way as to suggest a closer relationship."

"What makes you say that?"

"Does one carry on conversations with strangers while half-naked?"

"No, not even with relatives."

"Still, that is what you have done," Berteu insisted.

"Me? Half-naked. Not that I know of."

"At least barefoot."

"Not possible."

"And wrapped up in a red tablecloth."

It suddenly dawned on Schneffke what he was driving at. "Ah, now I'm beginning to follow you."

"And sporting a large Calabrese hat."

"Yes, yes, now I remember."

"So, what business did you have with the ladies?"

"Maybe you should ask them the same question?"

"About your involvement?"

"Monsieur!" Hieronymus objected loudly.

"What's wrong?" Charles asked bewildered.

"I want to know where you're going with this line of inquiry. You've done nothing but question me for the last half hour as if I owed you an explanation."

"I have good reason to."

"How come?"

"Those ladies are my sisters."

"Really? I don't see a resemblance."

"That's beside the point. My sisters had left here under peculiar, yes, even strange circumstances."

Schneffke pretended to be aghast. "Did they steal something?"

"No, nothing like that. They left without my permission."

"What does that have to do with me?"

"Yet you spoke to them afterwards."

"As I recall, it was only in passing."

"There was also a man in their company, a strong, domineering man. He's the one who whisked them away."

"Really? That's none of my business."

"Monsieur, it seems that everything which concerns me is of no concern to you."

"That's true. I wish that things were turned around, so you would pay attention to things that are of concern to me."

"Are you trying to be rude?"

"No, you're the one who's being rude."

Berteu blinked. "I only wish to know the part that is important to me. You were seen talking to my fleeing sisters and now you're staying here. Isn't that conspicuous?"

"It would be far more conspicuous if I had first come to stay here and then fled with your sisters. I never intended to stay here, remember. It was you who talked me into staying on."

"Still, as my guest, it is incumbent of you to be forthright with me, your host."

"I have every intention of doing so. But I object to being cross-examined like a criminal who stands before his judge." Schneffke had suddenly turned into a different man, confident and challenging, not the sort that Berteu was used to dealing with.

"Alright. I can see I've been a little hasty, perhaps even accusatory. Please, forgive my intrusive questions. Now then, you really don't know my sisters?"

"No."

"Then how is it that you spoke to them late at night?"

"Oh that. I simply got them mixed-up."

"Really?"

"I was expecting my bride to arrive that night. I was already in bed, when I heard a coach pull up. Naturally, I looked out the window, and by the lantern's poor light, I mistook the lady for my bride. In my hurry to see her I grabbed what was handy and rushed downstairs. That's when I found out I had made a mistake."

"Ah, so that was how it happened. Who's your bride?"

"A Polish girl from Paris."

"I see," Charles acknowledged, looking him up and down, not at all comfortable with the explanation. "And the fellow who was seen with my sisters, do you know him?"

"I've never laid eyes on him," Hieronymus answered truthfully.

"Then I'm forced to believe you."

"I don't care if you believe me or not. Besides, I have far more reason to mistrust you, my friend. Your family name is Berteu, right?"

"Yes."

"Yet you referred to the ladies as Charbonnier."

"I did, so what?"

"Why the different last name?"

"They're my stepsisters."

"I suppose I'm forced to believe you," he said imitating Berteu. "Still, it's none of my business. You can see that I'm in no wise happy with your accusatory manner. I'm an artist, not a vagabond. It's time I left. Since it's too late now, I will leave in the morning."

Schneffke did his best to look unhappy. This latest turn was not in Berteu's plans. He wanted the painter to stay and complete the restoration work, while at the same time keeping an eye on him.

"I have already apologized to you. Surely you can see that a brother can get worked up when his sisters leave his house, aided by a stranger."

"Well, yes, I too wouldn't have been too pleased. I wouldn't have allowed it."

"What would you have done in my stead?"

"I would have gone after him, to reclaim my sisters."

"I aim to do just that, but I haven't had the time. I intend to go after them tomorrow. Can I expect you to still be here when I get back?"

"Probably not."

"How about it, Monsieur? Won't you accept my apology? Let's have a toast and put an end to our discord."

Berteu held his glass toward Schneffke, who pretended that it wasn't easy for him to lay aside his hurt feelings. Yet in the end, he raised his glass and toasted to a renewed friendship.

"Well, why not. Let's remain friends," he said.

"And you will await my return?" queried Charles.

"Sure, and if not here, then in Etain, where I'll be waiting for my bride."

They sat together for a few more minutes, talking about unimportant things, and finally parted.

After Schneffke had left, Berteu pondered about the portly man. *He comes across as innocent,* he thought. *Should I trust him? He doesn't look that smart, but there's something about the way he handles himself that suggests he has plenty behind the ears.*[23.1] *I'll have to keep a close eye on him.*

Likewise, Schneffke, after he had entered his room, thought about his encounter with Berteu. *Quite the contemptible fellow,* he thought, *but he strikes me as being ten times dumber than he looks. Imagine him, trying to get information out of me, ha! It would take a much cleverer man than him. The night after tomorrow, I'll be keeping watch at the old stone quarry at Ortry. That's plain as pudding.*

CHAPTER TWENTY-FOUR

SCHNEFFKE'S FRIEND

Hieronymus Schneffke rose the following morning and partook his breakfast. It was then that he learned Charles Berteu had already left. He got busy with the restoration work right after breakfast. After making some progress, he headed toward the castle, where to his surprise, several windows were now wide open, and the curtains had been pulled back. As he entered Melac's house, he was welcomed by the overseer himself.

"Monsieur Schneffke, if you only knew what good news we had received late last night," Melac announced.

"I can't imagine," the astute painter replied.

"Well, humour me?"

"You're about to receive guests."

"Right you are. But who do you suppose is coming?"

"You seem to be airing out the place, so I can only assume it's for the owner's benefit. Am I right?"

"Yes, you've guessed it. We received the cable just before midnight," he announced, showing Hieronymus the telegram. It read as follows:

"We will be coming tomorrow. Count de Latreau."

"What do you say about that?" he asked, looking pleased.

"That you're looking forward to it. I can see it in your face. But something tells me I should be on my way."

"What for?"

"You won't have any time today for this painter."

"Oh, don't concern yourself with that. We've worked through the night. Mother and Marie are still over there, dusting the curtains. Do you want to come and have a look?"

"I'd be happy to."

Melac led him upstairs to the spacious rooms, where mother and daughter were working. Marie's face lit up when she saw them approach. Hieronymus didn't know what came over him, but the next thing he knew, he was high up on the ladder cleaning the drapes.

"Father, do you see what he's done with the curtains?" Madame Melac said, pointing to the painter.

"You mean in regard to cleaning them?"

"Yes, he's quite adept."

"Of course. He's quite the talented man. I can see by the way he works with them that he's supple and knowledgeable."

Surprisingly, the portly Hieronymus moved adeptly up and down the ladder, a far cry from his usual ways. He had no intention of tumbling or falling down. The work was completed by mid-day and the castle was ready for the count and his entourage. Back down at Melac's house, Schneffke was invited to lunch, and afterwards busied himself with the pastel painting. Marie kept him company and occupied herself with crocheting, while her grandparents returned to the upper rooms for tidying and finishing touches. She cast an admiring glance at the portrait from time to time and at the one who seemed to have eyes only for his work. At last, he laid his pastel pencil aside, stepped back from the picture and evaluated his handiwork.

"Are you finished?" Marie asked.

"Yes," Hieronymus said, still absorbed.

Marie walked up to him and stood by his side, allowing her eyes to take in the picture. "Isn't it wonderful, to be able to paint like that," she complemented him. "How can one convey such expression on canvass while it can be so difficult to put into words?"

He looked into her clear blue eyes. "Well, it's your smile that speaks to me, rather than words."

Marie turned red.

"Well, what I was thinking is this: when I look into those clear, loving eyes, then all I would like to do is... is to kiss you." It took him some extra effort to finish his sentence. Embarrassment clouded Marie's face, and it seemed as if she was about to turn away. "There, you see, Mademoiselle," he said. "You're upset with me, and now you're going to leave."

Marie quickly turned around. Her serious expression gave way to a smile forming on her lips. "Are my eyes really that clear and appealing?" she ventured.

"And how."

"So, then such a kiss would be considered as special?"

"Very special," he agreed.

"Hmm! I wasn't aware of that," she replied coyly.

"Good Lord! If I could only prove it to you."

"What for? I already am aware of it."

Hieronymus was temporarily at a loss for words. "You already know? Really? Do you have an admirer, a suitor?"

"No."

"Perhaps you've recently had one."

"No, not now or recently."

"Then how can you claim to know that your kiss is special?"

"Because I've already been kissed."

"Heavens! No lover, but already kissed? By whom?"

"Isn't it obvious? By my grandparents."

"Sapp—" he stopped in mid sentence, taking a deep breath. "What a fool I've been. I should have thought of that. But my dear Mademoiselle, that's quite different. Kissing one's father, or mother, brother or sister, even grandparents, isn't the same as kissing that someone special."

"It isn't? I don't understand you."

"I wish I could explain it, but in this case words simply aren't enough."

"What about through the medium of pastels?"

"No."

"Through the paintbrush?"

"Not even then."

"Then I have no choice but to forego the experience."

"Yes, it's a real shame," he lamented, throwing such a longing look at her red, beckoning lips, that Marie turned away from him. She sat down and picked up her crochet needle again.

Schneffke pulled up a stool and watched her small thick fingers as they nimbly worked the needle. But the more he watched, the more he thought about her. Marie momentarily paused in her work. With a far-away dream-like gaze, she looked out the window. Hieronymus didn't dare to interrupt her. Then she turned back to face him.

"Isn't it fortunate when a dream turns into reality?" Marie asked.

"Of course. Still, the fulfillment of this dream can't be termed unlucky."

"A person can't judge with such certainty."

"Pah! If the heart speaks, I trust in its message. Luck, after all, comes from following one's heart. And that's when it pains, when one has to leave his conviction because—"

"Because?" she asked, smiling.

"*Sapperlot!* Because I have to leave today."

"Today, already?" Marie asked surprised, her red cheeks visibly paler.

"Yes, today, Mademoiselle."

"Does it have to be so soon?"

"Unfortunately, yes. It can't be postponed."

"Yet yesterday, you never mentioned anything about leaving."

"Something has happened, which hastened my preparations for departure."

"Oh, no! Was it something that we—?"

"No, no," he interrupted her. "It's for a totally different reason."

"Will you ever return to this region?"

"I can't say. Once I've left, there doesn't seem to be much of a reason for me to return."

"But I can think of at least one," she added quickly.

"Which one?"

"The affair concerning Nanon and Madelon de Bas Montaigne."

"True. But who knows what course that business will take. My part will probably be a small one and relegated to the background. However, what is more likely is that I may soon return to France—as your enemy."

"No, never. I could never picture you as our enemy."

"What about in case of war?"

"No, not even then. You understand our inclination, in that we favor the Prussian cause. Are you certain a war will erupt so soon?"

"Yes, Mademoiselle. France has been pressuring Germany toward that end."

"How foolish. Dear God! I can only imagine the consequences of such a decision: the canons will roar, the bullets will whistle, and the sabres will rattle. And in its midst..." Marie stopped speaking, embarrassment spreading over her face.

"Don't stop. Please, continue," he pleaded.

"And in its midst, there you will be, carried along by the throng."

Schneffke's face shone with genuine delight. "You're thinking about me? About my well-being?" he asked.

"Yes. I don't know of a single individual who will be impacted in the same way."

"And if I were to fall? If you were to receive news one day, that I've been laid in a mass grave and—"

"Please, stop!" Marie objected. "That would be too much to bear." She covered her eyes, as if she had witnessed something awful. Moved with genuine concern, he walked up to her and gently pulled her hands away from her face.

"Mademoiselle Marie," he said softly, "will you forget me once I've left this place?"

"No," she whispered.

"Will you think about me?"

A roguish smile crossed her lips. "Should I?"

"Yes, yes indeed. It's my wish that you think of me often," he said and gingerly placed his arm around her waist, something she didn't resist.

"But what good is all that, Monsieur?" she asked playfully.

"Hmm. Isn't there anything else? What about our love?"

Marie hadn't expected that. "Our love? Are you serious?"

"Yes, yes, a thousand times yes. Marie, can't you see... that I'm in love with you?" Hieronymus blurted out.

"The skilful artist, in love with me, a simple, lowly farm girl?"

"Yes, you Marie. I love you, truly love you. And what about you? Will you give me your answer?"

Her face changed in an instant. "No," she replied, her voice sounding serious.

"What? You won't give me an answer?"

"I won't give you one, but you can take it," she replied, her playfulness returning. She puckered her lips, the ones he had desired all along.

"Heavens!" Hieronymus exclaimed. "You won't have to ask me twice, girl. That's the best answer yet. Come here!" He pulled her toward him, and kissed her once, twice, thrice, four times—and lost count. "He should see me now," he said without thinking.

"Who?"

"Monsieur Haller."

"Who is that?"

"A colleague of mine, a painter. It was on my account that he endured the famous downhill slide, which the governess—" Shocked at his carelessness, he stopped himself. He was on the verge of disclosing his latest romantic encounter.

"A slide on account of a governess? What do you mean?"

"Well, there once was this governess..." he admitted sheepishly.

"Ah, so that's how it starts, a most peculiar beginning."

"Well, that's a story for another time. But here I am, ready to do my bidding for you, in a foreign country no less."

"What a daring man you are, Hieronymus. Out of your love for me, I trust you will dispense with unnecessary dangers from now on."

"Out of your love, ha! I'm prepared to do much more. Still, I treasure your love and so—heavens, what's all that noise?"

They both heard approaching carriages outside, and the smacking of whips.

"It's our gracious master," Marie called excitedly. "I have to leave."

CHAPTER TWENTY-FIVE

AN UNUSUAL PROPOSAL

Suddenly, Hieronymus found himself alone in the house. "That went well," he muttered to himself, feeling pleased with how things had worked out. *Hopefully, she'll become my wife one day,* he mused. *Then she'll come to appreciate my finer qualities,* he mused.

As he looked out the window, he spotted a princely carriage pull up, followed by three coaches and a supply wagon. Two servants dismounted from the stately-looking carriage and opened the door. A refined older gentleman climbed down.

Clearly, the count himself, Hieronymus guessed. *A good-looking man. Handsome, proud, mellow and with a military bearing. And that must be his granddaughter, Ella de Latreau,* he surmised, as he watched her climb down from the coach.

"Heavens!" Hieronymus blurted out. "What an angel. A hourie[25.1] from Mohammed's seventh heaven." He was about to turn away when he spotted another woman step down. *Ah, here comes one more to my liking. Perhaps this is Alice, Count Rallion's secretary's sister,* he considered, thinking back to Tannert's story. *Now there's a nice-looking girl: Pretty, chaste, capable, and sumptuous like chocolate.* Hieronymus continued to watch as servants alighted from the other carriages.

Melac, along with his wife and granddaughter, stood in the doorway of the castle, ready to welcome their landlord and master. Count de Latreau and his granddaughter were well thought of by the Melac household, and to confirm their affection, they greeted them warmly by kissing both his and Ella's hand.

They led them upstairs into the salon. It took some time for the servants to unpack and bring things in order. With Alice by her side, Ella retired to her boudoir. This left her grandfather to ponder other matters.

Hieronymus, an astute observer, recognized right away that not all the coaches belonged to the count. He left Melac's house and approached one of the coachmen.

"Are you in the count's employ?" he inquired.

"No, Monsieur."

"Where else then?"

"With a firm in Metz."

"Ah. So, the count probably arrived by train and arranged for the rental of these carriages?"

"Yes."

"When do you head back?"

"Today, but not until we've fed the horses and allowed them a little rest."

"Would you have room for a passenger on your return trip?"

"Of course. Just conclude your affairs quickly because we'll be leaving in about half an hour."

Hieronymus discussed the fare and then rushed back to Berteu's house. It only took him a few moments to gather his belongings. He didn't bother to say goodbye to Madame Berteu and was inwardly rejoicing that he evaded the overbearing Charles and his intrusive questions. He returned to the castle where he collected his painting supplies. He stowed his belongings in the coach and was about to say his goodbyes when he was struck with a thought. He wanted to bid his farewell to the Melac family, but no one was in the house. The overseer was with the count, and Melac's wife and granddaughter were occupied with the countess. What was he to do? He acted like he always did—on impulse. Hieronymus climbed the castle's steps to the foyer, where he was intercepted by the watchful doorman.

"Who are you?" the man asked brusquely.

"Hieronymus Aurelius Schneffke, Monsieur," he replied. "I am an artist and I'm looking for Monsieur Melac."

"He is not available. He is engaged with His Excellency."

"What about Madame Melac?" Hieronymus suggested.

"She's occupied with the gracious lady."

"And Mademoiselle Melac?"

"She's also busy attending to the countess."

"*Sapperlot*! I don't have the time to go through every person engaged in this house. I'm leaving shortly."

"Monsieur, are you in that much of a rush?" the servant asked a little less severely, a smile forming on his lips.

"Yes, the coachman won't wait."

The doorman scratched his head. "Well, Melac can't be disturbed, and the same goes for Madame. Would it be agreeable if I managed to free up Mademoiselle?"

"Yes, yes, that should suffice," Hieronymus nearly blurted out.

"And where should I send her?"

"Down to her house. I will wait there."

"Alright. Leave it to me."

While the portly painter headed back down the stairs, the servant headed toward the countess's ante room. He spotted a maid sorting linen.

"Juliette, who's with the gracious lady?" he asked.

"Madame and Mademoiselle Melac."

"Would it be possible to speak to Madame?"

The maid shrugged her shoulders, but then left her work and walked into the adjoining room, returning shortly with Madame Melac.

"Madame," he addressed her, "there was a gentleman here who desired to speak with you. I gather it was urgent."

"Speak with me?"

"Yes, that's what I understood."

"Who was he, Pierre?"

"He had a long, cumbersome name, difficult to pronounce. Hier— or something. He claimed to be an artist."

"Ah, was he short and portly?"

"Yes, that's the man."

"Where is he now?"

"He is waiting in your house."

She left the foyer, heading downstairs, while Pierre watched her leave, an amused expression playing on his lips.

≈✠≈

Schneffke stood in front of a mirror and examined his likeness. He smiled, pleased with what he saw in the reflection. *Hmm, not a bad-looking sort*, he thought. *Whoever embraces me will have a hold of something. Zounds! Am I not the perfect match for Marie? Doesn't my figure complement hers? My height, waist, weight, and circumference, all of it fits. A kiss from that pretty girl is quite attainable. I don't have to jump up and risk tearing a seam in my pants, nor do I have to bend down, throwing my back out. And now comes the farewell. I guess—ah! I hear a woman's footsteps. I'm going to give her a big hug.*

Schneffke quickly stepped behind the door. When the lady opened it, he grabbed her around the waist.

"Marie, my dear sweet—holy paintbrush… what bad luck," he said, jumping back from the embrace. Instead of hugging his Marie, he was facing her grandmother.

Madame Melac was surprised. Yes, more than surprised, shocked in fact. "Monsieur!" she objected.

"Err… Madame," he replied, not knowing what else to say.

"You… you've just embraced me."

"Yes, unfortunately," he replied, the words tumbling out of his mouth.

"Unfortunately? Does that mean I'm not desirable enough?"

His temperature was rising. "Not for me," he replied, but then realized the rudeness of his response. The embarrassment showed on his face, and since she considered him to be a good man, a faint smile found its way to her lips.

"Not for me," she repeated. "Am I that repulsive?"

"No, not at all. I never meant to label you as unattractive."

"Alright. I take it that the embrace was meant for another?"

"Yes, Madame, for someone else."

"And perhaps this 'another' is called Marie? Were you referring to my granddaughter?"

"Yes, I was," he nodded sheepishly.

"Well, well. So that's who you wanted to embrace?"

"That was my intention, Madame."

"Then why did you send for me?"

"For you?" he asked, taken aback.

"Yes. Pierre specifically said you had asked for Madame Melac."

"Really?" Hieronymus replied, his mind going over the brief conversation. "If I could only get my hands on that conniver."

"Perhaps Pierre misheard you?"

"Impossible. I'm not mute and he's not deaf. I was very specific. I believe that fellow wanted to have a little fun at my expense."

"If that was his intent, then he succeeded admirably," she said, smiling.

"Maybe, but I don't care for such pranks."

"Likewise. However, since we can't change the outcome, we can at least sort this out."

"Hmm," he mused, looking at her skeptically. "What did you have in mind, Madame?"

"Something that any sensible man should do."

Hieronymus had already picked up his hat, ready for a quick exit should the unexpected occur. But when Madame Melac quietly took a seat and her face failed to convey any misgivings, he relaxed a fraction setting down his Calabrese hat.

"Um, Madame," he started. "Foremost, I have to ask for your forgiveness."

"I forgive you," she replied laughing. "There can't be many elderly women who wouldn't do the same. And besides, I have confirmation firsthand that I'm not a picture of ugliness."

"No, not in the least; otherwise, you wouldn't have the slightest resemblance to Mademoiselle Marie."

"She is the one whom I would like to discuss. So, it was Marie you were expecting?"

"Yes."

"But surely you know who you want to embrace?"

"Clearly those whom you like."

"Are you implying that—?"

"That I care about Marie? Yes, in fact, I'm in love with her."

Madame's jaw dropped. "But Monsieur, how long have you known Marie?"

"Only since yesterday."

"So, everything evolved so quickly?"

"Yes. I came, I saw, and I conquered."

Madame Melac laughed heartily. "You mean that you came, you saw, and won Marie over. Isn't that so?"

"Sort of like that. We've seen and conquered each other. We have traded our flags and climbed aboard our frigate, which will steam across the earthly seas of our lives."

"I can see you're accustomed to expressing yourself poetically, my good man."

"I've learned a thing or two," he said, smiling.

She laughed along with him, calming his earlier trepidation. "I gather you have already spoken to Marie about your future."

"Yes, quite a bit."

"When was that?"

"Earlier, just prior to the count's arrival, which by the way interrupted our conversation. He could have waited another ten minutes."

"Has Marie given you her consent?"

"Not exactly. Just a kiss."

"Really? She kissed you?"

"Yes," Hieronymus said. Then on impulse, he embraced her, and before she could object, he planted a kiss on her lips. "Something like this."

"Hold it!" she admonished him, laughing and pushing him back. "You strike me as Alexander the Great himself, conquering whomever you wish."

"It's a God-given talent," Hieronymus quipped.

"Still, I can't believe how quickly your relationship with Marie has evolved."

"I know. It surprised me as well. But while one man takes fifteen years to make up his mind over a woman, another has already driven his sixth wife to tears. Love comes to one like a tortoise, to another like a hare, and still to a third like a lightning bolt from heaven. All he sees are fireworks, struck by an unseen force that blinds him for life."

Madame Melac couldn't help but laugh at the poetic painter. "I have to say it again, that you know how to illustrate your pictures. A mild lyrical poet is lost on you, right?"

"Perhaps I'll become more forceful in my later years. For now, though, I will remain young and easy-going. Later, when life's lessons come along, one becomes sullen, ends up with gout and composes tragic life stories."

"I sincerely hope that you will remain young-at-heart."

"Then I can leave without any reservation for my future. But for now, Madame, let's put all this frivolity aside. Here is my hand. Are you upset with me that my heart has driven me to speak to Marie about my feelings?"

"How can I be upset? No one can suppress the inner voice of the heart. But one has the obligation to speak clearly and with reason."

"That was my intent all along."

"Do you believe that the voice of reason can find harmony with that of the heart?"

"I'm convinced of it."

She nodded. "Just one more thing. We live in France, while you reside abroad. Are you intending to take our only child and settle down far away?"

"Don't fret, Madame," he said shaking his head. "I often work for commission and am not bound to a specific town or country. Actually, I haven't had the opportunity to hear Marie's response."

"Really?" she asked, frowning. "How am I supposed to interpret that?"

"When we discussed the part about our love, she confirmed her love for me, but before we got any further, the count arrived with his entourage. And now I have to depart. So, as you can see, there really hasn't been an opportunity to speak about our future."

"I was under the impression all was in order."

"Not quite. I do, however, consider myself as belonging to Marie. When I return and find that Marie hasn't changed her mind, I will do my utmost to prove to you that I'm worthy of her. If you then give me your consent, I would be happy indeed."

"That is most honorable of you, Monsieur. You have my support." Suddenly, she was struck by a thought. "Does my husband know about your plans?"

"No."

"Should I tell him?"

"I will leave that up to you."

"Don't you want to speak to him before your departure?"

"I have to leave right away, and I don't know if he can spare the time."

"Yes, you may be right. He is still occupied with His Excellency and can't readily leave."

"Then I'm glad I've been able to convey my heart's desire to you. Will you permit me to write to Marie?"

"Of course, Monsieur. Hopefully we will see you soon."

"I would like that. I will write you in any case, since I want to advise you concerning the family Bas-Montaigne. But for now, here is my hand, signifying my appreciation and farewell at the same time. Be content in knowing that I am an honorable man, and you can trust me with your child."

"I do trust you. Adieu, Monsieur."

Madame Melac rose and offered her hand, which Hieronymus pressed to his lips. He was about to leave, yet she held him back with her words.

"Wait for one minute, Monsieur Schneffke. Surely the coachman can spare that much." With that comment, she turned and hurried back to the castle.

Sapperlot! Now she'll fetch the old man, Hieronymus lamented. *Ah well, I suppose it's only fitting that I speak to the patriarch of the family.* A few minutes went by and then the door opened. But it wasn't Melac who came hurrying through the entrance. It was Marie.

"Marie!" he exclaimed, pleasantly surprised. "Your grandmother has a lot more sense than that lackey, Pierre, the one who played a joke on us."

"Do you doubt her sincerity?"

"No, not after our talk. So, did she send you?"

She nodded. "Do you really have to leave right away?"

"Yes. The coachman is waiting for me."

"Will you write?"

"To whom, my angel?" he teased, pulling her closer. "Maybe your grandfather?"

"No, not him. Me!"

"I just have one request. Send me a real kiss."

Marie looked puzzled. "What do you mean?"

"Well, you draw the outline of your lips on paper. Then you write these words in the center: one kiss. And when the ink has dried, you touch the paper to your lips."

"Do you suppose my kisses have that much substance to them?"

"Let's find out right now." Hieronymus grabbed her and kissed her with urgency and passion. His experiment was short-lived though. The waiting coachman was getting impatient and interrupted their blissful interlude with a few smacks of his whip.

"Did you hear that, my love," Hieronymus said, forced to stop. "That man is obviously unhappily married, or else he would have given us a few more minutes. Be happy, my love."

"You too; and be faithful to me."

A minute later, the coach pulled out of the yard, carrying the lucky Hieronymus Aurelius Schneffke back to Metz.

❧❊☙

Charles Berteu had been away from the house for the better part of the day. It was late afternoon by the time he returned. His mother approached him, a worried look creasing her forehead.

"Charles, where have you been?" Louise asked anxiously. "I've been waiting and worried about you."

"Why?" he asked.

"Don't you know?"

"Know what? I've been busy at the mill. I just finished."

"You should have told me where you were going. I could have sent word to you."

"Was it that important?"

"Yes. Haven't you noticed that many of the drapes in the castle have been pulled back?"

"Of course, I have. The Melacs are probably cleaning the windows."

"Yes, but for good reason. The count has arrived."

That at last caught his attention. "You mean Latreau?" he asked, taken aback. "Is he alone?"

"No. He came with his granddaughter and a number of servants."

"Is he planning on staying for a while?"

"It would seem so."

"Hang it all! I knew all along he would come, but not this soon."

"He already sent for you."

"I was afraid of that."

"You're supposed to bring the ledgers and financial books. He wants to settle the accounts."

"*Sapperlot!* Father will turn over in his grave."

"Father was too careless. He should have handled it differently. Now we're finished."

"What do you mean? They can't pin anything on us."

"But what about your position?"

Charles waved his hand dismissively. "Our days here were numbered when Father passed away. Or did you think that the count would have kept me on as caretaker?"

"No, I suppose not. Now tell me honestly. Is there anything left over?"

"No. He spent it all."

"Oh, what an idiot!" she said bitterly.

"Who, me?" Charles replied irritated.

"No, your father."

"That's water under the bridge. We will have to leave, that much is clear. I'll just have to appropriate Nanon's inheritance."

"You won't get your hands on it."

"Pah! There are ways. I know of a man who can put her in the palm of my hand."

"Who could that be?"

"Never mind that now. I have to go up and meet the count." He collected several large ledgers and headed for the castle. Louise watched him with trepidation, as he mounted the steps.

❧✠☙

He returned after what seemed like hours, no longer carrying the books, yet his hunched shoulders suggested he was still carrying a heavy load.

"How did it go?" Louise asked with concern.

"Poorly."

"Has he already reconciled all the accounts?"

"No. He'll come across the loss later. But he didn't even welcome me in a favorable light. Even without the final tally, it's obvious that our time here will soon end. I'll have to head out."

"Dear God! You're not going to leave me behind, are you?"

"No. I will only be gone for a couple of days. Then I'll come back for you."

"Where are you going?"

"To Castle Ortry."

"Ah, to see the old captain? Surely, he will look out for us."

"Look out for us?" Charles scoffed. "That man is as unpredictable as the weather."

"I know. But he owes a lot to my dead husband," she offered, reminding Charles.

"Perhaps. Still, I can't imagine a less thankful man than Richemonte."

"Charles, it was he who had led your father astray. He won't let us perish, will he?"

"Morally, we wouldn't get far with him. He has a heart of stone. But I've kept a few secrets under wraps, secrets about his past that he wouldn't want to get out. He'll have to pay me to keep my mouth shut; whether in cash or —with Nanon. You can count on it."

TRANSLATION NOTES

I have taken the utmost care to render the original German text into a coherent and legible English format. Some of the passages were difficult to translate in the way they were presented, whether because of the sentence structure or by their sheer length. Karl May seemed to enjoy enveloping his readers with a series of interwoven thoughts—often in the same paragraph—plunging them deeper into the story through long sentences. You may read it in its entirety in German, all the while trying to catch your breath; but it just doesn't translate well into English.

In some cases, May employed old idioms or outdated sayings that I've coined as "Blücherisms", often stemming from the venerable Field Marshall Gebhard von Blücher. Although they heighten the dramatic moments, rendering them literally into English would have modern readers shaking their heads. This was especially prevalent in the first book, *The Prussian Lieutenant*. In the fourth book, *Captain Richemonte*, the sequel to *Buried Secrets*, May gives the reader a taste of the evil persona of Albin Richemonte. The book portrays a definitely darker theme, replete with henchmen, underground passages, train derailments, and much more.

Clearly, May delights in resurrecting old idioms and expressions from a previous era. Still, as much as possible, the final translation has to be faithful to the original. However, while the original story was penned in serial format over a span of two years, the current version comes in six separate books. The translator took a little (limited) liberty by adding further explanations, typically when setting a scene. This allows for better continuity from one book to the next, allowing the reader to follow the storyline without having to refer to previous chapters.

1.1   Sancho Pansa

Pansa was a fictional character from the play *The Ingenious Hidalgo Don Quixote of La Mancha,* by Miguel de Cervantes (1605). The implication here is that Schneffke is Haller's Sancho Pansa—in other words, his companion or sidekick.

2.1   Heinrich Heine

Heine (1797–1856) was a German poet and critic. He was widely acclaimed for his lyric poetry.

3.1   "In die Pfanne hauen."

Translation: "Cook our goose."

Interpretation: The old cavalry master was implying that the German forces were inferior and could be "blown away" by a superior French army.

3.2   Bajazzo

Within opera circles, this name is synonymous with the word clown. It usually refers to a colourful, visually stunning entertainer.

4.1   "Soutward Far the fair Espana"

"The Gipsy Boy," a poem by Emanuel Geibel, translated by F. H. Hedley (Trubney and Co., London.)

5.1 Blasewitz

The city of Blasewitz, became a suburb of Dresden in the 1900s. Rich in culture and diversity, it is situated on the Elbe River and was particularly prone to flooding during medieval times. A prominent resident was Johann Gottlieb Neuman (1741–1801), a composer and court conductor.

5.2 Franctireur

A franctireur, or franc-tireur was a French partisan soldier, or one belonging to a faction of troops engaged in forays, skirmishes, and upheaval. In its simplest form, a franc-tireur was a civilian who voluntarily enlisted to aid France's cause in the upcoming French-Prussian war. At their worst, franc-tireurs were seen as opportunists or highwaymen, only concerned for their own gain.

5.3 Matthäi the Last

This may be referring to Matthias the Apostle who replaced the ill-fated Judas Iscariot. Mathias, like the other apostles, succumbed to an early, horrible death for preaching the gospel in Jerusalem. Franz wasn't keen on dying and used an obscure reference to make his point.

8.1 Talisman

The term talisman usually refers to an object that is believed to possess magical powers. Typically, a talisman is treasured by the holder and likened to a good luck charm. A modern application would be a rabbit's foot or four-leaf clover.

8.2 "Deus ex machina"

Greek for, "God out of the machine". A somewhat unusual term that stemmed from ancient times. It often referred to a dramatic moment in a play, simulating actors appearing on a set via mechanical means. A more recent adaptation deals with a seemingly unsolvable problem in a story that is suddenly or abruptly resolved by an unexpected and unlikely occurrence. In this instance, Karl May is inferring that Countess Marion need only present Abu Hassan's edict to a local magistrate and she would not have to fear reprisals from Captain Richemonte.

9.1   Au Fait

A term referring to being current, or up to date. Au fait implies that a person is keeping up with the latest fashion, news, and entertainment.

10.1   Donner und Doria

Literal: Thunder and Doria.

Explanation: This minced oath, or expletive, was taken from Friedrich Schiller's story, "The Conspiracy of Fiesko of Geona." Literally, thunderclap or lightning. A modern rendering would be, "By Jove!"

10.2   Zündnadelgewehr

The first breech-loading rifle, invented by German industrialist, Johann Nikolaus Dreyse (1787–1867) became the weapon of choice for the Prussian military and was used extensively during the Franco-Prussian War of 1870.

10.3   "Beim Tisch schlafen"

Translation: Sleep at the table.

Explanation: During times of crisis, particularly during battles in war time, senior German military commanders were expected to be available at a moment's notice. A summons by the supreme commander Bismarck ensured they were never far away. Some generals were known to keep appointments all hours, even falling asleep at the dinner table.

13.1 **"Da haben Sie mit schlechten Pferden gepflügt"**

Translation: Plough with Inferior Horses

An old idiom from the time when farmers plowed their fields with teams of work horses. The meaning is obscure. From the context, it appears Franz was being admonished by the stranger (Gaston) for not being astute enough. Franz was a bachelor and apparently lacked in the essentials of matrimonial matters.

13.2 **Urian**

In German folklore, the term *Urian* also referred to Satan. See *Tragedy of Faust*, by Johann Wolfgang von Göethe:

Now to the Brocken the witches hie,
The stubble is yellow, the corn is green;
Thither the gathering legions fly,
And sitting aloft is Sir Urian seen:
O`er stick and o`er stone they go whirling along,
Witches and he-goats, a motley throng.

"Sir Urian" was an unwelcome guest whose presence or untimely visit implied that trouble or bad news wasn't far off.

16.1 **Hobble**

This term refers to the idea of hobbling or tethering a larger animal (cow or horse), allowing it limited movement for grazing, but not to the extent that it could roam freely. The tether could be something as simple as a rope or lanyard.

18.1 **Walk into a Closet**

An obscure idiom, one conveying the idea that no sensible man (or soldier) would risk walking into an unknown house or facility.

20.1   La Renommeé

A French Frigate that was transporting French troops in 1811. It was Attacked by English ships and captured. Franz Schneeberg makes a reference to the famous French ship, in a roundabout way letting Schneffke know that he connects him with the military.

21.1   Pfalz State

General Come de Mélac (1630-1704), a French career soldier under Louis XIV, caused untold harm on the German populace occupying regions within the Pfalz state.

23.1   "Faustdick hinter den Ohren"

Translation: He has plenty behind the ears.

Explanation: He's crafty, a sly old dog. Someone who can't easily be fooled.

25.1   Hourie

In Islamic religious belief, houris are women with beautiful eyes who are rewarded to the faithful Muslim believers in Paradise. The term is used four times in the Quran, where they are briefly mentioned. Source: Wikipedia

What follows is an exclusive peek from *The Foundling*, the next volume in *The Hussar's Love* series.

CHAPTER ONE

ABU HASSAN

If a traveller were to enter the city of Algiers by way of Bab el Qued Street and turn into Kasbahn Street, he would walk past one of the more infamous coffee houses of the former pirate town. However, the café's notoriety wasn't evident by its outward appearance. The building's façade was old and dirty. The stones were stacked precariously, one on top of another, and the entrance was narrow, much like the doorway of an ordinary hut. The entryway led to a long dark hallway that opened into a large open-air courtyard, surrounded by veiled ornate pillars which partitioned into small rooms, promising privacy. These rooms were set aside for special guests.

The middle of the courtyard contained a fountain which was shaded by the far-reaching branches of a sycamore tree. While foreigners sat in seclusion behind the portico drinking and smoking, the locals, dressed in their white kaftans, sat near the fountain, 'drinking' their *tschibuk* as the *Moor* likes to render it, and sipping their strong coffee, one cup after another.

Enjoying the pleasant evening breeze, they listened attentively to the performance of the *Meda*, a storyteller, who through his spell-binding craft took them on a spiritual journey to Damascus and beyond, fantasizing about tales that rivalled *A Thousand and One Nights*. The storyteller alternated between fantasy and reality, from embellishing local heroes to expounding on Mohammed the Prophet. He covered his caliphs, the Great Salladin, Tarik the Conqueror, and ending with stories about the Spanish *Moors* and their vast riches.

The *Meda* described the majesty and glory of antiquity, leading up to the treasures of the present time. If he was fortunate enough to have visited Mecca, the holy city, then he would describe the pilgrim's journey firsthand and if he managed to travel to the far reaches of the Sahara, then he would astound them even more with his tales. He talked of Samum of the Djinas, of evil spirits, and of the mighty lion, the Ruler of the desert. The *Meda*, eloquent and poetic, was not unlike the German poet of renown, Freligrath, who penned a poem about a *Moor*.

"His lengthening host through the palm-vale wound;
The purple shawl on his locks he bound;
He hung on his shoulders the lion-skin;
Martially sounded the cymbal's din.

Like a sea of termites the wild, black swarm
Swept, billowing, onward. He flung his dark arm,
Encircled with gold, round his loved one's neck:—
"For the feast of victory, maiden, deck!

"Lo! glittering pearls I've brought thee there,
To twine with thy dark and glossy hair;
And the corals, all snakelike, in Persia's green sea,
The dripping divers have fished for me.

"See! plumes of the ostrich, thy beauty to grace!
Let them nod, snowy-white, o'er thy dusky face.
Deck the tent,—make ready the feast for me,—
Fill the garlanded goblet of victory!"

And forth from his snowy and shimmering tent
The princely Moor, in his armor, went.
So looks the dark moon, when, eclipsed, through the gate
Of the silver-edged clouds, she rides forth in her state.

CAPTAIN RICHEMONTE

A welcoming shout his proud host flings,
And "Welcome!" the stamping steed's hoof rings;
For him rolls faithful the negro's blood,
And Niger's old, mysterious flood.

"Now lead us to victory,—lead us to fight!"
They battled from morning far into the night.
The hollow tooth of the elephant blew
A blast that pierced each foeman through.

How scatter the lions! the serpents fly
From the rattling tambour; the flags on high,
All hung with skulls, proclaim the dead,
And the yellow desert is dyed with red.

So rings in the valley the desperate fight;—
But she is preparing the feast for the night;
She fills the goblets with rich palm-wines,
And the shafts of the tent-poles with flowers she twines.

With pearls that Persia's green flood bare,
She dresses her dark and glossy hair;
Feathers are floating her brow to deck,
And gay shells gleam on her arms and neck.

She sits by the door of her lover's tent,—
She lists the far war-horns till morning is spent;
The noonday burns,—the sun stings hot,—
The garlands wither,—she heeds it not.

The sun goes down in the fading skies,
The night-dew trickles, the glow-worm flies,
And the crocodile looks from the tepid pool,
As if he, too, would enjoy the cool.

The lion bestirs him and prowls for prey,
The elephant-tusks through the jungles make way,
Home to her lair the giraffe goes,
And flower-leaves shut and eyelids close.

The maiden's fluttering heart beats high,
When a bleeding, fugitive Moor draws nigh:—
"Farewell to all hope now! the battle is lost;
Thy lover is captured,—he's dragged to the coast,—

"They sell him to white men,—he's carried——" O, spare!
The maiden falls headlong,—she clutches her hair;
All quivering she crushes the pearls in her hand,
She hides her hot cheek in the burning-hot sand.

PART II.

'Tis fair-day;—how sweeps the tempestuous throng
To circus and tilt-ground, with shout and with song!
There's a blast of trumpets,—the cymbal rings,—
The deep drum rumbles,—Bajazzo springs.

Come on! come on! How swells the roar!
They fly, as on wings, o'er the hard, flat floor;
The British sorrel, the Turk's black steed,
From plumèd beauty win honor's meed.

And there, by the tilting-ground's curtained door,
Stands, silent and thoughtful, a curly-haired Moor.
The Turkish drum he beats full loud,—
On the drum is hanging a lion-skin proud.

He sees not the knights and their graceful swing,—
He sees not the steeds and their daring spring;

The Moor's dry eye, with its stiff, wild stare,
Sees naught but the shaggy lion-skin there.

He thinks of the far, far distant Niger,
And how he once chased there the lion and tiger,
And how he once brandished his sword in the fight,
And came not back to his couch at night.

And he thinks of her , who, in other hours,
Decked her hair with his pearls and plucked him her flowers;
His eye grew moist,—with a scornful stroke
He smote the drum-head,—it rattled and broke."

Just as the storyteller reached the end of the poem, a new guest ventured into the courtyard. He stopped at the entrance and looked about, as if searching for someone. One of those seated at the fountain quietly stood up and meandered toward the stranger.

"*Sallam aaleikum*," the newcomer greeted.

"*Aaleikum sallam*," the other man replied with the familiar response. "How glad I am to see you."

"Allah has watched over me."

"Were you successful in your quest, Saadi?"

"Yes, my brother."

"Can you tell me where you were?"

"Of course, and much more. Come."

Saadi led his brother, Abu Hassan, through one of the porticos into a vacant room. They sat down on the plush cushions, waiting to be served. The *kawehdschi*, or innkeeper, instructed a servant to bring them tobacco and coffee.

"Now, fill me in," Abu said, lighting his *tschibuk*. "Where were you all this time?"

"You'll never guess."

"Just tell me."

"I was in the Aures Mountains."

"Up there? What business did you have there?"

"I went to visit the hut of the dead *marabout*."

"You mean the former Hajji Omanah?"

"None other."

"God is great. He lends his thoughts to his people. But I'm not all knowing and can't guess what you were doing there."

"I went to the holy place; I wanted to pray."

"That is pleasing to Allah. What else did you have in mind?"

"I wanted to see the marabout's corpse."

"What! Has a *scheitan* or devil possessed you? What were you planning on doing?"

"I wanted to unearth his remains."

"Saadi!" Abu exclaimed horrified. "Don't you know that a faithful Moslem will become unclean by doing so?"

"I know it. Still, it had to be done. I then spoke prayers of purification."

"Don't you realize that the one who desecrates the grave of a holy man subjects himself to Allah's wrath?"

"I know it."

"And still you followed through?"

"My motives were honourable, and Allah will forgive me."

ABOUT THE AUTHOR

Robert Stermscheg, born in Europe in 1956, was exposed to many wonderful writers – Edgar Rice Burroughs, Alexandre Dumas, even Karl May, to mention just a few. He appreciated how they opened up a whole new world to our imaginations through their portrayal of life.

His parents were of Austrian descent, and as a result of his father's occupation as an electrical engineer, he moved several times in his early childhood. His father kept a steady supply of books to broaden his education, including a repertoire of Karl May books.

The entire family moved to Canada in 1967, eventually settling in Manitoba. Robert was involved in chess, hockey, flying, but always kept up his interest in the German language. His passion to share the works of Karl May, largely unknown in North America at the time, resulted in his search for English translations.

After retiring from a satisfying career with the Winnipeg Police Service in 2006, he had the opportunity to pursue his dream—translating one of Karl May's novels into English. His wife, Toni, embraced his dream and encouraged him in the writing process. She supported him in this new venture by becoming a proof-reader.

He embarked on his first book, *The Prussian Lieutenant*, based on an earlier work by Karl May. Published in 2008 by Word Alive Press, it was well received locally, encouraging him to continue with the sequel, *The Marabout's Secret. Buried Secrets*, the third installment in *The Hussar's Love* series, was released independently several years later.

With the release of *Captain Richemonte*, Robert is eager to start work on the next installment, *The Foundling*.

Visit his website: www.robertstermscheg.com.

www.ingramcontent.com/pod-product-compliance
Lightning Source LLC
Chambersburg PA
CBHW031055080526
44587CB00011B/688